D1806220

P T FORSYTH

Theologian for a New Millenium

Edited by

Alan P F Sell

'102' Ecumenical Centre
Highgate, KENDAL, Cumbria
LA9 4HE Tel/Fax 01539 730250
Email manager@102ecumen.freeserve.co.uk

ISBN 0 85346 193 7
© The United Reformed Church 1999

Published by
The United Reformed Church
86 Tavistock Place, London WC1H 9RT

*All rights reserved. No part of this publication which is copyright ©
may be reproduced, stored in a retrieval system, or transmitted
in any form or by any means, electronic, mechanical, photocopying,
recording, or otherwise, without the prior permission of the publisher.*

Printed by Healeys Printers, Unit 10, the Sterling Complex,
Farthing Road, Ipswich, Suffolk IP1 5AP

Contents

Editor's Preface

As the twentieth century draws to a close there is welcome evidence that a theologian who was active when it opened is receiving a fresh hearing. Works by P T Forsyth (1848-1921) are currently being reprinted in Australia, England and the United States; Leslie McCurdy's monograph, *Attributes and Atonement*, is shortly to appear; and in 1993, in anticipation of the quincentenary in 1995 of the University of Aberdeen, and of the centenary of the award by that University of its honorary DD to its distinguished alumnus, Forsyth, a colloquium was held in the city of Forsyth's birth, the principal fruit of which is the collection of papers edited by Trevor Hart and published under the title, *Justice the True and Only Mercy* (1995).

This present volume is offered in celebration of the sesquicentenary of Forsyth's birth. It differs from the Aberdeen collection in two ways. First, whereas a wide variety of themes was treated in Aberdeen, these papers were delivered at a conference held in May 1998 at the Windermere Centre of the United Reformed Church under the title, 'P T Forsyth: Theologian for a New Millennium', where the unifying question which all contributors were invited to consider was, 'How far does Forsyth have a word for the Church as Christianity's third millennium approaches?' The resulting papers reveal that, while all the writers are indebted to Forsyth, some have more reservations concerning his continuing helpfulness than others. Secondly, whereas a predominantly academic audience was envisaged in Aberdeen, the Windermere papers, though rooted in sound scholarship, were written for a wider audience of ministers and church members. This is entirely appropriate, given that this was precisely the audience which Forsyth himself addressed most frequently and strove so earnestly to reach - as

Clyde Binfield makes clear in his study of Forsyth the college principal, itself a sequel to the same writer's contribution, 'P T Forsyth as Congregational Minister', to the Aberdeen volume. It is equally appropriate that while some of the present writers are employed in academic contexts, about half are in pastoral charge, and all are preachers.

The Windermere Conference was the brainchild of Alan Gaunt, who is to be congratulated on his enterprise in preparation and his diligence in leadership. All who addressed and attended the conference found it a most worthwhile occasion. In addition, Alan has kindly granted my request that his poem, 'For P T Forsyth, 1848-1921', be published herein. Having known Alan Gaunt since he and I shared a study in our first year at Lancashire Independent College - a mutually challenging experience from which, as it would appear, neither of us suffered any permanent harm - I was delighted to be invited to assist in the preparation of the conference and to see this volume through the press.

Alan P F Sell

Aberystwyth

For P T Forsyth 1848-1921

Eternal God, supreme in holiness,
whom all our self-made goodness must betray:
from your great majesty
pour out your light, expose our emptiness
and by your judgement, snatching pride away,
give us humility.

What but your holy love's stupendous grace,
which knew the outcome, could have left us free,
in disobedience,
to break away, to turn from your embrace,
and choose the shackles of sin's slavery,
the death of innocence?

Your holy love condemns us all, it slays
the self-claimed virtue that insults your name,
the worthless pride we wear;
your holy love alone has power to raise
our self-inflicted souls from death and shame,
to save us from despair.

Christ, lifted on the Cross for us, you died
to bear the judgement of love's holiness;
there, having heard Love's call,
you offered up, in being crucified,
Love's sacrifice of true obedience,
that would redeem us all.

The unspoiled bliss of Eden could not lift
the heart so high as these dead souls you raise,
nor could we ever grow
to reach the holiness we have as gift,
in which we share a depth of joy and praise
that angels never know.

Alan Gaunt, May 1977

1.

Peter Taylor Forsyth

Pastor as Principal

Clyde Binfield

What does it take to understand Peter Taylor Forsyth?[1] Take his official, that is to say his *Congregational Year Book*, obituary?[2] The 1922 *Year Book*, which covered 1921, was a slim volume reflecting hard times. This list of 'Ministers Deceased and Reported Since last Issue' contained sixty-one names (there should have been two more), and it was followed by fifty-three obituaries, some of them for men who had died the previous year. The average age of the sixty-one was seventy-one. The oldest was ninety-four and the youngest was thirty-nine. Forsyth was seventy-three. He had not retired, though for the past year he had been incapacitated, visibly wasting away. His obituary, although longer than the rest, was still spartan, but it was authoritative. Its author, HTA, was Forsyth's colleague and son-in-law, Herbert Thomas Andrews.[3] Andrews devoted the first of this three paragraphs to his subject's life, the second to his writings, the third and shortest to his theology. There it was: Forsyth in three paragraphs.

The life (1848-1921) was passed in Scotland, Germany, and England, chiefly London; twenty-eight years in formation and education, twenty-five in pastoral ministry, twenty years in theological teaching. Its distinctives were firmly etched: the postman's son born into Scottish Congregationalism (his father was an Aberdeen deacon) and educated in the Scottish way, locally and well (what Andrews carefully calls 'one of the public schools in Aberdeen', then at the Grammar School, and then at the University, 'taking a first class and winning distinction in classics' capped by an assistantship 'to the Professor of Humanity'). Germany followed naturally, although a British obituary in 1922 needed to choose its words with care: 'Later on he went to Germany and studied for a time under Ritschl at Gottingen, gaining a knowledge of German theology which became a powerful factor in his later thinking.' His English collegiate training is barely touched on

('Upon his return he entered New College, London'). His five pastorates, all English, are given: his 'chief work as a pastor' is confined to the last two. There is no reference to marriage or home life.

The writings ('Dr Forsyth began his career as an author') are deftly listed: the surprising beginning with children's sermons in *Pulpit Parable;* the book on *Religion in Recent Art* which won from G F Watts the acknowledgement that Forsyth understood his painting better than anyone else; and then the theology. Andrews gives the titles of ten books and alludes to a 'considerable number of smaller ones and many articles in theological journals.

The theology is caught in a short paragraph, bold, precise and suggestive:

> The central feature in Dr Forsyth's theology was the tremendous stress which he laid upon the doctrine of the Atonement. The Cross was to him the central fact of Christianity, and round that centre everything else revolved. It is impossible to exaggerate the effect produced by his prophetic championship of the Cross upon current theological thought.

Thus the *Congregational Year Book.* So what does is take to understand Peter Taylor Forsyth? Does it take Grace, or Belief, or Authority, or Love Holy at the Cross or the soul of Prayer? Or does it first take the knowledge that he was a man of his time, a Congregationalist, a minister of Word and Sacrament, and a College Principal, in that order but all four in interaction, and that he was a Scotsman?

He was a man of his time. That time (1848-1921) has been variously categorised in neat titles as the *Age of Great Cities, the Age of Improvement, the Age of Equipoise, the Age of Capital, the Age of Empire*, all of them ushering in *the Age of Extremes, the People's Century, and the Century of Total War.* We might also categorise it as the *Age of Best Purchase*, which saw his sort of churches reach and pass their zenith, tantalisingly close to its social, cultural, intellectual and political cutting edge and cut accordingly. Forsyth, as Victorian minister turned Edwardian Principal, was most representatively a man of his time.

He was a Congregationalist by birth and conviction. Those twin facts entailed some baggage: a measure of social insecurity balanced by a degree of spiritual superiority; a sense of personal election and consequent responsibility. You needed, because you were a Congregationalist, to know where you stood and why, in the light of your call as interpreted through scripture and realised in fellowship. You, though individualised, were never alone. Congregationalism, to use the language of Best Purchase, for such market-force talk came naturally to you, was value-added Independency.

He was a minister of Word and Sacrament. Regardless of when that precise phrase came into denominational currency, the concept fills his writing and it would not have become such a common phrase in Congregational (or United Reformed) churches without him. Comprehensive though it is, it needs filling out. A Congregational minister was ordained to a specific local pastorate and the ordination was confirmed on removal to subsequent pastorates by induction or recognition. From 1876 to 1901 Forsyth ministered in five such pastorates: Eastwood, Shipley (1876-79); St Thomas's Square, Hackney (1879-85); Cheetham Hill, Manchester (1895-99); Clarendon Park, Leicester (1888-94); Emmanuel, Cambridge (1894-1901). Each was urban, although all were socially and three were numerically respectable. Two were very new, one was quite new, and two were almost as old as Congregationalism. All, in conventional terms, were successful pastorates. In each his people admired him, some loved him and he drew lifelong strength from them. All were at the heart of what made his age, or ages, tick: Bradford, London, Manchester, Leicester, Cambridge; industry, commerce, civic spirit; and strong measures of cosmopolitan and metropolitan as well as provincial culture. In Bradford, London and Manchester there were Congregational theological colleges within easy reach; and London, Manchester and Cambridge were also, in their significantly different ways, university towns. It was a constantly changing scene. When Forsyth entered the pastoral ministry, one of his future churches had yet to be formed. When he exchanged his manse study for that of a college principal, two of his churches had already closed. Two survive, one in the Congregational Federation and one in the United Reformed Church.

His ministry was of Word and Sacrament. That was not just a matter of contractual convenience, a gentleman's agreement between the called and the calling. It implied shape, structure, and due authority. It implied churchmanship, intellect, and discipline. The Forsyth whom we celebrate and on whom I concentrate was a successful high Victorian Congregational minister, a man of note in his community and of rippling note in its wider networks, whose theology was bound to be a **preached** theology, a communication of tone, accent, words, rhetoric, distilled from a mind of unusual quality, seized by grace, fired in the crucible of personality and experience, shaped with an intensifying urgency in the 1890s. It was the growing denominational recognition of that shaping which had taken him to Cambridge in 1894 and which turned him into a London College Principal in 1901. His last two calls, like his first two, were, humanly speaking, the results of strategy not chance.

He was a College Principal. Congregational College Principals were a select band. There were eight in England, two in Wales, and one in Scotland. They had denominational clout which on the whole they retained to the 1960s. In Forsyth's day they, with a larger group of nationally known ministers, brothers beloved in pastoral charge, were Congregationalism's bishops, strategically placed men of spiritual, administrative and intellectually grasp. They had civic standing. They lived well, housed in such villages as quite grand churches might aspire to. They knew what and where the strings were and how to pull them. When they had time, and if they were not forever looking out for funds, they provided intellectual leadership. When they were not placating their committees, they were placing their young men whom they had trained with a hand-to-mouth sort of rigour. By most modern standards, but as is almost invariably the way with education, that training was at level best uneven, at worst unsatisfactory.[4] As is also almost invariably the way, there were some fine results. And there were a dozen constellations of small or struggling churches, radiating from the colleges, kept alive countrywide by these select young men in training.

Two aspects of this need emphasis. The first is the extent to which the College Principals were in the Congregational mainstream. Most of them (there were some telling exceptions) were men who had sustained successful pastorates and whose words carried weight on platforms and in committee rooms. In a remarkable number of cases pulpit and professional chair (or lecture desk) could have been interchangeable. During Forsyth's pastoral prime, it surely could have been so with Bowdon's Alexander Mackennal, Birmingham's R W Dale, Bedford's John Brown, Islington's Henry Allon, Norwich's George Barrett.[5] It certainly was with Cheshunt College's Henry Robert Reynolds, whose otherworldly wisdom was entirely belied by a notable town-centre pastorate in Leeds.[6] It was so with Joseph Parker, whose Manchester days were marked by the path-breaking experiment attached to his Cavendish Street Chapel, which J B Paton continued and transformed in Nottingham. Congregational ministerial training owes a great deal to Park, the quintessential pulpiteer; and Sheffield Congregational churches benefited for years from the Paton's young pastoral example in one of them before he turned to development of ministerial training in Nottingham.[7] In the twentieth century, Bournemouth's D J Jones was invited to become a college principal (and wisely declined); and while Campbell Morgan may not have been the best choice for Cheshunt College, Cambridge (but then the Great War makes a proper judgement impossible; and at least Campbell Morgan ensured that the College had its buildings), W B Selbie was an inspired choice for Mansfield College, Oxford.[8] More recently H F Lovell Cocks and John Huxtable might be placed in the same tradition, as indeed might J S Whale, whose brief pastorate at Bowdon was nonetheless in the grand manner, and who later turned down an approach from the City Temple.[9] Those names had in their day a national resonance, and not just in Congregational or Free Church circles. P T Forsyth was such a College Principal.

There is a second aspect. These men trained **young** men, in their twenties most of them. Forsyth's men could, therefore, be found on the United Reformed Church's roll of ministers into the 1980s, and in active Congregational pastorates into the 1950s.[10] The point is a simple but necessary one. The teacher's role even more than the pastor's is not so much determined over time as best appreciated in retrospect. The great teacher is a time bomb. The metaphor is infelicitous, but it fits Forsyth.

He was a Scotsman. Forsyth may not have seen much of his native country from the 1870s, but his Aberdeen DD, awarded pointedly in his first full Cambridge year, might remind us of two things. First, there was more opportunity for an Aberdeen postman's son to proceed **unhindered** to University, Germany, and an assured professional life in the middle-class suburbs of the world's foremost industrial (and imperial) national than there was, say, for a Bristol postman's sons. Secondly, Scottish Congregationalism was more significantly and constructively accented by Presbyterianism (and therefore by the Reformed tradition) than English Congregationalism was by Anglicanism. It was also newer. Moreover, relationships between Dissent and the Established Church differed between England and Scotland. Thus there were some inferiorities which Scotsmen could ignore more easily in England than the natives. Fairbairn at Bradford and Oxford is the prime example in the Congregational world.[11] Forsyth is another. The Scottish influence on English Nonconformity, as propagated in English theological colleges, merits study.

But was there, literally, a Scottish accent? Reminiscence suggests that there was, but I have yet to come across a direct or written reference to it. The *Christian World's* obituary noted that some of Forsyth's 'most intimate relationships were with laymen - Scottish laymen'.[12] His fellow Scot and fellow principal, A E Garvie, recollected Forsyth's 'Scotsman's reserve', and how 'he would sometimes allow himself a Scottish word or phrase which he knew I could fully appreciate, as his English friends could not'.[13] And one of his Scottish layman friends, Alexander Glegg, who had been a boy with Forsyth in Aberdeen, and in old age was Forsyth's college treasurer in London, later enlarged on this:

'Dr Forsyth was, I think, closest and clearest when speaking Scotch to Scotsmen. I have never listened to his equal as a reader of Scotch poetry or prose. The expression, pathos and power he put into the tendering, revealed his inmost soul. Like most Scotchmen he was reserved, but in his native dialect his own eyes moistened as well as those of his audience.'[14]

This is to say that Forsyth needed an audience and that he responded best to audiences with whom he felt at home. But there is more to it than that. Six months to the day after Forsyth's death, and on the eve of his birthday, a memorial tablet was unveiled at Hackney College. The inevitable speeches included one from a neighbouring minister, Macleod of St Andrews, Frognal. Perhaps it was simply the small change of platform good manners, but it is hard not to hear a also the tones of clan solidarity, intimating a cultural otherness.

'When I came here 20 years ago, I did not know a soul in London save my own people. They were good and generous enough. God knows; but I do not think I could have served them without Dr Forsyth. He made me feel he wanted me to make Hackney College my harbour of refuge.'

And there was a speech from a famous antagonist, R J Campbell. Campbell, an Anglican now, was careful to place Forsyth 'in a great successional, Scottish and English'.

'He brought to his work in the Congregational ministry in this country a mind and character made and moulded by a rich and massive spiritual tradition deriving immediately from three centuries of

Scottish religious idealism and strength of conviction. He never got away from it to the end of his life, and all his personal contribution to evangelical thought in his own and other denominations was coloured by it throughout. But, so far as England was concerned, he had mighty predecessors also upon whose inheritance he entered with an authority and influence as great as theirs. Congregationalism has always been fortunate in its outstanding men, its leaders and exponents, who have guided it councils and represented it to the world. In this respect Peter Forsyth is of the fellowship of Dale and Fairbairn, of Hannay, and Raleigh, and Allon, of Binney and Simon.....'[15]

With this Campbell, of all people, returns us to my contention that to understand Forsyth we must first place him as a man of his time, a high Victorian Congregational minister of Word and Sacrament turned Edwardian College Principal, a Scotsman who had lived in London for longer than he had lived in Aberdeen (and far longer than anywhere else), of wide experience and considerable contemporary influence, as providentially out of step as only a man so formed could be. Those eight names prove it, which Campbell brought to mind, as least four of them now forgotten though all meant much in their day. Dale, a Londoner; Allon, a Yorkshireman; Binney, a Northumbrian; Simon, of Welsh origins, though born in Stockport; and four Scotsmen; and only the Londoner and the Stockport-born Welshman found their chief work outside the capital.

Although the pastor and the principal, truly understood, intermingle, the rest of this paper concentrates on the principal because the pastor has been considered elsewhere.

It may be presumed that a successful college principal needs to bring to his task four qualities: a credible and attractive personality, intellectual ability, ministerial experience, and a teacher's skills. Forsyth's personality and intellect will burst out in what follows, but we should pause on three aspects of his particular pastoral experience. Since it was largely suburban, it might not surprise us that he has interesting things to say about women, and young people; and since the suburbs were in Bradford, London and Manchester (and, indeed, Leicester), it should not surprise us either that what he has to say is intertwined with the rich civic culture of Victorian England, Ruskin's England, that is to say, and William Morris's. Now transmute that experience into the teacher's skills. In Forsyth's day that meant a focus on the lecture. Concentrate less on the lecture's content (my present concern is not with syllabus[16]) than on its incidentals, so much larger than life when directed at what were usually small classes: the vehicle for personality, the debating point, the epigram, the legitimate opportunity (as a sermon might not be) for wit, even satire, the word-painting, the whole directed at particular hearers called to a defined future, young men, of disconcertingly varied ability, who have only their call in common. That call presumes in these young men a call to preach. By later standards this might seem a strikingly narrow remit. Even by some contemporary standards it was one in which practicalities - what doubtless we would call directly transferable skills - were conveyed, if at all, by osmosis. And Forsyth's horizons were so cosmic that he could be irresistibly scathing about mere practicalities, especially if they were immediate ones. So it needs to be stressed that his undertaking of the ministerial office was in fact almost unbearably comprehensive, his grasp of it informed by his experience. Given that his task was to educate men for contemporary Congregational ministry, he was a good principal by even the most gradgrindian present-day standards.

There can be no doubt as to Forsyth's high views of Congregational ministry. It was a logical concomitant of his understanding of authority and his concept of the Church.

> 'Christianity can only exist in the world as a Church and not as a mere spiritual movement in the midst of society. To own a Church authority duty …. is to enlarge oneself…. [T]he individual….must, therefore, allow great authority to the competent in correcting facts and to the Catholic tradition which runs through the Churches and braces them in eternal unity.'[17]

By 'the competent' Forsyth meant chiefly the ministry: 'the ministry, being specially appointed by the Church, had an authority in worship and teaching belonging to no layman who was without such appointment'.[18] Such a ministry was morally creative. It continually re-created the souls of men and women through the moral power of its message. The minister mediated God's initiative to His people, and the people's initiative to God, the former in his preaching (for there he represented God to the people; he conveyed Grace), and the latter in his praying (for thus he represented the people before God; he conveyed Faith).[19] How could such an office be diminished into a matter of 'tweed suits and red ties' (such as himself had once been know to wear), fitter for God's executives than God's gift.[20] There was an element of Moses in a Forsythian minister, descending on the Church with the Gospel, 'minister OF the Word, TO the Church, FOR the people'.[21] Worse yet, for free and independent Edwardian churchmen, such views presupposed a hierarchy: in Forsyth's words, one less of office than of 'competency, spiritual or intellectual'.[22] Views like that certainly set standards for any college that dares embody them, and Forsyth had no illusions about the immensity of his task:

'There is no more difficult position today, nor one which evokes less sympathy, than that of minister who had to stand between the world of modern knowledge on the one hand and the world of traditional religion on the other, and mediate between them. It is not a case of adjusting his own faith to the new knowledge. He has done that and can go on doing it. It is a case of adjusting the new knowledge to the untaught faith of others, and doing it in a way of reverence for truth, love for man and regard for the growth of living faith …. The premises are being rebuilt, but the business must be carried on and the builders must be competent to manage both without loss in the process, and with great gain in the end.'[23]

One needs to bear in mind here the **electric** emphasis which Forsyth places on faith, which points up what is paradoxically apparent in this extract - the carefully judged commercial tenor of this piece of up-to-date realism. There is an early contemporaneity as well as a cosmic urgency about the Forsythian style.

So, was he a successful principal in the eyes of those who immediately counted, his pupils, his colleagues and his council? Hackney, recalled his daughter (who was writing as a wife as well a daughter of the College), 'was a magnificent opportunity'.[24] Unlike its present buildings, the College itself was not new to Forsyth. When he had administered in the early 1880s at St Thomas' Square, in the real Hackney's heart, to what the *Christian World* called 'a select congregation drawn by his intellectual magnetism and broad views' (the church had a Literary and Social Union and used *Hymns Ancient and Modern* for its hymnbook), the College had been a near neighbour.[25] It had moved to West Hampstead shortly after Forsyth moved to Cheetham Hill. In Hackney it had made do with a terrace of plainly respectable houses. In Hampstead it was purpose-built, a striking, reticently Renaissance building on a good site. Downhill, to its west, grew a densely aspiring suburbia. Uphill, to the east, folk breathed a different air for there peeped a Kate Greenaway world of well-turned Arts and Crafts, ripe for Garden Cities. What man of intellectual magnetism could resist living next to Parsifal Road, knowing that a short walk away there was Kidderpore Avenue dedicated now to a women's college or higher education in best approved Queen Anne Revival?[26] To walk from his college to theirs was to walk from Bayreuth to a Raj transformed to womankind, from Kundry to Princess Ida. That was a Holy Grail indeed, and of all college principals Forsyth was the likeliest to be bewitched by it; but the man whose exposition of **Parsifal** remains an indispensable part of the true Wagnerian's travelling-bag, was the least likely to harbour illusions about the delights of his magnificent opportunity. [27]

Forsyth came in his early fifties to a building which was barely fifteen years old in the wake of a predecessor, Alfred Cave (DD, St Andrews), who had attempted with some success to update a relatively conservative evangelism for intelligent Congregationalists.[28] He had the considerable advantage of a much younger wife, whom her stepdaughter described as a woman of 'great charm, and even fascination, of looks and manner, incredible vitality, much wit and a born gift as a hostess'.[29] The College Treasurer spoke of her as a 'lubricant among the domestic wheels, sending them smoothly round'.[30] Given the edgy realities of life behind theological green baize doors, the testimony should be taken seriously. At the very end of his life, when it was clear that Forsyth must give up his remaining committees, Bertha Forsyth attended the Coward Trust's meeting to explain the situation on her husband's behalf.[31] It is hard for the late twentieth century mind to understand how Edwardian women, especially those who knew their place and seemed to keep to it, could yet achieve an apparently effortless equality.

Forsyth disliked business committees and he was, it seems, more of a name than a power on the Coward Trust. He equally disliked marking examination papers, whatever his 'delight in developing the training of ministers on academic lines'.[32] Those are his daughter's words, and she perfectly expresses the high ideal that a man who bears God's gift to His Church must be **competent**:' You are to here to graduate in Christ and his ministry', he insisted. That is why 'The carpet slipper standard of appearance or of mind at prayers or at lectures aroused his cutting displeasure'.[33]

It is Forsyth the principal rather than Forsyth the pastor who has been most consciously remembered, and the image which has been mediated over the years has been almost perversely consistent: a visitor whom hostesses regarded with apprehension, if not disapproval;[34] a brilliant man, therefore distant, yet delightful company, especially in smoke-filled studies; a man whose writing were - it was a well know fact - teeth-breakingly incomprehensible, yet capable of a terrifying clarity; whose spoken words riveted, yet were seldom remembered; whose famous obscurity was staunchly denied by those to whom he regularly lectured. The consistently contradictory testimony piles up. A 'prince of the Holy Church', described by B L Manning, who knew all about that sort of thing and had probably been chatting to Sydney Cave, a man who 'made dogmatic theology attractive even to undergraduates, and revived the Puritan tradition of the incomparable dignity of the preached Word'.[35] Perhaps he did:

> 'I remember hearing several sermons by the great Congregationalist theologian, Dr P T Forsyth, but not a word that he said or read can I remember. The

worst of it is, the first thing I remember about his is a joke. A minister staying in our home when I was a boy said Forsyth was always cold and wore ever so many thick overcoats. The tale went, he added, that Forsyth in a dream went to a certain very warm place, and there shouted angrily, 'Shut the door, there's a draught'. Forsyth wouldn't have minded even a wicked jest like that, for though congregations might not have guessed it, he was always making jokes himself. Dr Garvie says he was once with him and with Dr Rendel Harris. The latter was poking fun at a 'correct conduct' column in a religious weekly. I think the problem was 'If a bachelor minister has a spinster hostess and comes down to breakfast without his white tie, should she tell him, and how?' Forsyth settled this in a second. He said, 'She should suggest that the first hymn for the service should be *'Blest be the tie that binds"*.[36]

Stories like that are invaluable. They encapsulate Forsyth: the man of his time, itching to get in a truly dreadful pun; the nice sense of professional etiquette and place, the camaraderie in high altitudes; the affectionate en-mything; and the recognition that this doubtless great preacher was now a principal, that is to say academic. We expect academics to be incomprehensible (that Englishman's synonym for brilliant), but there is more to it than that. Academics sparkle with the old Adam in a way that is not quite Christian, and Forsyth, whose criticisms were most telling when he was most taken with that he was criticising, sparkled with the old Adam at his lecture desk. How could good Christians be quite sure that he was not bringing his lecture notes into their pulpit? His fellow Principals Garvie and Selbie alike felt that Forsyth allowed 'his delight in verbal antithesis' to deflect 'the balance of true judgement', putting him at the mercy of his own clever

phrases, and limiting his influence.[37] A successor principal,
Huxtable, delighted in the story told by him by yet another
principal, Lovell Cocks, of how Forsyth opened a lecture after
the pious review columns had been hit by the latest facile
shocker from R J Campbell: 'He's done it again, gentlemen!
Froth, gentlemen; froth!! Champagne froth, I grant you; but
froth, gentlemen, all the same'.[38] And his students were
hooked, as the journalist Harold Murray recognised: 'I can
only remember him as a rather severe-looking man in a coat
with a heavy astrakhan collar, who talked over our heads but
hundreds of his students would like think of him with
affection'.[39]

We need to pause on that. There is at Dr William's Library a
short and artless typescript in recollection of 'Dr Forsyth'. It
is unsigned, though its author was at Hackney between 1905
and 1920, and he can probably be narrowed down to one of
four candidates. One suspects that his study and his church
were neither very large nor very small, which makes Forsyth's
influence the more telling on such a journeyman minister.

> 'I have not met anyone whose personality impressed
> me more - or so much. At one time he gave a course
> of lectures at New College, to the students of both
> colleges.[40] Usually there was a considerable amount
> of noise going on in the lecture room, and frequently
> some ragging, before the lectures began. It was usual
> for the lecturer to come in at the last moment. On the
> occasion of the Doctor's first lecture, the New College
> men came in in groups, noisily talking and joking, as
> usual. They did not at first notice Dr Forsyth was
> already sitting at the desk. When they did so, there
> was a sudden silence, which was most eloquent. I do
> not believe any other member of the staffs of either
> college would have produced such a result…

I think we all regarded him as a good deal of a saint.
I certainly did so, and I still believe that to be true.
Week-night services were times of real experience to
us and frequently of heart searching. We felt that he
came to us straight from the Presence of God.

But not only the services. In the lectures too, again
and again he led us to the heights and gave us the
vision of things that were almost unspeakable. I have
known times - many times - when we all trooped
from the lecture room in profound silence. We did
not want to talk: we wanted to get away and think.'[41]

But this was the Forsyth who was also a fixture at the Friday
night common-room concerts, pipe in mouth, in his easy chair
by the fire:

'I remember one occasion - it was during the New
Theological Controversy - when Wicks, taking part
in a melodramatic sketch exclaimed: "My hair will
turn white! And what is the use of white hair, if you
cannot be a popular preacher?" I can still hear the
Doctor's chuckle.'[42]

Sparked by the old Adam, of course, for R J Campbell's
fabulous hair, white in the City Temple's great white pulpit,
was one of the beautiful sights of London. It was New
Theology's plume.

It was on another Friday night that our memory-laner, bounding
downstairs, four or five at a time, cannoned into the Doctor who
had just come through the door, coffee cup in hand. 'It was an
awful moment for me, but he merely asked if a concert was
being held that night. He had mistaken the date.'

'One very fine thing about him was that he never - to my knowledge - came into the students' quarters uninvited. He trusted us, and we respected his trust.'

Such memories are beyond price. Now that residential colleges are both unfashionable and impractical, we need to work our way into their intensities and their convictions; the rags, the heights, the power of personality, the fine-honing of call:

'About his books. I question whether those who know him only through his books could ever really know him. It was a surprise to me when I first discovered that many people regarded his books as difficult. To me they have always been the most readable of theological books. The explanation doubtless is that I had learned, a little at least, to know the man. He took pains to make his thought plain to us students. Though probably our understanding may often have been **mis**-understanding!'

That last sentence is inexpressibly moving and revealing. True teachers need to know how they may be **mis**-read and **mis**-heard.

One of that student's fellow Friday-night raggers, for they clearly overlapped, would have been Sydney Cave. Cave was less likely than most to be bowled over by Forsyth. He was to the pulpit born. He was a nephew of Forsyth's predecessor as Principal of Hackney; he was a product of the City of London School's Classical Sixth. And it was as a sixth former that he first met Forsyth, when he called on him with view to entering the College.[43] Cave too became the complete Forsythian. 'May an old student of his add a little?', he wrote, a College Principal himself now, to the *Christian World* when the news of Forsyth's death had broken.

'For we, who were trained by him, believe that he was the greatest of all as a College Principal Much has been said of his obscurity. I have heard no lecturer more lucid and attractive. His treatment of Christine Doctrine had, by the University regulation, to be historical, but even the dreariest period of theology became luminous under his guidance.

... But learned and brilliant as were his lectures, we owed to him a still greater debt. He was not a facile pietist, nor I suppose, had he a 'soul naturally Christian', but he brought to us an unforgettable impression of the majesty of God's grace and its adequacy to every human soul. All his work for us was sacramental. It conveyed God, and although some of may express our faith in somewhat other words than his, we know that it is chiefly through him that we cannot remember our Lord and his redeeming work without something of his awe and adoration ... some of us know that he has been the greatest influence in our lives, and that his influence is one which time cannot undo.'[44]

Nearly thirty years later Cave, successor now to both Forsyth and his uncle, wrote in the *Congregational Quarterly* on the centenary of Forsyth's birth, quoting with a now veteran principal's practised eye what Forsyth had written of his Hackney men, one of whom had been Cave himself:

'Their most plastic year has been wasted.... They are without what a universal religion requires - a historical background, a cosmopolitan horizon, the atmosphere of serious culture for conscience or imagination, which lifts piety to faith. It is pitiably hard for them to buckle down to accurate subjects.'[45]

Those words need to be borne in mind as I introduce another of Forsyth's Hackney men, class of 1912. This one too became a principal: H F Lovell Cocks.[46] Lovell Cocks was much in demand for his mastery of elegiac reminiscence. So in 1977 who better to delivery in Hackney's buildings the closing down Commemoration Address of what was now known as New College. He recalled the Hackney of his youth with its fond discomforts (bedrooms facing north east; ice to be broken in the morning water-jugs; gas in the corridors, candles in the bedrooms, oil lamps in the studies, 'provided and maintained at our own charges'; and food which precipitated a grandly quelled protest - 'Gentlemen, representations have been made to me that you are dissatisfied with the food provided in this College. Please do remember that this is not a hotel, it is a charitable institution. That will be all'. Then he surveyed the staff: Scullard, Andrews, Davies, Garvie too, each of whom years back he had mimicked with loving accuracy at the Friday-night concerts:[47]

'But for me and my contemporaries … the supreme experience was our contact with Peter Taylor Forsyth … at the peak of his powers … We … were proud of our Principal and pitied men who studied in other colleges under teachers who, however competent in their way, were not to be compared … We used to meet ministers … who asked us whether we could really understand Forsyth. 'Understand him?', we replied, 'of course we understand him!' And we did! Thank God, we did! He was a brilliant and exciting teacher. His lectures were luminous. But for all the power and profundity of his formal teaching, what is impressed most deeply on my memory is our Wednesday evening sessions, when, after prayer, Forsyth would prop a few scraps of paper against the big pulpit bible, and for forty-five minutes would

> think aloud on a theme … 'winding into his subject
> like a serpent', as Goldsmith said of Burke, opening
> to us new vistas of truth and setting the whole within
> the text of the Gospel … it is to Peter Forsyth that I
> owe my theological soul and my footing in the
> Gospel.'[48]

Now contrast that reality with its accompaniment as each
Sunday the Hackney students, frock-coated, top-hatted, starch
white-collared, walked down long hot, dusty, country lanes to
'serve the mission stations of the old Village Itinerarancy
Society'. Lovell Cocks was one of them, prayed over, as he
recalled, by a village deacon after service one summer Sunday
in 1914: 'O lord, this 'ere Kaiser's a-breathin out threatenins
and slaughter. **You** deal with 'im Lord. Just you **deal** with
'im!' And then, by who knows what association of ideas, he
went on: 'And this young man who's been preachin' here
today, O Lord, **save** him!'[49]

Those are the polarities, which Forsyth, postman's son turned
professional, pastor turned principal, played into a
congregational, catholic unity.

In 1922 there were fifty-eight men listed as ministers in good
standing with the Congregational Union of England and Wales
who had been at Hackney during Forsyth's principalship.
That is almost as many as the *Year Book's* list of 'Ministers
Deceased and Reported Since Last Issue', but it is not a large
number, even if allowance is made for those who had died, or
moved overseas, or left the Congregational ministry for other
churches or other occupations. There is some evidence that
numbers were increasing, or at least consolidating, and that
the Great War had less effect on them than might be thought.
Nonetheless the figures clinch the case for the merger with
New College which Forsyth had always favoured and which

happened in 1924. Not too much can be made of the emergence of a Forsythian type of Hackney man and certainly no party-line appears, though the range of pastoral experience to which Forsyth's men were called is striking, and so is the cumulative evidence of solid worth. Here were men, some of whom flashed and sparkled, who adorned their calling. They all add weight to the enjoyable reminiscence.[50]

There is, however, a range of evidence, which applies to Forsyth more than to most principals: the quality mediated through what he wrote. What he wrote inevitable remains our most direct surviving evidence and since it was to a marked degree what he said it cannot be ignored. Moreover, his lesser works can be just as speaking as his best; and he was a marvellous recyclist - the same things, only different, pop up repeatedly.

The evidence begins long before he became a principal because from the first he brought to his public and pastoral ministry precisely that 'cosmopolitan horizon', that 'atmosphere of serious culture of conscience or imagination', which he later feared was so lacking in his Hackney men. And he brought it above all to those key congregational components, the young, the female, and the working.

Some of the evidence is fugitive - the postcard to a bereaved church member, the letter to a young woman applying for church membership; but that postcard and letter were kept by their recipients.[51] His attitude to women, the young, and to culture, gleams through his *Pulpit Parables for Young Hearers* (1886) and *Religion in Recent Art* (1889) in which he transmutes his clearly recognisable sources into pure, if evolving, Forsyth. It is academic larceny of the best kind. There is, incidentally, in both of them a poignant clue to a later Forsyth, which may help to explain why no party-line can be

easily discerned in his Hackney men. His collaborator in
Pulpit Parables, who also read the text of *Religion in Recent
Art*, was J A Hamilton whom Forsyth had come to know in his
Shipley days when they were neighbours in Saltaire.[52]
Hamilton's publications were limited to children's stories and
books for young people. Forsyth was good at that: Hamilton
was better. Years later, when Campbell wrote *New Theology*,
to whom did he turn to read his text? J A Hamilton.[53]
Liberalism was a more consistent part of Forsyth's being than
has been fashionable to recognise; and his excoriating
criticism of liberalism was part of that closeness.[54] Campbell's
presence at the unveiling of Hackney's plaque to Forsyth was
testimony to that.

To young culture Forsyth added the civic sense, the historical
sense, and the consequent high sense of the Church, which he
saw as integral to each minister's equipment. His experience
at Cambridge had convinced him of that. There he found both
incomparable stimulus and an exclusion, which no Scotsman
could tolerate. It exploded into two sets of lectures, *The
Charter of the Church* (1896) and *Rome, Reform and Reaction*
(1899). Here were imperial manifestos for an Edwardian Free
Churchman. The Congregational Colleges of the new century
needed such a man.

And such a man was bound to compromised. As Gladstone
had skimmed along the edges of intellectual, and therefore
moral, catastrophe in politics, and Lloyd George more so later,
so did Forsyth in theology. How else do we explain *The
Christian Ethic of War* (1916), that un-put-downable book
which we wish he had not written, yet which only he could
have written, repetitive, flawed, bad-tempered, celebrating all
its author's powers and his limitations, directed, or rather
misdirected, at what he was closest to understanding, the
pacifism of old friends and one of his Cambridge

successors?[55] By contrast, for the inspired communicator at his best, we turn to *The Work of Christ* (1910), his method gleaming out of those lectures to Campbell Morgan's young admirers summer camping at Mundesley which Sydney Cave remembered as Forsyth at his most compelling.[56] And as summation, not least because of its sequence of perorations and his personal apologia as preacher and teacher, there must be *Positive Preaching and the Modern Mind* (1907).

The **modern** mind? Surely Forsyth is the Edmund Burke of British theology. Burke saw himself as a working politician. Forsyth was a working minister. That is not how most others have seen either, but both practised what they preached. To reach into Burke's logic, therefore, one has first to recognise his rhetoric, his workaday tools, and their assumptions, the pictures that he quite consciously sought to create in the minds of his readers or hearers. That is integral to an understanding of Forsyth's logic, too. The rhetoric of both men has impressed itself on select generations of Liberals and Conservatives alike, even though both are placed on the conservative side. Both too were dinner-gongs. Though Burke's speeches to the Commons are universally admired as models of the art, members unaccountably remembered that it was dinnertime whenever he rose to speak. Was it like that when Forsyth's name appeared on posters, or his person on platforms? Like Burke, Forsyth wrote on aesthetics before he turned to his life's work; indeed he took Burke as epigraph in *Religion in Recent Art*.[57] And Burke's style surfaces with Ruskin's, its tones working in with the more obvious accents of contemporary theologian, rapidly assimilated, transformed but never repudiated, informing the language of a man who has manifestly experienced what he teaches, and what he criticises, and what his hearers are or have been.

Here is a man properly qualified by experience to teach those aspects of the individual, and society, and the Church, with which the preacher is duty bound to engage both as minister and citizen. Here is also a man who can put doubt, liberalism and its limits, art and music, illness and bereavement, in their place, as all round human beings should but as few are able, because his own life has ranged through each and he can put what he has found into words - rhetoric properly understood. They are the words moreover of a man who has been what most of his students have been and what one and another of them might become, of godly but poor stock, church member, minister, chairman of the County Union, and of the Congregational Union itself. And they are also the words of a man who powerfully mediates an alternative Congregationalism, in tension with, parallel to, and yet also entwined with the liberalising Congregationalism, which was more generally representative of his contemporaries. It was here that his role as teacher was most powerful. Forsyth is formative in helping us to understand the development of the Congregational temper which made possible not just the New Genevans of the 1930s and 1940s but also the United Reformed Church of the 1970s.

The measure of his contribution to this process can be grasped by looking at the signatories of the Call to Reformation addressed in 1939 'To the Ministers of Christ's Holy Gospel in the Churches of the Congregational Order'. They were B L Manning (the solitary layman), J D Jones and John Short (past and present ministers of famous churches), and five college principals, E J Price of Bradford, Micklem of Mansfield, Whale of Cheshunt, Lovell Cocks of the Scottish Congregational College, and Cave of New College, London. Two of them, Lovell Cocks and Sydney Cave, had been Forsyth's pupils, and Cave was now occupying Forsyth's study. Three of them, Manning, Whale and Cave, had overlapped as members of Emmanuel Church, Cambridge, where Forsyth's ministry had long worked itself into myth and of which Forsyth remained a member until 1917 (and J D Jones, as it happens, had been considered by Emmanuel in 1894, although it was Forsyth who accepted the call, and he preached the sermon at Forsyth's funeral). In the previous year one of them, Whale, had contributed a foreword to Forsyth's reissued *Work of Christ*, one copy of which was distributed by the Coward Trust to each student in the English Congregational Colleges.[58] Too much should not be read into this. In a smallish denomination such inter-layerings are as inevitable as they may be coincidental, and the differences between Forsyth and the Call's signatories were numerous. Nonetheless the congruencies are inescapable.

And to sum up? Two points might be made. The first is that, whatever his traceable influence, it should not be presumed that Forsyth would himself have been a New Genevan or an architect of the United Reformed Church, though it might be felt that any criticisms of his would have been the sharper for his understanding. The second is to resurrect that favourite device, which is to ask whether Forsyth was a Barthian before Barth. That question presupposes the answer 'no', prefaced by a moment of judicious doubt. The question, however, cannot be so easily dismissed. The **disposition** was certainly there, and it was inevitably transmitted.[59] In 1947 as Anglican clergyman, F W Camfield, edited a tribute to Karl Barth, *Reformation Old and New*. The volume had three Congregational contributors. Two of them, Daniel Jenkins and W A Whitehouse, were notable young New Genevans. The third was Lovell Cocks.[60] Camfield himself had been a Congregational minister for nearly thirty years before he conformed to the Established Church, and ten years earlier he had exemplified the exhilarating polarity within his old denomination when his paper "The Barthian Challenge" followed Thomas Wigley's "Faith, Fact, and Knowledge" at the Oxford Congregational Theological conference. Wigley was liberalism's standard bearer, leader of the "Blackheathens". Camfield was quite the opposite. One Oxford participant, who found neither sympathetic, noted that they were 'the solitary representatives of their position.... their singleness in the Conference ... perhaps proportionate to their numerical support in the denomination'.[61] Even so Wigley and Camfield were ministers of apparently thriving churches. They were also near contemporaries. Wigley was a Cheshunt man, for whom Campbell Morgan had evidently not been a formative influence. Camfield was a Hackney man, whose first pastorate was at West Hampstead Congregational Church, next door to his old College, and his old College Principal.[62]

It is a question of **disposition**; but this brings to mind George Steiner's comments that "To ready Barth ... is ... to be in dialogue with a human presence of rare intensity".[63] So it also is when one reads Forsyth; and to be in dialogue is beyond all else in a truly class-room activity. Peter Taylor Forsyth, minister of Word and Sacrament, was in his element when pastor as principal.

Notes:

1   This paper should be read in tandem with C Binfield, *P T Forsyth as Congregational Minister* in Trevor Hart (ed*) Justice the True and Only Mercy: essays on the life and theology of Peter Taylor Forsyth,* T & T Clark, Edinburgh 1995, pp 168-196, which is itself an enlargement of C Binfield*, Principal when Pastor: P T Forsyth 1876-1901,* in W J Shiels and Diana Woods (eds*) The Ministry: Clerical and Lay, Studies in Church History 26,* Basil Blackwell, Oxford, 1989, pp 397-414.

2   *Congregational Year Book* 1922 pp 104-5.

3   Herbert Thomas Andrews (1864-1928) 'had the unique distinction of being the only elementary schoolboy who ever won a classical scholarship at Magdalen College' (*Congregational Year Book 1929 p 208).* He taught New Testament and Exegesis at Hackney and New Colleges from 1903, moving from Cheshunt where he had professed Church History and Historical Theology. He married, as his second wife, Jessie Forsyth, the only child of P T Forsyth.

4   See K D Brown, *A Social History of the Nonconformist Ministry in England and Wales 1880-1930,* OUP, 1988.

5   Alexander Mackennal (1835-1904), minister at Bowdon Downs 1877-1904; Robert William Dale (1829-95), minister at Carrs Lane, Birmingham 1854-95; John Brown (1830-1922), minister at Bunyan Meeting, Bedford 1864-1903; Henry Allon (1818-92), minister at Princes Street, Norwich, 1866-1910. All are to be found in A Peel*, The Congregational Two Hundred 1530-1948,* Independent Press, London, 1948.

6   Henry Robert Reynolds (1825-96), minister at East Parade, Leeds, 1849-69; president, Cheshunt College, 1860-94. Ibid, pp 203-4.

7   Joseph Parker (1830-1902), minister at Cavendish Street, Manchester 1849-69; John Brown Paton (1830-1911), minister at Wicker, Sheffield 1854-63; principal, Nottingham Congregational Institute (later Paton College), 1863-98. Ibid, pp 208-210.

8   John Daniel Jones (1856-1942), minister at Richmond Hill, Bournemouth 1898-1937. In the 1890s, while at Newland, Lincoln, he lectured in New Testament and Church History at the Nottingham Institute; William Boothby Selbie (1862-1944), minister at Emmanuel, Cambridge 1902-09, was principal of Mansfield College, Oxford, 1909-32 (Ibid, pp 271, 280-1); for George Campbell Morgan (1863-1945) and the building of Cheshunt College, Cambridge, see C Binfield, *Holy Murder at Cheshunt College: The formation of an English Architect: R P Morley Horder 1870-1944* in *Journal of the United Reformed History Society* vol 4 no.2, May 1988 pp 103-134. Campbell Morgan was president of Cheshunt 1911-14 while continuing to minister at Westminster Chapel 1904-17, 1932-43.

9   Harry Francis Lovell Cocks (1894-1983) ministered at Headingley Hill, Leeds (1927-32) and was principal of Scottish Congregational College 1937-41 and Western College, Bristol, 1941-60; William John Fairchild Huxtable (1912-90) was minister at Palmers Green 1942-53, and principal of New College, London 1953-64; John Seldon Whale (1986-1997) ministered at Bowdon Downs 1925-29

and was president of Cheshunt College, Cambridge, 1933-1944.

[10] Lovell Cocks was the last surviving Hackney man to have experienced Forsyth in his prime but the *United Reformed Church Year Book* for 1981 listed three men, W J Bremner (d. 1988), R A Hopley (d.1984) and J W Thompson (d.1988) whose course began towards the end of Forsyth's principalship and they retired from pastoral work in 1960, 1965 and 1975 respectively. Robert Hopley certainly bore the marks of Forsythian ministry, but although the *Year Book* obituary states that he was at Hackney from 1919-1925 his *Reminiscences of Student Days* (in the possession of his son) make it clear that he entered New College, lodging in a hostel for Indian students and only later in residence at Hackney. His chief memories are of Garvie, and Forsyth is not mentioned in his reminiscences though he has frequently cropped up in Hopley's conversations and notes and his copy of J K Mozeley's *The Heart of the Gospel* has on its fly page: 'To Mr R A Hopley from E B Forsyth, June 1925'. I am indebted to the Revd Micah Hopley for this information.

[11] See Elaine Kaye, Mansfield College, *Oxford: Its Origin, History and Significance*, OUP, 1996, pp 61-6, 91-110 for Andrew Martin Fairbairn (1838-1912), principal of Airedale College, Bradford 1877-1886 and Mansfield College, Oxford, 1886-1909.

[12] *The Christian World*, 17th November 1921, p 4. I am indebted to Mr John Creasey for this reference.

[13] Ibid,, Alfred E Garvie (1861-1945) was principal of New College, London, 1907-22 and of Hackney and New Colleges, 1922-33.

[14] *The Addresses delivered at the Unveiling of the Tablet to the memory of Rev Peter Taylor Forsyth, MA, DD, May 11th 1922* (Sir) Alexander Glegg became Chairman of the Council of CUEW and of its General Purposes Committee. While one son, Grahame Robertson (b 1879) followed him in prominent Congregationalism, his younger son, Alexander Lindsay (b 1882), a linoleum manufacturer, followed more breezily evangelical paths as president or chairman of the National Sunday School Union, the Christian Endeavour Union, the Bible Testimony Fellowship, the Advent Testimony Movement, the Evangelical Union of South America and much else. This doughty philanthropist wrote pamphlets with decidedly unForsythian titles: *Life with a Capital L, Youth with a Capital Why*, and *Conquering the Capital I*. His golf handicap was 12. Thus *Who's Who*, 1948, p 1052.

[15] *The Addresses…* op cit, pp 5-10. Antagonism had flared between Campbell and Forsyth with the publication of Campbell's *The New Theology* (1907). There was a public truce in 1911. Alexander Hannay (1822-90) _was the Secretary of the Congregational Union 1870-90; Alexander Raleigh (1817-80), was minister of Hare Court, Canonbury, 1858-75, and Allen Street, Kensington, 1875-80; Thomas Binney (1798-1874) was minister of Kings Weigh House 1829-69; David Worthington Simon (1830-1909) was successively principal of Spring Hill College, Birmingham 1869-84, Congregational Theological Hall, Edinburgh 1884-93 and Yorkshire United Independent College, Bradford (1893-1907).

[16] Forsyth taught Apologetics, Dogmatics, and Homiletics.

[17] P T Forsyth, *The Principal of Authority*, Hodder & Stoughton, London, 1912, pp 369-70.

[18] Ibid, p 321.

19 W L Bradley, *P T Forsyth, the Man and His Work*, Independent Press, London, 1952 p 238.

20 Quoted in W B Glover, *Evangelical Nonconformists and Higher Criticism in the Nineteenth Century,* Independent Press, London, 1954 pp 241-2.

21 P T Forsyth, *The Church and the Sacraments* 2nd Edition, Independent Press, London, 1948, p 11.

22 P T Forsyth, *The Principal of Authority*, 2nd edition, Independent Press, London, 1952, p 283.

23 P T Forsyth, Introduction to J Monro Gibson, *The Inspiration and Authority of Holy Scripture* (1912),quoted in Glover, op cit,,p 138.

24 Jessie Forsyth Andrews, *Memoir of P T Forsyth* in *The Work of Christ*, 2nd edition, Independent Press, 1938, p xix.

25 *The Christian World,* 17th November 1921, p 3; A Mearns (ed) *London Congregational Directory and Church Guide*, 1889, p 85.

26 For the building of Hackney College see C Binfield, 'Hackneyed in Hampstead: The Growth of a College Building', *Journal of the Untied Reformed Church History Society* Vol 4, No 1, October 1987, pp 50-71: Westfield College, in Kidderpore Avenue, eventually had a chapel (in a singularly austere meeting-house style) and some other buildings by Morley Horder, architect of Cheshunt College: see Janet Sondheimer, *Castle Adamant in Hampstead: A history of Westfield College 1882-1982,*: Westfield College, London, 1983.

27 See the chapters *Richard Wagner and Pessimism* and *Wagner's Parsifal*, in P T Forsyth, *Religion in Recent Art: Being Expository Lectures on Rosetti, Burne Jones, Watts, Holman Hunt, and Wagner*; London and Manchester 1889 pp 234-61; Dr G F Nuttall draws my attention to "the considerable number of books on art and architecture" bearing Forsyth's name in what had become New College's library.

28 Alfred Cave (1847-1900), principal of Hackney College 1881-1900. *Congregational Year Book*, 1902 pp 161-4.

29 Jessie Forsyth Andrews op cit,, p xvii.

30 *Christian World*, 17th November 1921, p 4.

31 J H Thompson, *A History of the Coward Trust. The First Two Hundred and Fifty Years 1738-1988*, Journal of the United Reformed Church History Society Vol 6 (Supplement 1), May 1998, p 82.

32 Ibid, p 80; Jessie Forsyth Andrews op cit, p. xix.

33 Ibid.

34 It was remembered in a household belonging to another Congregational College that he wrought havoc on his eiderdown by pinning it down so that it would not fall off when he stirred restlessly in the night. Personal Information.

35 B L Manning, *This Latter House. The Life of Emmanuel Congregational Church, Cambridge 1874-1924*, W E Heffer, Cambridge, 1924, p 28.

36 H Murray, *Preachers Only*, Nottingham, nd, pp 29-30. The author Harold Murrray, was a journalist who was ministerially well-connected. James Rendel Harris (1852-1941), the Quaker scholar, was reared in a Congregational family with numerous Emmanuel connexions: he was loved by the younger generation

for his genuinely – and intentionally – funny power of prayer. Stories abound of how Forsyth felt the cold. Emmanuel's pulpit canopy is said to have been added to combat the draughts which he felt while preaching. Clearly he had an extraordinary metabolism. His successor at Cambridge recalled how two large vases of cold water were kept in the vestry, into which Forsyth would thrust his bare arms to cool himself down after a service. Personal information.

[37] Murray, op cit, p 30; W B Selbie, *Congregationalism*, London, 1927, p 175.

[38] W J F Huxtable, *P T Forsyth: 1838-1921, Journal of the United Reformed Church History Society*, Vol 4 No 1, October 1987. p 73. The son of one of Forsyth's students recalled Forsyth's comments to his father after sermon class: "That was psychology baptised: but it was infant baptism". A biting criticism and yet offering encouragement, as well as raising questions (as is the way of debating points) about Forsyth's view of baptism. (Conversation 12th May 1998 with Revd Alan Green).

[39] Murray, op cit,. p 30.

[40] New College was down hill from Hackney, at Swiss Cottage. A block of 1930s flats marks the site. Throughout Forsyth's time at Hackney the two colleges shared staff and frequently shared lectures; this practice was strengthened by wartime constraints after 1914. The union of the two colleges proceeded doggedly after Forsyth's death: the same principal (Garvie) from 1922; legal union, as Hackney and New, in 1924 (but Garvie was not going to move house); geographical union from 1934 when Sydney Cave, Alfred's nephew and Forsyth's pupil had become principal of what was now New College, though in Hackney's elegantly enlarged buildings.

[41] *Dr Forsyth*, typescript, Dr William's Library. I am indebted to Mr John Creasey for drawing my attention to this. It is undated and unsigned; Jessie Forsyth Andrews wrote on it in pencil 'Elliott?' Though there was no Elliott at Hackney 1905-10, H F Croft, Samuel Tonkin, F Wheatcroft, and W H Wigley all left in 1910 and the author is likeliest to be one of them.

[42] Wicks was Sidney Frederick Wicks, whose first pastorate was Robertson Street, Hastings (1910-11). He left pastoral charge for YMCA work in 1918 and ceased to be listed in *Congregational Year Book* after 1921.

[43] For Sydney Cave (1883-1953), president of Cheshunt College 1920-33 and principal of Hackney 1933-53, see *Congregational Year Book,* p 506.

[44] *Christian World*, 1st December 1921.

[45] P T Forsyth, *Reconstruction and Religion*, in F A Rees (ed) *Problems of Tomorrow: Social, Moral and Religious,* London, 1918, quoted in S Cave, Dr P T Forsyth: the Man and His Writings, *Congregational Quarterly*, Vol XXVI No 2, April 1948, p 111.

[46] See above note 9.

[47] H F Lovell Cocks, *The Address Delivered at Commemoration, 1977*, in *New College, London Annual Report 1976-1977*, pp 8-11. Herbert Hayes Scullard (1862-1926) taught Church History at Hackney and New 1907-26; and William Archibald Davies (1880-1966) taught Hebrew and Old Testament 1913-46.

[48] Cocks, Ibid,. pp 10-11.

[49] Ibid, p 9.

50 The 1922 figure does not of course include those ordained 1922-23 who entered Hackney in Forsyth's time. The 1915 *Year Book* lists 35 so the 'wastage' between 1902 and 1922 was slight. In 1905 Hackney listed 21 and New College 41; in 1910 the numbers were 32 and 45; in 1915, 30 and 52; in 1917 (the last *Year Book* listing), 24 and 23. Hackney unlike New was residential. Forsyth's men ranged from the unabashedly liberal Ernest Barson, 'of Penge' (left 1905) to the unswervingly Barthian F W S Camfield (left 1913). The former stayed, and flourished, in Congregationalism; the latter became an Anglican. See below note 61.

51 Thus his unpublished letter of 28th October 1900 to Edith Roper of Cambridge: ' My dear Edith / I am sorry you are so unwell. I wish I could have called on you on Thursday. But I am still a victim. I hope you will soon be about again. / It is a happiness to me to know that you wish to join the Church. I think that need not wait till you are able to see me. The deacons meet tomorrow and I should like to nominate you at the Church meeting on Wednesday 31. You have grown up among us and you know what this step means. In those circumstances the desire is sufficient qualification. I will see you of course before you are received but <u>if I do not hear</u> from you before tomorrow night I will add your name to the others who wish to be put forward for membership. And I trust that this will be a comfort to you in your illness and you will know that it is the Lord himself who has guided you to this step and moved your heart to take on you [?] his name. And so may he keep you always. / With my kind regards / Faithfully yours / P T Forsyth / I will speak of the other matter when I see you.'

52 John Arthur Hamilton (1845-1924), minister at Saltaire 1878-96, Penzance 1897-1924, see *Congregational Year Book,* 1925, p 147; see also P T Forsyth, *Religion in Recent Art*, 1889, p X.

53 R J Campbell, *The New Theology*, Chapman and Hall, London, 1907, p vii.

54 Before 1907 he was on excellent terms with Campbell, whom he had wished to follow him at Emmanuel; and those Liberal standard bearers, Baldwin Brown and Bernard Snell, both of Brixton had officiated at his first and second marriages respectively; it was Brown's recommendation which took Forsyth to his first pastorate in Shipley, and Forsyth's style has echoes of Brown's. The friendship between Snell and Forsyth perhaps dated from when they were both ministers in Manchester, 1886-88.

55 The pacifism of Henry Child Carter, minister at Emmanuel from 1910, and the formation of the Fellowship of Reconciliation, were particularly hard for him to take.

56 *Christian World*, 1st December 1921. It is conceivable that Cave, then out in Travancore, had missed the 1910 Expositor's Library edition. For Cave wrote in 1921 'I wish that his lectures to us on the Work of Christ had been published or even now could be'. Or is this an example of Forsyth's recycling? Forsyth regarded his Mundesley lectures as the highest vulgarisation; was what Cave had heard a year or so earlier more rigorously focused on the Hackney mind? Anyway, Cave's wish was eventually heard and the *Work of Christ* (or at least the Mundesley lectures with that title) was reissued in 1938 with a foreword by Cave's successor at Cheshunt, J S Whale. The cyclical rediscovery of Forsyth had begun.

[57] 'Art is man's nature'*: Religion in Recent Art*, 1889, title page.

[58] See above note 56, and J H Thompson, *Coward Trust*, p 88; for the Call see C Binfield, *A Learned and Gifted Protestant Minister: John Seldon Whale, 19th December 1896 – 17th September 1997*, in *Journal of the United Reformed Church History Society*, Vol 6 No 2, May 1998, p 125.

[59] Thus see J Thompson, '*Was Forsyth really a Barthian before Barth*? in T Hart(ed) *Justice the True and Only Mercy*, Edinburgh, 1996, pp 237-255 (and note *inter alia* Markus Barth, 'P T Forsyth: the Theologian for the Practical Man', *Congregational Quarterly*, Vol xvii no 4, October 1939, pp 437-42).

[60] R Tudur Jones, *Congregationalism in England 1662-1962*, Independent Press, London, 1962, pp 437-42.

[61] G F Nuttall, The Theological Conference II, *Congregational Quarterly* Vol XV, no 4. October 1937, p 503; the Conference is described pp 498-505. Wigley had been minister at Blackheath since 1927 and Camfield at Southernhay, Exeter, since 1934. John Thompson notes the phrase, 'Barthian before Barth', was apparently coined in the foreword to Camfield's *Revelation and the Holy Spirit: an essay in Barthian Theology*, 1933, p vii, (Thompson, op cit,, p 237).

[62] Camfield ministered at West Hampstead 1913-19; no manse in Parsifal Road for him however; he lived (not unsuitably perhaps) in Pandora Road. In 1948 he contributed 'Peter Taylor Forsyth' to *The Presbyter, A Journal of Reformed Churchmanship*, Vol 6 no 2, pp 3-10, in which he reaffirmed his personal debt to Forsyth. I am indebted to Revd Micah Hopley (who retains his father's marked copy of Camfield's paper) for this reference.

[63] G Steiner, 'To Speak of God,' *Times Literary Supplement*, 19th May 1995, p 7.

2.

P T Forsyth

The Preacher's Theologian

Alan Gaunt

P T Forsyth did not make me a preacher. My background in family and Church, coupled with the only subjects I seemed to have an aptitude for at school, with temperament, and with perhaps a measure of narcissism, all contributed to it. God, however, made me as I am, and, if it were not primarily the grace of God in Christ that decided the issue, I ought never to have been a preacher at all. That said, though, I have to add that P T Forsyth has had a lasting and profound effect on the sort of preacher I have been. If I were asked to account for that statement in a systematic way, I do not think that I could. I can only account for it in a preacher's way.

In *Preaching and the Modern Mind* Forsyth said of the preacher, 'He may be quite unfit to lecture in theology as a science...' So I am: but here is the paragraph in which he made that statement:

> It is not simply faith as a personal experience that is the burthen of the preacher, but faith as a knowledge, the inner objective content of faith, the thing in faith which always creates the experience of it; in a word, the person, will, and action of God in Christ. It is there, in the objective personal content of faith, and not in the subjective personal experience, that the authority of the preacher lies. His experience may make him impressive at times, but it is his faith that gives him permanent power. That power really lies not in the preacher but in his Gospel, in his theology. For the preacher it is most true that his theology is an essential, perhaps the essential, part of his religion. He may be quite unfit to lecture in theology as a science, but he is the less of a preacher, however fine a speaker, if he have not a theology at the root of his preaching, and its sap circulating in it. And if he is a pastor, producing his effect not by a few addresses but by a cumulative ministry, all this is still more true.[1]

That, I think, is the primary thing that Forsyth did for me. He made me aware that there must be an objective theology at the root of my preaching, that the sap of theology must circulate through it, and that this is all the more necessarily true in the context of pastoral ministry. Pastoral ministry begins, continues and ends with the proclamation of the theology. I am convinced that whatever natural sympathy or compassion I may have possessed, the real sympathy and compassion that I have been able to exercise in ministry has been rooted in, and sustained by, the theology of the Gospel which I have been given to proclaim. And in so far as people have been helped, inspired and even changed through my ministry, it is because of that theology, that inner objective quality of faith: the person, will and action of God in Christ. All this, of course, ought to be taken for granted, but I am not sure that it is.

That assertion about the basis of preaching and pastoral care has done three essential things for me. Firstly, in pointing me to this rock, Forsyth confirmed me in the faith that holds me. It was in *The Work of Christ* that he said,

> We do not preach impressions, or even our experience. These make but the vehicle, as it were. What we preach is something much more solid, more objective, with more stay in it; something that can suffice when our experience has ebbed until it seems to be as low as Christ's was in the great desertion and victory on the Cross. We want something that will stand by us when we cannot feel any more; we want a Cross we can cling to, not simply a subjective Cross.[2]

That is a preacher's way of putting it, and from personal experience one knows that it is that solidity and objectivity which make it possible to preach with real power, when the heart is aching and the preacher would rather run away, or might even be tempted to desecrate preaching, by resorting to personal animosity. That has always been the ground on which I have stood: the realisation that my faith could be knocked out of me by systematic brain-washing, or some depth of grief and despair I have never yet experienced, but I would still be held: because my faith is not in my faith, but in the crucified and resurrected Christ: 'the same yesterday, today and for ever.'

Secondly, in pointing me to this rock, Forsyth showed me where I could stand to view the landscape round, in such a way that disturbing new theologies, new interpretations or challenges to faith from within or without, instead of shaking, frightening or misleading, could be taken on, absorbed, dealt with, and used to deepen understanding; and other theologians, with big names, could be read with discernment and discretion without being swallowed whole. Also, with that, came the realisation that there are other teachers: teachers from other faiths, and from no faith, through whom the Spirit of God can speak to me, not only with challenge, but with comfort and reassurance too! Preaching in the City Temple, Forsyth once said, that the religion of Christ '...is absolute and final. Yet it does not damn other religions, but only the evil and the inadequacy in them.' It goes without saying, and Forsyth did not say it on that occasion, that it damns the evil and inadequacy in Christianity too. Of other religions, he did say,

> It interprets them, transfigures them, gives them to themselves. It judges them into their true place. It criticises them in the sense of appreciating them. It does not denounce them. It does not say that all religious founders outside him [Christ] are thieves and robbers. I do not believe Christ ever said that.[3]

It is in this light that I have come to say of myself: precisely because Christ, and who he is, is absolutely central to my life, I cannot hit other people over the head with my faith, and say 'you must believe what I believe.' I can only say, 'Here I stand' and proclaim the Gospel that has been given to me.

Thirdly, in pointing me to this rock, Forsyth liberated me: made me realise that I could launch out from it, into my own theological adventures, being imaginative and experimental, discovering for myself truths that I may not have known before; arriving at truths that seemed new, even at times heretical, to me, only to discover subsequently that they were ancient truths of faith, firmly grounded in the Scriptures.

It is true that other theologians could have taught me these things, and others have confirmed me in them, but it was from Forsyth that I learned them, although I was not aware of being taught; and it was Forsyth's teaching which, to quote Christopher Fry's Moses, in *The Firstborn*, 'slipped quietly in to become my nature.'[4] If I had never read another word of his, and never read *Positive Preaching*... again, having read that book at the right time in my life, having been so theologically uneducated and naive, the essence of it would have remained with me, as it has. There were things there which, if I knew before reading the book, I did not know that I knew; and if I did know, he put them into the right words, so that I could make them my own. Re-reading the book yet again some time ago, after an interval of some years, I realised how much which I had always thought of as my very own I had taken, if not word for word then thought for thought, from it.

There was a time, at the age of four, when I realised, not through intellect or piety, that Christ was central to my life. It was in the primary department at Sunday School, when a teacher said, 'God so loved the world that he gave His only begotten Son.' I realised then whose I was. About ten years later, probably in a rather maudlin sentimental way, I knew myself called to the ministry. I knew what I had to be. Then, another ten years, at the age of twenty four, after five years in college, and being already ordained, I discovered the theology of P T Forsyth in *Positive Preaching and the Modern Mind.* And from that, having known whose I was and what I was to be, I realised how I was to be. Like William Wordsworth:

> ...I made no vows, but vows
> Were made for me: bond unknown to me
> Was given, that I should be, else sinning greatly,
> A dedicated Spirit.[5]

And, like Wordsworth, I have walked on

> In thankful blessedness, which yet survives.[6]

A dedicated spirit, yes, but dedicated to what? To what Forsyth calls the great fundamental sacrament of the Word, of which he says,

> It is an act and a power; it is God's act of Redemption before it is man's message of it. It is an eternal, perennial act of God in Christ, repeating itself within every declaration of it. It was a work that redeemed us into the power of understanding its own word. It is an objective power, an historic act and perennial energy of the holy love of God in Christ; decisive for humanity in time and eternity; and altering for ever the whole relation of the soul to God, as it may be rejected or believed. The gift of God's grace was, and is, His work of the Gospel. And it is this act which is prolonged in the word of the preacher, and not merely proclaimed. The great, the fundamental sacrament is the Sacrament of the Word.[7]

Looked at from the mundane level of sermon after sermon, week after week, that is an astounding statement; but, if I did not believe it, I do not see how I could have gone on week after week, making sermon after sermon. For me, this belief remains central. In a sense it makes me what I am: and to the extent that I, as a preacher, am true to this, the Word is broken and shared, and nourishes Christ's people; and nourishes, too, people who have not known themselves as Christ's. I know that is true, because I have seen it: I have seen lives change, and spirits grow up in faith.

All this, of course, implies that preaching is not lecturing, and not entertainment. Forsyth says,

> ...only an age engrossed with impressions and careless about realities... could regard the preacher's prime work as that of converting the world, to the neglect of transforming the Church. It is only such an age that could think of preaching as something said with more or less force, instead of something done with more or less power... In true preaching, as in a true sacrament, more is done than said... No true preaching of the Cross can be other than the Cross in action. No true preaching of the Cross can be other than part of the action of the Cross. If a man preach let him preach as the Oracle of God, let him preach as Christ did, whose true pulpit was his Cross, whose Cross made his disciples apostles, in whose Cross God first preached to the world, whose preaching from the Cross has done for the world what all His discourses - even His discourses - failed to do...[8]

> A true sermon is a real deed. It puts the preacher's personality into an act. That is his chief form of Christian life and practice.[9]

That is not a fashionable position to adopt in these days, when an article in the *Free Church Chronicle* can be written and read without trembling, which suggests that in the Church of the future there may be no preaching at all; in these days of ministers' profiles and CVs; when ministers are interviewed, as though by employees, with a view to being employed, and justifying their pay! But if we are not, first and foremost, servants of the Word, why are we in this ministry at all, when there are so many worthy occupations, so many ways of serving our fellow human beings and fulfilling our Christian commitment?

But here I stand, believing still, as Forsyth declares:

> The preacher's word, when he preaches the Gospel and not only delivers a sermon, is an effective deed, charged with blessing or judgement... And it is known to be real by the insight of faith, however many counterfeits there are, with no insight but only zeal, and sometimes with nothing but stir.[10]

The Word made flesh comes first; and our grasp of the Word, or the Word's grasp on us, is not dependent ultimately on the Bible. It was largely through the Bible and its stories that I was nurtured into faith; and I am grateful that it never occurred to me, at any time in my life, that the Bible had to be swallowed, gulped down, as literal truth, or that, if anyone had the effrontery to suggest that Adam and Eve were not really the first man and woman, the truth of the whole Bible was being undermined. Whatever our understanding of the way the Bible was given to us, whatever theory of inspiration we may have, I think I always knew that the Bible is not the Word. Yet, from my earliest memories of hearing Bible stories and fairy stories, I never recall a time when I was not aware that the Bible stories had an extra dimension.

Forsyth confirmed this for me, in his assertion that the Bible is not the Word, but is itself preaching: God being made known to humanity in human ways, through human beings. It was ever thus, and this is what the Bible itself confirms, that God has never been revealed, except through human beings. Even if we hold a natural theology, and find God in nature, it is we human beings who find God there, and the God we find there is the God we are looking for. Forsyth said,

> We do not treat a preacher fairly when we judge him by statements, logic, anecdotes, or phrases. We must judge him by his positive and effective message. The preacher claims to be thus understood... He asks that we will give much more attention to his message than to his methods. And if his methods eclipse his message he feels, or ought to feel, that he has failed. He has preached himself. His idiosyncrasy has stepped in front of his Gospel. Well, what the preacher claims from the public in this way, the Bible claims from the preacher. Measure it by its message, not its phrase, its style, its incidents, episodes, views, or faults.[11]

This is so liberating! It relieves us of the tremendous burden of believing that a horror story here, a psalmist's bitterness there, and what it seems Paul had to say about women somewhere else, have to be uncomfortably gulped down, like nasty medicine! The horror story, the psalmist's bitterness, and what seems like Paul's sexism, are intended to point us to something beyond themselves, even though sometimes they may inadvertently, or even wilfully, step in front of the Gospel of God's Holy Love, and the Word made flesh in Christ. How else would the Gospel have convinced us, for example, that slavery was an affront to God's Holy Love, as is the subjection and oppression of women? One day the Gospel may convince us absolutely of the evil of war.

The Bible is the preacher for preachers. It speaks to
them above all, and with a word and not a creed. It
makes believers into preachers or agents in
proportion as it lays hold of them. Its first congenial
appeal is not to the scientific theologian. It handles
his ideas, but it does not speak his methodical
language. St Paul, for instance, was no dogmatician
in the sense of Aquinas or Melanchthon. He was
comparatively careless about the correct form of his
belief, what could be called its orthodoxy (indeed he
was the great heretic of his day), and he was lost in
the experimental reality of it. He was the first of
Christian theologians only because he was the
greatest of Christian experimentalists. To express a
reality so unspeakable he strained language and
tortured ideas, which he enlisted from any quarter
where he could lay hands on them.[12]

So the Bible is a preacher to preachers, teaching them that the
communication of God's mercy,

is not formal but dynamic, not scientific but
sacramental. The theologian has charge of the Gospel
as truth, the preacher has it in his charge as grace.[13]

Yes, and what Paul did is what Forsyth did, and what we as
preachers are to do. My imagination is liberated here: not so
that I can take texts out of their context, to hang on them my
own thoughts or even my own fantasies. This, too, I learned
from P T Forsyth.

One of the great tasks of the preacher is to rescue the
Bible from the textual idea in the mind of the public,
from the Biblicist, atomist idea which reduces it to a
religious scrap book.[14]

This is why I have been committed to preach, always, not from texts but from passages; even, over a period of time, through whole books: cultivating, as Forsyth put it, 'more the free, large, and organic treatment of the Bible.' The Bible is great imaginative literature, and it is as such that it does its work! A snippet here and snippet there, a sentence or phrase recalled, may sometimes be of great encouragement, and may even have converting power; but Forsyth says,

> Bible preaching means leading people into the Bible
> and its higher powers. It is not leading them out of
> the Bible into subjectivities, fancies, quips or
> theories...[15]

Though every portion of the Bible is not great literature, if it were not, with its single parts, a body of great literature, it could not be worthy of the Gospel we find in it. For the community of faith, it is more than great literature, but it could not be that more if it were not great literature first. And so, responding to it,

> Let the preacher's suggestion teem by all means, as it
> will teem in the quickened vitality given to his
> personal resources by the Word of Life. Let the gift of
> his fancy be stirred up, as well as all his other gifts.[16]

That, for me, has been so exciting; and it is, of course, so dangerous too, which is why there must be safeguards:

> Let every suggestion keep its true place in the
> economy and proportion of faith. Let it wear the
> clear livery of the Gospel and conspire to lighten and
> magnify that! It is into the Bible world of the eternal
> redemption that the preacher must bring his people.
> This eternal world from which Christ came is

contemporary with every age. To every age it is
equally near, and it is equally authoritative for every
age, however modern... The only preaching which is
up to date, for every time, is the preaching of this
eternity... the eternal of holy love, grace and
redemption, the eternal and immutable morality of
saving grace for our indelible sin.

In connection with all this, he says, that 'the preacher is the
organ of the only real and final authority for mankind.'[17]

Hubert Cunliffe-Jones wrote of Forsyth's theology, that 'its
intellectual construction, built on moral passion, though
stimulating, and a warning against shallow theologies, does
not grapple with the intellectual problems which had emerged
by the 1960s.'[18] I am sure that is true, although some of the
intellectual problems of the 1960s may now be old hat, whilst
Forsyth's warning against shallow theologies is as pertinent as
it ever was. There are perhaps even greater intellectual, moral
and ethical problems to be grappled with now than most of us
ever dreamt of in the 1960s, and even greater need to avoid
shallow theologies; especially those shallow theologies which
would futilely attempt to shelter behind ancient certainties,
from all the exciting but highly dangerous possibilities of the
new millennium!

There are those who would suggest, or even insist, that the
Bible, and the Gospel it proclaims, are quite outmoded and of
no value whatsoever in the working out of the great issues that
we are faced with. The Canadian novelist, Robertson Davies,
in a lecture in the New York Metropolitan Museum of Art,
said, 'In our time, when religion and knowledge of the Bible
have sunk into eclipse, and mythology where it exists at all has
become an incomprehensible tangle, the language which
painters once used with such eloquence is almost forgotten.

Do I regret it? Yes, I do, because faith and mythology summed up in themselves vast wisdom which we neglect at our peril. The Bible, which has now sunk to the level of a book of admonition and law in the hands of people who profess to take it literally, remains, perhaps, the greatest compendium of history, philosophy, and fruitful reflection available to us.'[19]

I do not think that P T Forsyth would be too distressed by Cunliffe-Jones' summary, but he would be concerned by the truth of what Robertson Davies was saying. More than ever, I think, he would have been insisting that the Bible is contemporary with every age: and not only because it is a compendium of history, philosophy and fruitful reflection, but because it is the preacher's charter, and the preacher is still, however unfashionably, 'the organ of the only real and final authority' for the human race.

We are, of course, up against it as we approach the new millennium. When so much is happening around us and to us, in a world which is changing so rapidly, the whole notion of preaching at all, to mere handfuls of people, with the Bible as our charter, must seem completely futile to those who do not believe in it. Yet, here we stand. Here I stand, anyway, and can do no other; still claimed for this futile exercise: the responsibility laid on me, not chosen by me. If it is futile, then it must be as the Cross of Christ was futile!

Obviously, our preaching must be touched and its meaning changed, transposed, into the key of the times. I know what Forsyth meant when he suggested, somewhere, that the preacher should read the newspaper standing up. He is more and more right about that. In a very real sense there is less and less of human reality in the newspapers; and it remains true that all of human reality is in the Bible. We should still, metaphorically at least, read the newspapers standing up. I listen to the Today programme shaving. Forsyth did not mean that we should keep ourselves ignorant of the great issues of our time. As preachers, few of us can be experts in computer science or genetics, but simply to go on preaching as though enormously exciting and highly dangerous changes were not happening would be criminally naive. Yet, the great need at such times, when so many things are happening around us and to us, must be a message, which is searchingly inward, coming with moral authority.

Forsyth said,

> The law of being is a moral law. The nature of reality is not only experience, as the modern drift of thought teaches, but it is moral experience. It is will's action. It is decision.[20]

What could be more necessary in times when so much is happening around us and to us, over which we have no control, but that we should rediscover our own moral freedom.

> I am a sinful man. My new ideal does as much to oppress me as to exalt me, and often much more. The more it teaches me to see, the less I am able to do. The more it smiles on me as my ideal, the less it seems as if it could ever become mine. It is lovely, but it has no arms. It does not grasp, it does not save. O wretched man! How shall my ideal become my destiny, and my vision my goal? How can my sinful self become my true free moral self? I want a power to give me not vision nor truth nor conviction alone, but myself... I want relief from myself. I must be redeemed from myself into the moral freedom I have now learned to crave.

He quotes Tennyson:

> O for a man to arise in me
> That the man I am may cease to be.[21]

Iris Murdoch puts it rather differently, in the thoughts of John Ducane, in her novel, *The Nice and the Good*. Dangerously trapped by the tide in a cave, 'He thought, if I ever get out of here I will be no man's judge. Nothing is worth doing except to kill the little rat, not to judge, not to be superior, not to exercise power, not to seek, seek, seek. To love and to reconcile and to forgive, only this matters. All power is sin and all law is frailty. Love is the only justice. Forgiveness, reconciliation, not law. To kill the little rat.'[22] Later in the novel, in the course of investigating the death of a civil service colleague, Ducane finds himself in a cellar where his colleague had practised black magic. And there he realises, 'Perhaps there were spirits, but they were little things. The great evil, the dreadful evil, that which made war and slavery and all man's inhumanity to man lay in the cool self-justifying ruthless selfishness of quite ordinary people, such as Biranne and himself.'[22]

Hell is not other people; hell is self! P T Forsyth speaks for me when he says, 'I am a sinful man!' I could certainly wish that it were true in my daily life, that a man would arise in me, so that the man I am may cease to be. And yet grace is at work! We preachers have a tremendous advantage, having to give so much of our time and attention to the Scriptures, and the proclamation of the Gospel! I realise that even if my preaching were never to have any effect on anybody else at all, it has its effect on me! Whatever is true of my daily life, I know that, in preaching, there is a man who rises in me, so that the man I am does cease to be! Others have experienced it too: that saying of things you never knew you had to say, that you can hardly believe you have said. You cannot see where they have come from. If you had no copy of them or if you lost the copy, you would never be able to work them out again. Yet those words, which are not your own, are more your own than anything else you have ever said.

It is in this sense that Forsyth deliberately misquotes, Coleridge's *Ancient Mariner*:

> He is the first that ever burst
> Into that silent sea.[23]

Of course, every creative artist has experienced this. It is not confined to preachers, and it may be open to discussion as to whether, in every case, the experience is the fruit of the Holy Spirit, or whether the creative imagination is a purely psychological phenomenon. Though how else could the Spirit of God speak to us, except through the human mind? Forsyth says, so far as preaching is concerned,

> When God comes to us He brings more than a mere extension of our previous horizon, a supplement to nature, or a development of it. It is not a mere enrichment of our previous mentality... It is not education. It is revelation. It is not giving effect to our native power, and enlarging us to the destined fullness of our hidden resource... It is a fresh spontaneity of His, a new creation, a free gift.[24]

Through preaching, doctrines I never knew existed became my own, and, because I came upon them, as though the first that ever burst into that silent sea, they became, and have remained, more my own than anything I might ever have received at second hand! As Forsyth says, we are to be original in the sense that our truth is our own, but not in the sense that it has been no one else's.

There is, however, more to be said. 'Practice what you preach' may be an obvious maxim, but if a preacher can live up to his or her preaching, he or she is not worth listening to, because we preach, not ourselves, but Christ. Having said that, being under the authority of Christ, we find, as Forsyth puts it, that his is the authority 'that gives us to ourselves, and puts us in possession of our moral freedom.'[25] Yes, I am being given to myself. I am, as it were, seeing myself in the mirror of Christ; myself as I really am, and there I am being introduced, as it were, to that man who is arising in me, so that the man I am may cease to be. I make no claims as to my own virtue. I am conscious of too many weaknesses of the flesh; of emotional immaturity, self-centred sensitivity, unholy dissatisfaction, and unhelpful volatility; and yet I am also aware of grace at work, and of attitudes that have crept quietly in to become my nature. In spite of the man that I am, I am being set free towards true obedience, the obedience of love to love, by the grace of Christ.

I always remember what Forysth says:

> Your faith is faith in him as acting, rousing your faith, creating it, and not merely receiving it. In your faith you are more conscious and sure of Him than you are of your faith. For your faith, you well know, may fail Him, but you know still better that he will not fail your faith. And you are more conscious and sure of Him, as the source and cause of your experience, than you are of the experience itself…[26]

So preaching is central: not only because of what it does for me, but because it does the same for those who are willing and able to hear it. It brings Christ to them, as the source and goal of their faith and the ground of their experience; it introduces them, in the mirror of Christ, to the woman and the man who rises up in them, so that the woman or man that they are may cease to be! It gives them to themselves. In this, the preacher is responsible to them; but the preacher's prior responsibility, for their sake, is to Christ.

> The preacher reflects the faith of the great true Church, but neither the faith nor the view of those around him. He is not giving expression to the average opinion of his congregation, or his denomination.[27]

We are not crowd pleasers; we are not entertainers; we are not employees, indeed, with our employers' demands to meet: we are servants of the imperious Gospel of Christ, and; our preaching is, Forsyth says,

> …the chief part of our evangelical ritual, the part which gives the law to all worship, since the message is what stirs worship and makes it possible. Our chief praise is thanksgiving for the Gospel. And our prayer is Christian only in the name of Gospel. Preaching is 'the organised Halleujah of an ordered community.'[28]

This is a very high doctrine of preaching, hardly believed in, I think, today. Was it ever? Forsyth spoke at some length about the triviality, uncertainty and complacency from which we suffer. I think, perhaps, of that trinity, that triviality is the Father, uncertainty the Son, and complacency the unholy Spirit. The two proceed from the one. 'There may be evil spirits,' as Iris Murdoch's Ducane thought, but there is no worse enemy to faith, hope and love than triviality.

Forsyth was aware of it in 1907, although he knew nothing about the mass media: about broadcasting's tremendous power for good and its capacity for trivial escapism, not to mention computer games and the inter-net.

I am afraid that, for the general public, religion has become associated with the small and negligible side of the soul. Nowhere has mediocrity its chance as it has in religion. Nowhere has the gossipy side of life such scope. Nowhere has quackery of every kind such a field and such a harvest... When Paul, the persecutor, goes the length he does in considering the weak brother it is a very great trophy of the moral victory of Christ, and it prescribes a principle of Christian ethic. But it is a total inversion of that ethic when the weakling sets up a claim, and demands as a right what the apostle gave as but a grace. That is overweening in the weak, and it is fatal for the Church.[29]

'Start where the people are,' we are told. How can we start where the people are, when our responsibility to them is to point them beyond themselves to Christ? Yet we do start where they are, when we stand before them, like Moses stretching his staff across the sea, saying in effect, 'Follow me or perish.' We start where they are, when we go ahead of them, like Jesus setting his face towards Jerusalem, leaving them to follow, if they will, troubled and perplexed. Forsyth spoke of consideration turning to pampering and making 'Christian pity the factory of moral paupers with the paupers' audacity.'

'Give us variety,' they say; 'Give us modern songs,' not really meaning 'modern' but simplistic; and if there must be sermons, make them short.

Or, on the other hand, the Church's worship, which should gather and greaten its soul, is sacrificed to its work. You have bustle all the week and baldness all the Sunday. You have energy everywhere except in the Spirit. The religious material is tugged and

> stretched to cover so much that it grows too thin for anything and parts into rents and rags. We are more anxious to cover ground than to secure it, to evangelise the world than to convert it. It is faithless impatience of the youngest, thinnest kind.[30]

> We must regain our sense of soul greatness, and our sense of its eternal price. If we measure things by the Cross, which is the price of salvation, and the touchstone of spiritual reality, God cares more that we should be great than that we should be happy... that we should trust and help than that we should enjoy![31]

Forsyth has always provided one great corrective to my own understanding and my preaching. I am always tempted to emphasise God's love in Christ. Why should that be a temptation? Surely God's love is what Christ is all about! But one is tempted to make love lovely! 'All you need is love'! Is that really true? Violet Elizabeth Bott would lisp: 'Love ith all! Love ith all!'[32] Love is all! But what love! The love of God, Forsyth taught me, is inseparable from the holiness of God! And the essence of the love of Christ was in his passion to honour God's holiness! God, the Father, did not say to Jesus, 'in order to honour my holiness, you are going to have to be crucified.' But Jesus said, by his whole life, 'no sacrifice is too great for the honouring of God's holiness,' and the price of holy love for him was the Cross.

So I came to realise that, far from pampering the sinner, the love of God was that holiness, which is more piercing and painful, and more demanding, to the sinful soul than mere punishing anger can ever be! Judgement and love are not separate. The damning judgement of holiness, leading to our free and loving submission to that holiness, is the only way to the realisation of mercy! Therefore the Cross is central, because the Cross is where that holiness is satisfied! Prompted initially by Forsyth, I can preach no sermon now without the Cross in it! Resurrection without the Cross is merely a sentimental fairy tale: a response to Danny Kaye's song; 'Give me a happy ending every time!'

As I draw towards a close, I recall that I said that Forsyth liberated me theologically. But to be theologically liberated is not necessarily to be theologically Liberal. I have always disliked theological labels, and the party, even the sectarian spirit, that tends to go with them, whether they are put forward as claims or applied as negative criticism: such as Catholic, Evangelical, Liberal or Conservative. Forsyth said,

> The first requisite for the ministry of a Church is a theology, a faith which knows what it is about, a positive faith, faith with not only an experience but a content, not glow only but grasp, and mass, and measure.[33] ...A positive theology is an evangelical theology.[34]

His understanding of Liberalism was that it made the modern mind the supreme court, and that nothing should survive in Christianity which was not congenial to it.[35] He believed (and has he been proved wrong?) that Liberalism tended to destroy positive belief, distinctive experience, and aggressive, that is evangelical, Christianity. A positive theology emphasises the primacy of the given. And what is given is the great revelation of God in the Cross, and the great gift of the Cross is the Holy Spirit, and the revelation is holiness, holiness working out as love.

> The primacy of the given is only another way of expressing the final authority of grace. The question of the hour, for all life, and not only for the religious,

is that of authority - the true effective authority. Where is it? At the last it is here. It is in God's eternal, perpetual act and gift of grace, met by the absolute obedience of our faith. Faith is absolute obedience to grace as absolute authority. Personal faith in the holy, gracious God of Christ's Cross is the one creative, authoritative, life-making, life-giving, life-shaping power of the moral soul.[36]

Something like that unfashionable stance, which can find itself the butt of confident intellectualism and fashionable conservatism, is what I hold. The faith that I proclaim has been given to me. I believe that it demands that I use my mind, and it liberates my imagination. My mind is exercised by the realising of it in my own understanding, and my imagination on the proclamation of it. I do not make it: it makes me! It is not an edifice that I build for myself, like some tower of Babel; not a message of some Sea of Faith elite, but, as Forsyth says,

We preach an historic message from God to humanity, and not a message of historic humanity to itself; a real rescue by a hand from heaven at our utmost moral need, and not a scaling of heaven by our intrinsic moral strength.[37]

Finally, in the saying of all this, I have to add that Forsyth has influenced my style. Every good practitioner develops his or her own style; and style in all creative enterprises arises out of passion. And passion is what I find on almost every page of Forsyth's writing that I have ever read. There is almost a stream of consciousness quality about it, though not in any surrealist sense. He is the arch-realist. His imagination is rooted and grounded in his positive Gospel. It is liberated by it, but also controlled by it. If his writings were described as fireworks in a fog, we probably ought to say, 'Thank God for the fireworks!' But once upon a time, a naive young man who had read barely any serious theology came to *Positive Preaching and the Modern Mind*, and found himself captured by it, carried along by it, excited by it: and not as though he were watching a firework display, with bangs and flashing lights, gone as soon as come; but catching on to ideas, which were to remain with him for years and to be developed and built on by him. As I said before, they were put quietly in to become my nature.

Most of Forsyth's books were unrevised lectures; but even as lectures they were more like preaching. How different would his style have been, had he set himself to revise his lectures into solid theological tomes? He wrote, I believe, in the tradition of Paul: starting from the firm ground of the given faith, and doing his theology at white heat. Passion speaks to passion, and passion expresses it again! So, Forsyth's own flow is not so much systematic, as a sort of sweeping logic, in the way that Coleridge's conversational monologues would meander here and there, so that his hearers would think he had lost his way, until he arrived back at his theme, and they could see that he had known where he was going all along. The logic of a flowing stream working its way round promontories, and over rocks and stones, coming into the deep, broad river, flowing inexorably on towards the great sea.

For that very reason, I find Forsyth not always convincing on the printed page. In what some consider to be his greatest book, *The Justification of God*, I find passages that were probably very impressive when heard, which in cold print seem exaggerated! Perhaps he even felt that himself, because at one point he says,

> These... may seem extreme views, couched in
> extravagant rhetoric which jars upon minds of a
> different type, training or experience, minds arrested
> on the sanity instead of the tragedy of the world.[38]

Yet even when I feel like one of those arrested minds, I know
that he is speaking truth for me; and, when all is said, I have
been taught, and I have grown; and I realise that, had I heard
his voice filled with his passion, speaking the words, my
whole moral being might have been joyfully carried along on
the excitingly turbulent stream.

His style might not suit modern congregations. Though, if he
were here, preaching as he preached then, we might be
surprised! He would be loath to limit himself to ten, fifteen or
twenty minutes! Modern congregations might have difficulty
concentrating, and following his longer sentences; and yet I
would like to believe that, in my own way, I have caught, or
been given, something of his passion, his freedom of
expression, his searching, and the quality of sudden
realisation! I would like to believe that those things will never
be lost to preaching, or from the pastoral ministry; and that
there will always be those in congregations, who listen, hear
and realise themselves found, lifted and carried, joyful, on the
stream of proclamation towards the great sea!

So, unsystematically, incompletely and inadequately, I try to
account for the way in which P T Forsyth has influenced the
sort of preacher and minister I have been and am. He has,
without doubt, been this preacher's theologian!

Notes:

1   P T Forsyth, *Positive Preaching and the Modern Mind*, Hodder and Stoughton, London, 1907, pp 201ff.

2   P T Forsyth, *The Work of Christ*, Independent Press, London, 1946, p 49.

3   P T Forsyth, 'The Fatherhood of Death' in *Missions in State and Church*, Hodder and Stoughton, London, 1908, pp 17f.

4   Christopher Fry, *The Firstborn,* 2nd edition, Oxford, 1946.

5   William Wordsworth, *The Prelude,* Book 4, lines 334-7.

6   Ibid, Book 4, line 338.

7   *Positive Preaching and the Modern Mind*, Hodder and Stoughton, London, 1907, pp 6f.

8   Ibid, pp 80 f.

9   Ibid, p 22.

10 Ibid, p 83.

11 Ibid, p 17.

12 Ibid, pp 17ff.

13 Ibid, p 19.

14 Ibid, p 28.

15 Ibid, p 29.

16 Ibid, pp 32ff.

17 Ibid, p 41.

18 H Cunliffe-Jones, *Christian Theology since 1600*, Duckworth, London, 1970.

19 Robertson Davies, 'Painting, Fiction and Faking' in *The Merry Heart*, Viking, 1996.

20 P T Forsyth, *Positive Preaching and the Modern Mind*, Hodder and Stoughton, London, 1907, footnote p 49.

21 Ibid, pp 52ff.

22 Iris Murdoch, *The Nice and the Good*, Chatto & Windus, 1968, World Books edition, 1969, pp 267ff and 290.

23 P T Forsyth, *Positive Preaching and the Modern Mind*, Hodder and Stoughton, London, 1907, p 54.

24 Ibid, p 54.

25 Ibid, p 64.

26 Ibid, p 68.

27 Ibid, pp 94ff.

28 Ibid, pp 94ff.

29 Ibid, pp 170ff.

30 Ibid, p 171.

31 Ibid, p 174.

32 Violet Elizabeth Bott is a friend of William Brown in various of Richmal Crompton's *William* stories.

33 P T Forsyth, *Positive Preaching and the Modern Mind*, Hodder and Stoughton, London, 1907, p 199.

34 Ibid, p 203.

35 Ibid, p 216.
36 Ibid, pp 213ff.
37 Ibid, p 218.
38 P T Forsyth, *The Justification of God*, originally published 1917, quoted from 1948 edition, p 150.

3.

Authority & Freedom
in the thought of
PT Forsyth

Kirk Summers

Authority:

What we usually mean by authority is this. It is another's certainty taken as the **sufficient** and **final** reason for some certainty of ours, in thought or action.[1]

Freedom:

In the strict Christian sense religious liberty means freedom before God, in God, no condemnation, freedom of intercourse with God, unhampered by guilt and the demands of a law which God has now made His own charge and become responsible for in Christ. It is the son-ship of faith, the being at home, not in society, but in the Father's house and kingdom.[2]

Authority

The Cross as the Locus of Authority

There is a network of radio stations throughout Canada that pride themselves on being - *'Your authoritative news voice'*. In the city of Toronto, where I went to theological college, the authoritative news voice remains CRFB. They are an all news radio station - with aggressive and opinionated talk show hosts and reporters checking in from all over the world - with 'news every hour on the half hour or when it happens' - alert, aware, confident - *Your authoritative news voice'*. Says who and by whose authority? Well, says the radio station of itself. But is it really *'Your authoritative News Voice?'*

For P T Forsyth, true, full and complete authority rested in the Cross of Jesus Christ, Son of God, crucified and risen. So deeply believing in and trusting this, Forsyth put pen to paper in such a way that led one commentator on his work to say: "It is impossible not to be stimulated and challenged by a personality of such intellectual energy and vision who glorified so wholeheartedly in the Cross of Christ.[3]

With this energy and conviction, this vigour and passion, knowing the answer before the question[4,] Forsyth asked - "Where are we to take our bearings and find our true north? Where shall we rest our lever?" [5] , knowing that the authority that we need is one that has to with life, and not merely with thought.[6] Certainly not first from the local radio station bent on the news, but in the Cross of Christ, "Forsyth centres in the cross, which is the place where, once and for all, something is not merely shown, but done by God".[7] To this belief he held fast throughout his life - the belief permeating everything he had to say and everything he had to do as a servant of Christ. In his text *The Cruciality of the Cross* Forsyth writes:

Our faith begins with the historic Christ … We begin in principle if not in method, with Christ the crucified'.[8] 'You do not understand Christ till you understand his Cross … It is only by understanding it that we escape from religion with no mind, and from religion which is all mind, from pietism with its lack of critical judgement, and from rationalism with its lack of everything else'.[9]

Beyond doubt or exception for P T Forsyth the whole of Christ's life and teachings must be interpreted by His death on the Cross. [10] Further, not only the whole of Christ's life and teachings, but indeed all that is life in every time must be interpreted by Christ's death on the Cross.

'You cannot sever the death of Christ from the life of Christ. When you think of the self emptying which brought Christ to earth, His whole life here was a living death. The death of Christ must be organic with His whole personal life and action. And that means not only His earthly life previous to the Cross, but His whole celestial life from the beginning, and to this hour, and to all eternity. The death of Christ is the central point of eternity as well as of human history. His own eternal life revolves around it. And we shall never be so good and holy at any point, even in eternity, that we shall not look into the Cross of Christ as the centre of all our hope in earth and heaven'.[11]

'If there is any authority over the natural man, it must be that of its Creator; and if the New Humanity has any authority over it, that authority must be found in the act of *its* creation, which act is the Cross of Christ.[12]

Sure that the God of the cross was the only one who has the power of all things,[13] time and again Forsyth expressed his desire to not 'sever the Cross from the whole moral fabric and movement of the universe and make it a theologian's affair'.[14] Rather, he presented all of creation understood in the light of redemption, contending 'that salvation is redemption in, and with, the created order, not out of it'.[15]

To Forsyth, Christ becomes for humanity the test of all else. He is, in this capacity, 'the evangelical principal of Authority. The seat of authority for the whole human conscience, and therefore, the whole of human history, especially in the future, is the Redeemer'.[16] Forsyth asks - 'Where is the ultimate authority for belief and life? If humanity's supreme need is for an authority,[17] then where is that authority to be found, where is to be seated?[18] The cross was to Forsyth the 'final scat of authority'.

> The track that I … pursue of course starts from a unique emphasis upon the Cross of Christ as the ultimate act of universal moral reality, and the final seat of authority in history, and the whether we regard it as an act condensed at a focal point of time, or the same act "functioning" by the Spirit in the Church's detailed experience'.[19]

For him 'the cross was the pivot on which the whole of Christianity turned'.[20] Where is authority to be found for faith and life? It is to be found in the Gospel of the redeeming and reconciling grace of God in Christ.[21] It is … the nature of the cross and the God there revealed which finally shapes Forsyth's conception of authority and the locus of its action'[22] a shaping that insists that Christ is not only the Omega, to whom our thought must finally come and in bondage to whom it must finally be made captive if it is to be truly free, but

Christ is also the Alpha, the beginning: and if we do not truly start with him, there is little chance that we will truly end with him.[23] For this Forsyth was insistent:

> '(W)e must begin with the end, taken as a gift. We must carry it back to the beginning. The purpose is not revealed in the process, but the process in the purpose ... The savage does not explain the saint, but the saint the savage. Creation does not explain Christianity, but Christianity creation ... For (God) is the end, He does not simply cherish it, and He does not simply declare it, and He does not simply produce it. He is our peace. We began in Him in whom we end. We die in our nest. The light of our first sight came from Him who is the object of our last faith. Our greatest destiny is as certain as He is absolute and holy. But we possess such a God, the Reality of reality, and the Act in all action, only in Christ, the historic Christ on His Cross. Though God is hinted freely in the world, we possess Him securely and finally only in Jesus Christ, the Redeemer, the Redeemer of the conscience, the Holy Redeemer'.[24]

> 'To live is Christ'.[25]

Behind all that was Forsyth and his thought - historical, present and visionary - all that was his action - preacher, pastor, principal - lies the theme of the Cross. 'Everything that is the proper concern of a Christian theology and living was examined by Forsyth and illuminated for him within the shadow of the cross of Christ, a cross that casts a shadow only because behind it is the bright light of the gracious God who has visited and redeemed his people'.[26]

Authority and Freedom

Behind that Cross is God. Forsyth, though humble in his humanity, viewed everything from God's heart and mind asking as it were: 'What did the cross mean to God?', and concluding in response that, 'Nothing can make us free which does not secure in advance the freedom of God'.[27] 'The permanent thing in Christianity must be that which gives its chief value to God'.[28]

> 'The first thing is not how I feel, but it is, How does God feel, and what has God said or done for my soul? When we get to real close quarters with that our feeling and response will look after itself'.[29]

An example of Forsyth's commitment to see things from the standpoint of God, and be in 'close quarters' in this way, is found in the ninth chapter of his 1917 book *The Justification of God*. This book is based upon a series of 'Lectures for War Time on a Christian Theology'. The ninth chapter is entitled, 'The Eternal Cruciality of the Cross for Destiny'. There these words are found:

> 'This misery of ages, I have said, vanishes from human thought or feeling, till some experience like war carried some idea of home. But there is a consciousness too, which it is all and always present. And in the full view of it He has spoken. As it might be thus: 'Do you stumble at the cost? It has Me more than you - Me who see and feel it all more than you who feel it but as atoms might. "Groaning all and moaning, none of it I lose". Yes, it has cost Me more than if the price paid were all Mankind. For it cost Me My only and beloved Son to justify My name of righteousness, and to realise the destiny on My

creature in holy love. And all mankind is not so great and dear as He is. Nor it its suffering the enormity in a moral world that His Cross is. I am no spectator of the course of things, and no speculator on the result. I spared My own Son. He carried the load that crushes you. It bowed Him into the ground. On the third day He rose with a new creation in His hand, and a regenerate world, and all things working for good to love and holy purpose in love. And what He did, I did. How did I do it? This you know not how, and could not, but you shall know hereafter. There are things the Father must keep in His own hand. Be still and know that I am God, whose mercy is as His majesty, and His innocence is chiefly in forgiving, and redeeming, and settling all souls in worship in the temple of a new heaven and earth full of holiness. In that day the anguish will be forgotten for joy that a New Humanity is born into the world'.[30]

The Cross therefore, and everything else, was all embraced by Forsyth in an understanding asserting that what happened at the time and place of Jesus' death, and resurrection, was first for God and by God, and that therefore the freedom of the human enterprise, however defined and expressed, is therefore not of self, but ultimately of God, and exists in purest form as freedom to do what God pleases.[31]

'Our chief concern is…. that of the ultimate truth in God's final revelation of Himself, where not only our last reality comes by our Liberator, but He is Himself our only freedom. If we have not the warrant of our religious freedom there, we have it nowhere. As churches we are entitled only to such freedom as that inspires, demands or implies'.[32]

To Forsyth, Christian freedom is always 'founded freedom',[33] freedom founded on the gospel of grace.[34] He wrote:

> 'Our theology is not a fixed system we must accept but a gracious experience which we must declare, not the mould but the image of the Church's spiritual life. It therefore advances with it, but always by the power which makes a man a Christian and the Church the Church, the power of our regeneration in the grace, cross, resurrection and Holy Spirit of Jesus Christ our Lord and Saviour. Rooted in that freedom we theologise as it compels, for it is the compulsion of a new freedom and not of a new scheme, of a final gospel and not a fixed law. We believe by the divine might of that founded liberty, and certainly do not believe as we please. We think most freely when our first concern is to be bound to our freedom in redemption'.[35]

> We exist for the freedom of a truth we have already found, and which began by finding us'.[36]

> 'Man's freedom has its origin in God's creative act and its life in His sustaining providence. God's autonomy has its ground in itself but it underlies and guarantees all ours'.[37]

> 'There are many ways in which freedom is given by being limited, but chief among them is that it is something that has to be given from without. Above all, it must be given by God, and that means by the Christ of the apostolic redemption'.[38]

What Forsyth saw was:

'that man's freedom and happiness are never more surely lost than when the ultimate perspective, the ultimate sovereign values, are sacrificed to them. The supreme object of existence for man is not man, but God: not man's kingdoms, but the Kingdoms of God.... Public freedom at last depends on spiritual freedom, and spiritual freedom is not in human nature but in redemption. This was to be his insistent, repetitive witness'.[39]

Therefore, the whole sense of authority resting in the hands and hearts of God rests there not in isolation from the realisation that 'man belongs to the cross much more than the cross belongs to man'.[40]

'We think of God, we entertain the idea of God, as we think anything else that is reasonable. But what everything turns on for the truth of the notion is the discovery of a right and a claim on it. It thinks us, it does not merely think itself in us. We are its humble creatures and not merely its proud organs'.[41]

'Forgiveness arose at no point in time. Grace was there even before creation. It abounded before sin did. The holiness, which makes sin sin, is one with the necessity to destroy sin in gracious love.'[42]

Griffith was right when he warned that with regard to Forsyth's 'approach to the question of authority ... that Forsyth will demand (of the reader) some fairly close thinking'.[43]

Forsyth saw that '(t)here is only one think greater than Liberty, and that is Authority',[44] and that humanity needs the latter before the former. And, though it be greater, it is clear throughout Forsyth's writing that neither authority nor freedom as he sees them exist in isolation from one another.

They are not alternatives. Neither are they some form of opposition: freedom it not to be achieved in freedom from authority. In truth is, in Forsyth's thought, authority and freedom are mutually involving. Further, for Forsyth, any notion of freedom which does not conceive it as arising from a divine action, and as therefore dependent upon a prior authority, is finally the denial of the gospel by divine grace. [45]

This being said, Forsyth had several notions of freedom and not all of them were always kept entirely separate from each other. He also had a tendency to use liberty and freedom as both interchangeable and distinct terms, stating on the same page in *Faith, Freedom & Future* - 'liberty means the liberty of each … to be free and liberty means freedom before and liberty meant freedom'.[46]

Almost as though knowing he was leading the reader into some despair, Forsyth rescued his perspective from the depths of misunderstanding with the following summation. It is to the summation that we must hold fast to realise what he was struggling to say about authority and freedom - all kinds of freedom, but first of all the freedom from God to be with God:

> '… a liberty conferred, not won: …. And for us, this must always be the case. We do not stand simply for civil liberty, but for civil liberty on a spiritual and evangelical base; not for a free state, but for a free state as the product of a free church of men whom Christ has set free. This is always the genius of our existence. Our secret is our inward and spiritual freedom. And the power in that secret, the power which as a historical fact produced civil liberty, was nothing else than the gospel of justifying and regenerating grace in Jesus Christ our Lord and God. It can never be anything else at last. Nothing else exists which gives the guilty conscience experimental and practical

freedom with God, and so makes his own freeman with men. And what has been here said about civil liberty applies to theological also. It is secondary, though an inevitable product. It is not the reason for our existence'.[47]

Further:

'(U)nqualified religious liberty is but love in a mist, and it ends in the convictions of ghosts, the energy of eccentrics, the anarchy of egoists. It is going behind a long history and victory, which it ignores and wastes, in order to start a new spiritual struggle for existence from the very foundation and to make a ring for a conflict of warring religious possibilities out of which the gospel may emerge or not. Liberty can only exist as qualified. Everything turns therefore on what qualifies the liberty. And there again, everything must depend on what creates the liberty. For in all spiritual freedom its only final authority is its source. Its normal principle is in its origins. And the source of Christian liberty is not any natural right … Christianity is not a divine charter for natural independence - for the recalcitrant, the turbulent…. It was born … in something that created a new liberty, and did that only by first creating a new and greater obedience. It put in our hands a new and greater trust than our freedom, something which made us free and able not only to serve, but to serve it'.[48]

'It follows from Forsyth's understanding of the cross that the true liberty is not freedom from, but for and under the gospel'.[49] It was Forsyth who said: 'Secure that God be free. Seek first the kingdom of God, and all other freedom shall be added to you'.[50]

Sin

According to Forsyth, to be truly free is to seek first the kingdom of God, otherwise freedom is sinful. Forsyth saw the matter of God's authority in relation to the reality of humanity's sin, and general overall shortcomings, strongly stating God's abhorrence of sin.

> 'The power in God can convert suffering to a sacrament, but it must destroy sin. It can transcend and sanctify suffering while the suffering remains, but sin it must abolish. The Cross of Christ can submerge suffering, and make it a means of salvation, but with sin it can make neither use nor terms; it can only make an end of. God in Christ is capable of suffering and transmuting sorrow, but of sin He is incapable, and His work is to destroy it'.[51]

> 'Displace the centrality of sin in the natural world, or of holiness in the supernatural, and Christianity…. is a kind of rebus, an incoherent drama where you see a lifeboat launched to save a painted ship upon a painted ocean.'[52]

Not surprisingly, believing as he that '(t)he wrongest thing in the world is its sin',[53]' and that '(t)o make little of sin is to diminish the holiness of God.'[54] Forsyth was sufficiently awakened to his own sin to recognise his need to recognise and receive the Authority of God's Word in Christ. Neither the 'ship' nor the 'ocean' that Forsyth saw were painted, but real. And in response, he gave everything he had as time and time again he launched the lifeboat of which he wrote, and to which he dedicated all that was his life and work.

And to this end it seems that in order for Forsyth to talk adequately about what God did, he found it necessary to talk about what humanity did wrong, or at least did not do well, or not at all. Of its malaise and its inability and unwillingness to see beyond itself, Forsyth said in 1900:

> 'The trouble of the time is this - that we are more universal in our thought and experience than we are in our faith. Our experience is wider than our faith. Death is wider than grace. Our ideas are wider than our real religion. Our culture is wider that our actual creed. Our crises overwhelm our Christ. Men range the world with ships, trains and wires. They range the universe with microscope, telescope and spectrum. They explore human nature with the aid of genius, and they go far in that knowledge of the soul which comes of culture. History and geography and science and literature serve us, as they never did before ... We go far, but do we go deep? We have more experience than we have faith to carry. If masses are under-educated, masses are over-educated. Their resources submerge their conscience. And their right conscience itself outruns their ethics. Men see a right, which they cannot make a habit, or pass into public use. Their knowledge of the world is so great it actually belittles their world. The more they know of it the less they think of it. Prosperity brings leanness of soul and meanness of ideal. The more they know of man the less they respect man. The more they see the less they believe. The more they experience the less their faith in the great faiths, hopes and gospels. They like broad views, often because these seem to make less demand on their bankrupt souls'. [55]

It is apparent from these words of Forsyth, that one of the things humanity did wrong in his eyes was simply to permit itself to get a full grasp of the nature of God and, from that nature, the extent to which God had gone to redeem His creation.

'Most of the failure to recognise the divine greatness of Christ arises in the end from a moral failure to appreciate Him as a personal Saviour, and that failure rises from a defect in the estimate of the sin from which He saves. A lofty ideal is not mighty to save'.[56]

On a personal level he appears to be very sensitive, though not excusing, the difficulty a person may have in truly and willing to 'recognise the divine greatness of Christ', and the even greater difficulty of estimating 'the sin from which he saves'. In his 1909 book *The Cruciality of the Cross* Forsyth went to great lengths to express his belief that even as 'the atoning cross is central for the New Testament gospel, it is central to Christian experience'.[57] He even concedes that that experience need not necessarily be overly cross consumed as with 'respect to personal experience' he asks: '(D)o we deny all true faith which does not grasp the atoning Cross?', and in response says: 'Surely not, so long as that Cross is not denied or denounced; and so long as the experience of particular individuals is not made the measure of the message of the Church'.[58]

Not much of a concession, for even here, as everywhere, and 'with a consistency almost unbelievable, Forsyth takes every topic with which he deals and examines it in the light of what it means in a world where there has been an empty tomb'.[59] Though willing to listen to voices that would say otherwise, one gets the impression that his time of listening would not have been that long. Everything goes back to the Cross. Knowing that, he expects people to live according to that. 'We are mastered, but not concussed', he said. [60] Yet, again, on the personal level he does seem to have a more sympathetic or at least attentive ear, acknowledging for instance that.

'There are thus a thousand influences of no quite ignoble sort which may arrest a man's total committal of himself and his kind to the new creation in Christ's Cross. And it seems a reasonable self-respect which solicits him to reserve a plot of freehold in his interior where his house is his castle, and he can call his soul his own … he struggles, sometimes pathetically, to set up what is impossible morally as mathematically - a subsidiary centre; which is a contradiction in terms. There is but one centre, one Lord, one Cross, one faith, and one Spirit of a new life in Jesus Christ.[61]

And further to the pastoral tone of his call to people to realise their sin and come to know Christ as crucified and risen Saviour, Hunter presents the following question and answer, grounded in Forsyth's work:

'But how is a man to be brought to a proper sense of his own sin and guilt? Not, said Forsyth, by constantly flailing him with a sense of guilt. It was the vision of God's holiness which brought home to Isaiah his sinfulness. Therefore better far to show man the holiness of that God who by His very nature cannot palter with sin, and how in the gracious gift of His Son and the atoning cross He has judged sin and redeemed sinners'. [62]

Forsyth could also be, and often was, a man who voiced words full of criticism and rebuke. In 1901 he wrote:

'We have moved our faith's centre of gravity, and we have detached it too far from the experiences which gather specially around the Cross and Resurrection. We cultivate the pieties and are strange to the hells and heavens that open about that historic moment'.[63]

'We have lost the idea that there is greater power at work even in the natural world than the might of the cosmic process, glorious states, or brilliant genius. And that is the power of sin, which has in it to bring all these things to dust with the alliance of time... In these moral measurements of the universe which give us final values, this (sin) is the ruling power unless it finds its master'.[64]

For Forsyth there was absolutely no question as to what that power is:

'The power, which masters the world's sin, is the real omnipotence of the universe. And the true sense of what power is, comes home to us only in our sense of forgiveness and redemption. And that sense issues for us from the two acts of the death and rising of Jesus Christ ... We only believe by the power of His resurrection ... My point is that what we lack in our faith and pay for in our effect is that element of power which makes faith the continued action in the Church of the greatest exertion of omnipotence ever known - the resurrection of Jesus Christ from the dead'. [65]

The Cross Still Authoritative

In giving explanation for the title of his book, A M Hunter writes:

'On the memorial tablet to Peter Taylor Forsyth in New College Chapel (London, England) there stands the epitapth - and none could be more apter: *PER CRUCEM AD LUCEM* - 'through the Cross to the Light'.[66]

In every step along the way, such seems to have been the road that Forsyth travelled. Further, appreciating the good intention of the man himself it is no wonder that he would be about wishing well and wanting the best for his neighbour. Even as his writings are read here and now - one hundred and fifty years to the day of his birth - one can almost feel the man's determination to make the love of God in Jesus Christ known to all people for the good of all people and all to the glory of God. And we remember that Forsyth said of God in his life and ministry in every form: 'He has told me to treat every man as savable'.[67] To that end, Forsyth knew that it took an authoritative voice and presence to bring about a positive resolution in difficult times - such as the sin of humanity - sin seen as an affront to God's holiness, and humanity 'not simply as stray sheep or wandering prodigals, but as rebels - rebels taken with weapons in their hands'.[68] We are the problem and through Christ alone, the focus of the solution'.[69] The locus of authority to bring about the solution is the Cross.

'No reason of man can justify God for His treatment of His Son; but whatever does justify it justifies God's whole providence with the universe, and solves its problem. He so spared not His Son as with Him to give us all things. The true theology of the Cross and its atonement is the solution of the world. There is no other. It is that or none'.[70]

'What then does (Forsyth) have to say of the atonement as God's act? The Cross is an atonement God made to God's holiness - made by God himself. Who covered the sin of man? The all-seeing God himself. The atonement was made to God but by God. The real objective element is that God made the atonement and gave it finished to man'.[71] The Cross does not in the New Testament exhibit God as accepting sacrifice so much as making it'.[72] Making a personal comment in this regard, Forsyth stated:

'We are more sure of Him than our own experience
… The **first content** of my religious experience is
not myself so or so … not myself in a certain frame,
but God in a certain act, as giving Himself, as thus
grasping, saving, new creating me'.[73]

Freedom - Church and State

That focus, no matter what road Forsyth decided his mind
should journey, always remained the main and essential one.
From art, to politics, to education, to social welfare, to youth
work, to whatever, the historic cross of the crucified and risen
Christ remained the authority over all, in all and through all.
Even when Forsyth appears in his writing to be making a
concession to the harsh realities of the world as they stand in
opposition and all the authority and triumph therein, he brings
his thought around to confirm what we would come to expect
and, as noted above, there shall in the end be no concession.
An example of one such journey is found in his discussion of
'Plebiscite and Gospel' [74]…where he addresses the
relationship between church and state. States Forsyth:

'We have two democracies - a natural and a spiritual.
The natural cannot survive without the spiritual. And
the spiritual is only saved by that in its constitution
which is not democratic, by an authority that does not
proceed from the community; it is not amenable to its
vote'[75]

'In a Church, the majority principle is only adequate
and safe if it be a majority in a society composed of
people who care supremely for some given, settled and
final thing, which majorities have no power to decree
or alter, and which neither the present nor the future
has any right to control, only the duty to obey'.[76]

'For the State, unlike the Church.... has no changeless trust from the past ... Its ethic is utilitarian for public good in the long run. It advances by steps which are valuable only as they serve a final moral ideal which is not in the charge of the State'.[77]

Forsyth's great concern for and interest in the relationship between church and state is especially seen here in relation to the state's use of its freedom as it seeks to lead the people to upholding a moral and ethical way. Clearly and succinctly Forsyth made known in his writings who is in charge - which is ultimately authoritative as such efforts are undertaken.

'Freedom does not mean the same thing in religion as politics. It has different postulates in each case, and a different ethic. A State polity cannot rest on Christian ethic till the State is composed of regenerated Christian men. And the only thing that can make public freedom safe at last is its control by the freedom of the soul in its most private, intimate and final relation with God in Christ. The development of freedom is a slow process of adjusting the law of natural society to the Christian idea, and securing permanence for the cohesive instincts of human nature by the supernatural unity of its re-creation in the Son of God'.[78]

'The Church dissolves, and its effect on freedom is lost for the State, when it ceases to be evangelical in the great apostolic and Reformation sense of being regenerate by the cross of the risen Christ'.[79]

'We observe that *the democracy will recognise no authority but what it creates; the Church none but*

what creates it; and the collision is sharp ... It occurs
to many to question if democratic liberty, fraternity
and equality are the be-all and end-all of moral
humanity; to ask where place is left in that list of
rights for duty, and especially for man's first duty of
obedience with heart and soul and strength and mind.
... Christ gave no sign that He came to set up a final
and millennial state of democratic liberty; that He
was chiefly concerned with something which had an
eternal right to rule and use liberty of every kind; and
that if political liberty could ever be finally shown
incompatible with His ideal purpose and action, then
political liberty must go down, like every other
natural instinct or ambition similarly incompatible'.[80]

From the quotation above is once more evident that 'authority'
for P T Forsyth is a God given, Christ centred, Spirit fed, Word
inspired, Cross grounded thing. 'What we really rally to is not
the facts of the Bible or the Church, but their central, creative
and therefore controlling fact - the Gospel in living power'.[81]

In Forsyth's discussion of a kind of hierarchy of authorities
and of his acknowledgement of natural patterns of authority,
including the authority of all, of most and of the few, the same
message is heard.[82] The[86]discussion is found in his text *The
Principle of Authority.[83]* It represents yet another valuable
effort by Forsyth to write down how everything in the world
fits in, only to conclude that it all fits in right where he said it
did from the very start.

'If there is any authority over the natural man, it must
be that of its Creator; and if the New Humanity has
any authority above it, that authority must be found
in the act of its creation, which act is the Cross of
Christ'.[84]

Still, despite the now obvious conclusion, the many paths Forsyth took to get there provide for us not only a greater insight into the depth of the man's faith and thinking, but also of our own need to have an ever growing ad alert sense of why we do what we do, and from that, of which direction we choose to direct our own lives. In the process of arriving his position Forsyth rejected the ideas that God has to reconciled, stressing that the satisfaction made by Christ flowed from the grace of God and did not procure it, denying that redemption cost God the Father nothing, stressing that the Son could not suffer without the Father suffering; affirming that satisfaction had to made to God's wounded honour, stressing that it is God who requires atonement, not his attributes, and that the Atonement has anything to do with a transfer of guilt.[85]

Faithfulness

Human freedom does exist and Forsyth knew that it had to be acknowledged lest people come to think of the human enterprise as robotic. 'Our faith, like our freedom, is a creation of God - yet so that we are responsible for both'.[86] People make choices, some good, some not so good, and Forsyth never forgot that though he wished it were otherwise people keep sinning despite the Cross - with all its moral victory, triumph and powerful rule of the world and grasp on its destiny. People keep on employing their freedom to make a mess of things. Perhaps nothing flies in the face of beauty and strength of Forsyth's great perspective on God that the consistent fact that there is so much ungodliness in the world.

And so he wrote, with a good preacher's passion:

> 'It is no light problem that faces the Creator in His
> world. There was never such a fateful experiment as
> when God trusted man with freedom. But our

Christian faith is that He well knew what He was about. He did not do that as a mere adventure, not without knowing that He had the power to remedy any abuse of it that might occur, and to do this by a new creation more mighty, marvellous and mysterious than the first. He had means to emancipate even freedom, to convert moral freedom even in its ruin, into spiritual. If the first creation drew on His might, the second taxed His all-might. It revealed His power, as moral majesty, as holy omnipotence, most chiefly shown in the mercy that redeems and reconciles. To redeem creation is a more creative act that it was to create it. It is the last thing omnipotence could do. What is omnipotence but the costly and inevitable action of holiness in establishing itself everywhere forever. The supreme power in the world is not simply the power of a God but of a holy God, upon whose rule all things wait, and may wait long. It is no slack knot that the Saviour has to undo. All the energy of a perverse world in its created freedom pulled on the tangle to tighten it. And its undoing has given the supreme form to all God's dealings with the world. But at the same time the snarl is not beyond being untied. Man is born to be redeemed. The great and final assurance we need is that God will save, must save, has saved His own holy purpose, gospel and glory; and that history is the action of that salvation, surely however obscurely, irresistibly however slowly. With that faith we are sure of man's future. And only so. Man could never come to himself till God came to His own. If we first hallow God's Name, as Christ first did, as God in Christ did, we are delivered from all evil, and all things are ours.'[87]

Here in these words it becomes apparent again as always that P T Forsyth was a deeply faithful man - 'faith being to be sure of things we hope for, and to be certain of things we cannot see' (*Hebrews 11:1*). Not surprisingly he saw his faith as a gift from God. He wrote in 1907:

> 'It also pleased God by revelation of His holiness and grace, which the great theologians taught me to find in the Bible, to bring home to me my sin in a way that submerged all the school questions of weight, urgency and poignancy. I was turned from a Christian to a believer, from a lover of love to an object of grace'.[88]

It is therefore also rightly acknowledged that through the experience of personal redemption Forsyth arrived at his principle of religious authority.[89] Yet, even though there is evidence of his deep faith in the Cross of Christ, crucified and risen, and even though he has made it so clear that 'there is nothing so good and wholesome for man as the Kingdom of God and its holiness, which Christ first sought and won,'[90] and even though he has a clear and consistent sense of authority in these and all matters, there still exists the sad truth that people do and say things that hurt themselves and other people and are all against the will of God.

Forsyth knew this and knew it well and in response to this truth his writings, and all the more the man himself, present a call to faithfulness - for those of the faith to be faithful. In 1911 he wrote:

> 'It is required that a man first be faithful and then be free … Faith is an obedience before it is anything else'.[91]

And in 1913:

'A strong faith is engrossed with the reality of God's
crucial and creative action, whether on history or on
us, more than with our sense of it, or our perception
of the way it takes.[92]

In further making his point, and as is often the case, his
essential thoughts lap over one another in writing, for in the
text *The Justification of God* we find the very essence of his
text *Faith, Freedom and the Future*. Though writing of
matters relating to the First World War, Forsyth's words ring
true for all times when sin seems to be getting the upper hand
and the message of Christ appears to be but a faint voice from
another time. Saying this, it is right to present P T Forsyth as
a theologian for the next Millennium. The words to follow
can inspire for all time in all places all people, whether the sin
they know or create is deeply personal or corporate, whether
one struggling with the next direction for some social order, or
the Church, or a person as he or she is striving to be as they
were meant to be: Wrote Forsyth in 1917 –

'We are now in a crisis that no individual can
measure, nor his piety deal with; and it is beyond any
philosophy or idealism of a time. It needs the faith of
an agelong holy Church to grasp it. Would that the
Church's faith could always handle it in the true
power of that crisis greater still which made the
Church - in the power of the Church, Cross and
Gospel. An awful crisis of wickedness like war can
only be met on the Church's height and range of
faith, and it forces us up to levels and aspects of our
belief, which our common hours of moral slackness
too easily feel extreme. Nothing but the great
theologies of redemption are adequate to the great

tragedies of the world … We cannot love God too much, nor believe too much in his love, nor reckon it too holy. A due faith in Him is immoderate, absolute trust, and it has a creed to correspond. Only an immoderate belief is true enough for the extraordinary tragedy of the world - the kind of belief in which Christ conquered the whole crisis of the world not to say of Eternity … No language is extreme which does justice to His conquest of His trial as the Act in which God's grace subdues the whole evil of the world, universe forever'.[93]

'The only moral authority that can save society is one that thus asserts itself in the individual conscience by its saved experience of a universal redeemer'.[94]

It is not surprising that in the prologue to the text *The Principal of Authority*, he stated: 'The question of authority, which in its religious form is the first and the last issue of life',[95] and that much further on in the same text:

'The question of the hour, for all of life, and not only for the religious, is that of authority - the true effective authority. Where is it? At last it is here. It is God's eternal, perpetual act and gift of grace, met in the absolute obedience of our faith. Faith is the absolute obedience to grace as absolute authority. Personal faith in the holy, gracious God of Christ's Cross is the one creative, authoritative, life-making, life-giving, life-shaping power of the moral soul'.[96]

Such authority - with its triumph and its victory - is authoritative only in as much as it is ultimately loving an gracious - for without either, along with all the other 'fruits of the Spirit' - it has no might, no power - no ability to speak well to the people and to lead them where they should go. 'What we really rally to is not the facts of the Bible or the Church but their central creative and therefore controlling fact - the Gospel in living power'.[97]

In a 1906 paper, *'The Authority of the Cross'*, by Robert Mackintosh, with annotations by P T Forsyth, Mackintosh wrote:

> 'We have all heard of the formula which states the essence of Protestantism as twofold; there is the formal and a material principle - justification by faith, the authority of Scripture. I think we might define Dr Forsyth's view of authority by saying that he invites us to regard one principle (justification by faith) as playing both parts. Indeed how could Protestantism be firmly based if it see-sawed between two authorities? I need not remind my audience that, with Dr Forsyth, the question is not merely about Protestantism, but about Christianity. With him, as with the reformers, faith which is the faith by which a sinner casts his reliance upon the redeeming death of Christ - no less than that, and (perhaps) nothing more'.[98]

There follows Forsyth's annotation:

> 'Agreed!'[99]

So strongly feeling this way, he exhorted people to ask of themselves - 'Are you, within your methods and organisations, well calculated to serve in a distinctive way the Gospel that God has given, and to secure its authority?'[100] He especially asked this question of the Church, and in 1901 he not so gently mocked the Church at large for its complaint that it had 'a lack of power'[101] - lack of authority - and that therefore it couldn't be expected to thrive. In addressing the complaint, he declared: 'In admission, of course, the greatest of all powers is God, is faith, is the Cross. We concede that without saying, and we believe we believe it. But practically we retract the admission'.[102]

Speaking to the retraction tendency he wrote:

'Again, we feel the power of heroes, emperors, geniuses, even when we have more of the imperial than of the heroes, or the inspired. We feel the power of the personality, of eloquence, of sentiment. We recognise the vast power of money, the unprecedented part played by finance in the social economy and the modern time. We have a momentary and reactionary passion of belief in institutions, in institutional politics or piety. We know the power of science and its organisation of knowledge. We have a sense never before given to the world of cosmos power, the collective force and energy of a perfectly coherent universe. These are but examples of power on the vast scale which we all feel, and they are in striking contrast with our sense of power which we associate with faith, or answer in it. Yet if in our faith we do not feel and own a power infinitely greater than any of the historic or cosmic forces of the time, our religion has but a limited future and every effort we make to organise it into line with the powers which we secretly and practically call most effective, is bound to end in deep disappointment.... (F)rom the New Testament point of view the seat of chief power and authority in the universe is the cross of resurrection of Jesus Christ'.[103]

Forsyth's great anguish - filled outpouring of thought during the First World War - is captured in his 1917 text *The Justification of God.* Throughout the text he makes known his belief that human freedom has been badly used.[104] However, God did trust humanity with freedom, and the consequences of doing so frustrated Forsyth time and time again. Once more, more than fifteen years later, he remained particularly unimpressed with the Church, citing its 'failure as an International Authority',[105] more especially its failure during war times. From his perspective the failure rests in the Church's wrong assessment of its 'first work or first business'[106] - 'to return and readjust its compass at the Cross, to rise above both the precepts and the principles Christ taught to the power He put forth there for the world's regeneration, and to recover a Christian ethic, not interim but final'.[107]

Final, asserted Forsyth, *Final.*

> 'The most universal thing in the universal Christ is His cross. Everywhere, according to God's ubiquity, immanence, or what you will, His holy love is invincibly at issue with death, sin, and sorrow. Everywhere is redemption … The purpose of salvation is the principle of creation; and the ruling power of the world is the purpose of God'.[108]

To let Christ be your 'authoritative news voice' is to let His love and mercy be the things that govern your life and guide your use of freedom. It angered Forsyth when life was perceived as to function the other way.

> 'Anthropocentric religion means egoist religion. It is a religion whose God revolves around man … it caters to individual or racial egoism, because it has come to regard God's love as the greatest asset of man instead of man's trustful obedience as the supreme worship and due of God'.[109]

'God is not the world's great asset but its eternal Lord … To move the centre of supreme concern from God to man is false religion, whose nemesis is slow but sure'.[110]

'To make the development of man the supreme interest of God … instead of making the glory of God the supreme interest of man, is a moral error which invites the only treatment that can cure a civilisation whose religion has become so false - public judgement … A society, whose God is less than holy represents in the end a godless civilisation … Man's holiness is not spiritual eminence, nor mystic remoteness, nor religious facility; it is more insight and practical experience of love's miracle of majesty and mercy combined only in an atoning Cross. Religion in losing the note of the holy, and its supremacy, loses the note of authority, which in the end, is to lose all'.[111]

There is throughout Forsyth's thought a sincere and real sense of establishing a fair, decent, just and true moral order. Striving for this he was involved in the world in which he lived, believing as he did that the authority of the Cross lives in the present, not the past. It was in no way his way nor his desire for any other person to live '(a)s if Christ came but to promote moral excellence, service, and happiness, and the offence and tragedy of the Cross had now ceased'.[112] The very dimension of that authority grounds and exercises a 'vibrant moral authority,[113] such authority being expressed in upholding and enriching a clear and consistent sense of the will of God on earth as it is in heaven, with the responsibility for doing so resting with the Church.

'Today, as ever, the Church has to control, lead, and secure human freedom. And today, as ever, not by idolising freedom, but by its old method of authority, by providing an authority whose very nature creates freedom - the authority, that is, not of the Church itself but of its Gospel and Saviour'.[114]

Conclusion

Today we celebrate P T Forsyth and his voice from the past, more recently than we might at first imagine and we hear that voice saying - 'Remember Christ is your authority - even as you listen to the radio and watch the TV - nice invention - and go to your football finals and rugby matches and ice hockey games - even as you decide what to do with you everyday - remember Christ is your authority. First listening to Him and first seeing Him with eyes of heart, expend your energy first wanting to be for Him. Under and for His Cross live and with the Christ of this Cross go forth to embrace change and great challenge and be about that which is your daily round, your freedom having been used to let Christ be your authoritative voice - the voice coming from the One Who has, and you have let have, the greatest authority in your life'. As Brown rightly says,

'(E)very word Forsyth ever put on paper was an occasion to celebrate the reality of the good news and call attention to the fact that something had really happened, and that therefore nothing could ever be the same again. This is one reason Forsyth is an exciting theologian; he is so obviously caught up in what he is writing about and so aware that the issues he is describing are momentous'.[115]

It is, therefore, from Forsyth's appreciation, some say to the point of 'fanatical insistence',[116] of God's authoritative voice in his life that his thought expounds a wanting for that same voice to be heard and received in the lives of other people. Forsyth appeared to know full well that in and from his freedom he too was able to say no to this authority, to turn it away and to live believing that it will not be permitted to have any effect upon his life. He was not so bold and certainly not so arrogant as to think or to articulate a way of believing that saw himself as better than the other - but rather to see his righteousness, his authority and his freedom all as finding substance and root in the gift he had received and accepted from a gracious, redeeming and loving God.

Not everyone agreed with Forsyth on these matters of authority and freedom: some people perhaps simply because they didn't know quite what he was talking about, having maybe given up before they could find out where he was really coming from, quite literally, in the first place. That is an understandable position for many to have found themselves in. Criticisms of his style are not entirely out of order, yet they do not outweigh the great collection of thought that he has left for future generations to ponder, and the great gift he gave as '(h)e was struggling to say what cannot be said'.[117] It is said that '(d)uring his lifetime he swam against the current theological trends ... and was out of step with his own theological generation',[118] leading no doubt to people dismissing his thought just because it was not in fashion. But how many people really did dismiss his thought, and are we entirely sure that he was as much the 'odd man out' as we are lead to believe? His distinguished pastorates, his principalship, his presidency of the Congregational Church of his day, his extensive publications, and the absence of a clear, definitive account telling of his unpopularity leave the issue somewhat open for this author. Griffith notes with less certainty that others, 'In his day, Forsyth was listened to with respect that his parts and powers commanded, but it seemed that the flowing tide was against him and that his brave protest must be left stranded in a channel from which water has retreated'.[119]   Although it has been said of Forsyth that he 'recognised that a popular following was not the index of the truth of the free grace of God',[120] we can well imagine that he would have preferred more people to have both embraced and supported what he had to say and why he was saying it.

Further, others saw other things as more significant than the Cross, such as the incarnation,[121] the church, personal experience, intellectualism and knowledge, the conscience and things spiritual and experimental.[122] Forsyth's writings address all of these perspectives, yet never in an accommodating way. This being said, perhaps his unwavering grounding or everything in the Cross and his constant call for a 'practical establishment of (God's) Holy goodness in the face of everything'[123] was just too unwavering and constant for them, for it really never seems to stop. Still, they sure knew where he was coming from and why.

In closing we remember that he said :

> 'We have the ground of all things in the goal of all things. The total effect of Christ's redemption is not to be sought in the soul alone, as if it were only by His action on the soul and its exaltation to command a still alien and hostile universe (as the martyr does not feel the fire) that He secured the great consummation. For the whole of creation groans for the Redemption, and is included in the process which works to the manifestation of the Sons of God. And the miracles of Christ show that His work is not simply to empower the soul to rise over an inferior

creation and beat down Nature under its feet, but that it is also to involve Nature in the grand co-operation of all things in the everlasting kingdom'.[124]

All things. The whole creation. The grand co-operation of all things. Yes, he was constant and unwavering in his grounding of everything in the Cross - everything. From all authority. From it all freedom. From it the very nature and calling to the Church. Here, surely, is a word for the new millennium.

Notes;

1. P.T Forsyth, *The Principle of Authority in Relation to Certainty, Sanctity and Society*: Independent Press, London, 1952,p 313 (1st edition 1912).
2. P T Forsyth, *Faith, Freedom and Future*, Hodder & Stoughton, London, 1912, p 201
3. P E Hughes, *Forsyth, 'Theologian of the Cross'*, in *'Christianity Today'* December 23, 1957, p 4.
4. P T Forsyth, *Positive Preaching and Modern Mind: The Lyman Beecher Lecture on Preaching, Yale University,* Hodder & Stoughton, London, 1907, p viii. Here Forsyth states: 'It has cost the writer much to find his way so far. And he has a long way to go. But he believes he has found the true and magnetic North'.
5. Ibid p 229
6. See Gwilyn O Griffith, *The Theology of P T Forsyth,* Lutterworth Press, London: 1948) p 30.
7. Alan P F Sell, *P T Forsyth as Unsystematic Systematician,* in Trevor Hart (ed), *Justice the True and Only Mercy,* T&T Clark, Edinburgh, 1995, p 136.
8. P T Forsyth, *The Cruciality of the Cross* London, Independent Press, 1948 p 17 (lst ed 1909)
9. Ibid
10. See W L Bradley, *P T Forsyth, The Man and His Work*, Independent Press, London 1952, p 150.
11. P T Forsyth, *The Work of Christ*, Expositor's Library, Hodder and Stoughton, London, 1910, p 153.
12. P T Forsyth, *The Principle of Authority, op cit,* p 58.
13. See Colin Gunton, *The Real as the Redemptive: Forsyth on Authority and Freedom,* in Trevor Hart (ed) *Justice the True and Only Mercy, op cit,* p 52
14. P T Forsyth, *The Justification of God: Lectures for War-Time on a Christian Theodicy*, Hodder and Stoughton, London, 1917, p 192.
15. See Colin Gunton, *The Real as the Redemptive: Forsyth on Authority and Freedom, op cit,* p51.
16. W L Bradley, *P T Forsyth, The Man and His Work, op cit,* p 82.
17. See P T Forsyth, *The Principle of Authority, op cit,* p 289.
18. See Gwilyn O Griffith, *The Theology of P T Forsyth, op cit,* pp 31-34.
19. P T Forsyth, *The Principle of Authority, op cit,* p 57.
20. A M Hunter, *Sin and Salvation: the Sin of Man,* pp 57-59.
21. Gwilyn O Griffith, *The Theology of P T Forsyth, op cit,* p 34.
22. Colin Gunton, *The Real as the Redemptive: Forsyth on Authority and Freedom, op cit,* p 47.
23. R M Brown, *A Handbook of Christian Theology* P T Forsyth, pp 144-165, Editors: Martin B Marty and Dean G Peerman, Cleveland World Publishing 1965.
24. P T Forsyth, *The Justification of God: Lectures for War-Time on a Christian Theodicy,* Latimer House, London, 1948 p 56.
25. Ibid, p 190.
26. R M Brown *A Handbook of Christian Theology, op cit,* p 145.
27. P T Forsyth, *Positive Preaching and Modern Mind, op cit,* p 142.

28 P T Forsyth, *The Justification of God: Lectures for War-Time on a Christian Theodicy, op cit*, p 185

29 P T Forsyth, *The Work of Christ, op cit*, p 41.

30 P T Forsyth, *The Justification of God: Lectures for War-Time on a Christian Theodicy, op cit*. pp 164-5.

31 See also 'The Cross, The Great Confessional' chapter 5 *The Work of Christ*, and Donald G Miller, Browne Barr, and Robert S Paul, *P T Forsyth - The Man, the Preacher's Theologian, Prophet for the Twentieth Century, A Contemporary Assessment*, Pickwick, Pittsburgh: 1981 p 3.

32 P T Forsyth, *Faith, Freedom and Future op cit*, p 340.

33 Ibid, p 290.

34 Literature Review, *The Expository Times*, Vol.LXVII, No7, p 203.

35 P T Forsyth, *Faith, Freedom and Future, op cit*, p 120

36 P T Forsyth, *Theology in Church and State*, Hodder and Stoughton, London, p 201.

37 P T Forsyth, *Positive Preaching and Modern Mind, op cit*, p 69.

38 P T Forsyth, *The Principle of Authority, op cit*, p 250. (See also *Revelation Old and New*, p 54 :'All the power and greatness of the Kingdom is derived from the King. We do not make Him our King, but He did make us His realm. We are not our own.')

39 Gwilyn O Griffith, *The Theology of P T Forsyth, op cit*, p 26.

40 P T Forsyth, *The Taste of Death and the Life of Grace*, James Clark, London, 1901, p6.

41 P T Forsyth, *The Principle of Authority, op cit*, p 102.

42 P T Forsyth, *The Work of Christ*, Independent Press, London, 1938, p180, (Ist edition 1910)

43 Gwilyn O Griffith, *The Theology of P T Forsyth, op cit*, p 30.

44 P T Forsyth, *The Principle of Authority, op cit*, p 17.

45 Colin Gunton, *The Real as the Redemptive: Forsyth on Authority and Freedom, op cit*, pp 38-42.

46 P T Forsyth, *Faith, Freedom and Future, op cit*, p 201.

47 Ibid. p 207-208.

48 Ibid. p 207.

49 Alan P F Sell, *P T Forsyth as Unsystematic Systematician*, in Trevor Hart (ed), *Justice the True and Only Mercy, op cit*, p 138. *(*See also P T Forsyth, *The Principle of Authority, op cit*, p 219)

50 P T Forsyth, *The Principle of Authority, op cit*, p 254.

51 P T Forsyth, *The Justification of God: Lectures for War-Time on a Christian Theodicy, op cit*, p 135.

52 P T Forsyth as quoted without reference in Gwilyn O Griffith, *The Theology of P T Forsyth, op cit*, p 35. (See also *Sin and Salvation: the Sin of Man*, Hunter pp 57-59.

53 P T Forsyth, *The Justification of God: Lectures for War-Time on a Christian Theodicy, op cit* p 167.

54 P T Forsyth, *The Work of Christ, op cit*, p 129.

55 P T Forsyth, *The Taste of Death and Life of Grace*, as found without page reference in H Escot *P T Forsyth and the Cure of Souls* George Allen & Unwin

Ltd, London, 1970, p 33 (lst ed 1948 - *P T Forsyth - Director of Souls.*

56 P T Forsyth, *The Person and Place of Jesus Christ* Congregational Union of England and Wales and Hodder & Stoughton, London, 1909, p 73 (see also p 219).

57 P T Forsyth, *The Cruciality of the Cross, op cit,* p 40.

58 Ibid, p 41-42.

59 R M Brown *A Handbook of Christian Theology, op cit,* p 148.

60 P T Forsyth, *Positive Preaching and Modern Mind, op cit,* p 64.

61 P T Forsyth, *The Cruciality of the Cross, op cit,* pp 47-8.

62 A M Hunter, *Sin and Salvation: the Sin of Man,* p 59.

63 P T Forsyth, *Revelation Old and New, Sermons and Addresses,* Inedpendent Press, London, 1962, p 57.

64 Ibid, p 57.

65 Ibid, p 57.

66 A M Hunter, *Sin and Salvation: the Sin of Man,* p 60.

67 P T Forsyth without reference in W L Bradley, *P T Forsyth, The Man and His Work, op cit,* p 134

68 P T Forsyth without reference in A M Hunter, *Sin and Salvation: the Sin of Man.*

69 Colin Gunton, *The Real as the Redemptive: Forsyth on Authority and Freedom, op cit,* p 58.

70 P T Forsyth, *The Justification of God: Lectures for War-Time on a Christian Theodicy, op cit* p 122.

71 A M Hunter, *Sin and Salvation: the Sin of Man,* p 62.

72 P T Forsyth, *The Cruciality of the Cross, op cit,* p 93.

73 P T Forsyth, *The Principle of Authority, op cit,* p 372.

74 *Plebescite and Gospel, The Contemporary Review, vol. C* July – December, 1911, pp 60-76.

75 Ibid, p 61.

76 Ibid, p 62.

77 Ibid. p 65.

78 P T Forsyth, *Faith, Freedom and Future, op cit,* pp 153-154.

79 Ibid, p 157.

80 Ibid, pp 192-3.

81 Ibid, p 297.

82 See Colin Gunton, *The Real as the Redemptive: Forsyth on Authority and Freedom, op cit,* pp 52-3.

83 P T Forsyth, *The Principle of Authority, op cit,* pp 313-4.

84 Ibid, p 58.

85 L Bradley, *P T Forsyth, The Man and His Work, op cit,* pp 149-152.

86 P T Forsyth, *The Principle of Authority, op cit,* p 52

87 P T Forsyth, *The Justification of God: Lectures for War-Time on a Christian Theodicy, op cit* pp 124-126.

88 Plebescite and Gospel, *The Contemporary Review, vol. C* July – December, 1911.p 67.

89 W L Bradley, P T Forsyth, *The Man and His Work, op cit,* p 136. (see also Miller , 11-17)

90 P T Forsyth, *The Justification of God: Lectures for War-Time on a Christian Theodicy, op cit*, p 124.

91 *Plebescite and Gospel, The Contemporary Review, vol. C* July – December, 1911, p 67.

92 P T Forsyth, *The Principle of Authority, op cit*, p 81.

93 P T Forsyth, *The Justification of God: Lectures for War-Time on a Christian Theodicy, op cit*, p 126.

94 P T Forsyth, *The Principle of Authority, op cit*, pp 298-99.

95 Ibid, p 1.

96 Ibid, p 213.

97 P T Forsyth, *Faith, Freedom and Future, op cit*, p 297.

98 Robert Macintosh, *The Authority of the Cross*, in *Congregational Quarterly*, Vol XXI, No1, January 1943, pp 210-11.

99 Ibid, p 211.

100 P T Forsyth, *Faith, Freedom and Future, op cit*, p 208.

101 P T Forsyth, *Revelation Old and New, Sermons and Addresses, op cit*, p 55.

102 Ibid p 56.

103 Ibid p 56.

104 P T Forsyth, *The Justification of God: Lectures for War-Time on a Christian Theodicy, op cit* p 123.

105 Ibid, p 98.

106 Ibid pp 101 & 104.

107 Ibid p 104.

108 Ibid, p 123.

109 Ibid. p 106

110 Ibid, p 116.

111 Ibid. p 118.

112 P T Forsyth, *Faith, Freedom and Future, op cit*, p 275.

113 W L Bradley, P T Forsyth, *The Man and His Work, op cit*, pp 22-27.

114 P T Forsyth, *The Principle of Authority, op cit*, p 8.

115 R M Brown *A Handbook of Christian Theology, op cit*, p 164.

116 Davies in the foreword to P T Forsyth, *The Justification of God: Lectures for War-Time on a Christian Theodicy, op cit*, p 6.

117 Donald G Miller, Browne Barr, and Robert S Paul, *P T Forsyth - The Man, the Preacher's Theologian, Prophet for the Twentieth Century, A Contemporary Assessment,* Pickwick, Pittsburgh: 1981, p 18.

118 R M Brown *A Handbook of Christian Theology, op cit*, p 147.

119 Gwilyn O Griffith, *The Theology of P T Forsyth, op cit,*

120 R M Brown, *A Handbook of Christian Theology, op cit*, p 147.

121 *(Not surprisingly Forsyth insisted that only the Atonement gives the incarnation its base ad value in any moral and religious sense "Without it, it is but a philosophic scheme"* (Sell 137)

122 See: A E Garvie, *The Christian Certainty Amid the Modern Perplexity*, Hodder & Stoughton, London, MCMX; T H Hughes, *The Atonement: Modern Theories of the Doctrine*, George Allen & Unwin Ltd, London:1945; J H Rogers, *Forsyth's*

Critique of the Dominant Theological Tendencies of His Time, The Theology of P T Forsyth, pp 14-24 ; J K Mozley, *Some Tendencies in British Theology:* SPCK 1951, London ; B M G Reardon, *Religious thought in the Victoria Age: A Survey from Coleridge to Gore,* Longman 1980; A P F Sell *Theology of Turmoil,* Baker Book House, Grand Rapids, Michigan, 1986.

[123] P T Forsyth, *The Justification of God: Lectures for War-Time on a Christian Theodicy, op cit* p 98.

[124] P T Forsyth, *The Principle of Authority, op cit,* p 206.

4.

P T Forsyth

Holy Love and the
Cross of Christ

W Bryn Williams

Having been invited to participate in this Conference on P T Forsyth (1848 -1921), A Theologian For a New Millenium' we revisit a committed believer, a preacher, and an intellectual who spoke with the voice of his time, yet spoke prophetically concerning what he called in the *Cruciality of the Cross*, 'current and weak religion.'[1]. What was lacking in the New Theology he says here is 'that element supplied in the atoning cross as the reconciling judgement of the world'[2], but is he a theologian for a new millennium? In this short paper I will attempt to say something of this man, his period, his contemporaries, his work and his legacy and then maybe, try to consider his ongoing contribution to the discipline of theology and the practical work of proclaiming the Gospel.

As a student and a young minister he acquainted himself with the prevailing theological trends of his age, drawing much from F D Maurice (1805-1872)[3] who stressed that socialism should come under the influence of Christian thought and that Christ's kingdom was universal to mankind in general. During this time he responded positively to the New Theology and would regularly host liberally - minded theologians and preachers in his pulpits, but in 1896 at the Congregational Union meetings held in Leicester, he said:

'There was a time when I was interested in the first degree with purely scientific criticism. Bred among academic scholarship of the classics and philosophy, I carried these habits to the Bible, and I found in the subject a new fascination, in proportion, as the stakes were so much higher. But, fortunately for me, I was not condemned to the mere scholar's cloistered life. I could not treat the matter as an academic quest. I was in a relation of life, duty and responsibility for others. I could not contemplate conclusions without asking how they would affect these people and my

word to them in doubt, death, grief or repentance....
It also pleased God by the revelation of His holiness
and grace, which the great theologians taught me to
find in the Bible, to bring home to me my sin in a
way that submerged all the school questions in
weight, urgency, and poignancy. I was turned from a
Christian to a believer, from a lover of God to an
object of grace... I withdrew my prime attention from
much of the scholar's work and gave it to those
theological interests imbibed first from Maurice, and
then more mightily through Ritschl, which came
nearer to life than science, sentiment or ethic can
ever do. I immersed myself in the logic of Hegel,
and corrected it by the theology of Paul, and its
continuity in the Reformation, because I was all the
time being corrected and humiliated by the Holy
Spirit... My faith in critical methods is unchanged...
But the need of the hour is not that... What is needed
is no mere change of view, but a change and a
deepening in the type of personal religion, amounting
in cases to a new conversion.'[4]

Also at the Boston International Congregational Council in
1899, on the theme of *The Evangelical Principle of Authority*,
he was to begin his address by saying 'The Cross is the final
seat of authority, not only for the Church, but for all human
society.' The response to this address was total silence at first
and then the vast audience almost spontaneously turned its
long applause into the singing of the hymn (which he
suggested) *In the Cross of Christ I glory.*[5] One cannot speak
of *Holy Love* and *Cross* without speaking of atonement, and
during this paper when either is mentioned the other is also
implied.

In his introduction to his work on the doctrine of the atonement, T H Hughes says that, 'One of the most disturbing features in the progress of knowledge is to discover terms that at one time fitted the ideas they thought to express, but which fit them no longer.'[6] He suggests two reasons why this might be the case. First, there is, in reality, no one teaching concerning the atonement. The Christian Church, at its Councils, has never made a definite pronouncement with regard to this doctrine. There are, 'therefore no stereotyped words, or sacrosanct terms, which can hinder us from expressing our thoughts in our own way.'[7] Hughes' second reason is that the doctrine of atonement is more dependent on the experience of Christian men and women than almost any other primary truth of the Christian faith. For him, this doctrine must be experienced to be understood and interpreted. Experience must be first, and interpretation must follow. Truth 'has to be lived through before it can be understood.'[8] This, for Hughes, is even more profoundly true with regard to the atonement: 'Something must be experienced in the soul and must become a fact of consciousness, before there is any probability of it being understood or adequately expressed.' [9] Is this the case with Peter Taylor Forsyth? We shall see.

As we visit P T Forsyth and his dealings with the doctrine of the atonement it is good to prepare before any visit, and part of our preparation before we visit is to consider how the Christian Church has historically viewed this doctrine. Christians believe that Jesus Christ, by dying a shameful and cruel death upon the Cross in about AD30, atoned for the sin of humanity, and made salvation available to the end of time. But how was this salvation secured? Was it by substituting Himself for the transgressions of mankind? In 1910 Forsyth writes:

'Christ and His Cross come nearer and nearer, and we do not realise what we owe Him until we realise that He has plucked us from the fearful pit, and the miry clay, and set us upon a rock of God's own founding. The meaning of Christ's death rouses our shame, self-contempt, and repentance. And we resent being made to feel ashamed of ourselves, we resent being made to repent. A great many people are afraid to come too near to anything that does that for them. That is a frequent reason for not going to church.'[10]

For Anselm in the eleventh century there was only one dogma, the incarnation; thus he wrote, *Cur Deus Homo, why God became man?* which was a defence of Christianity. But within this apologia James Denney, a contemporary of Forsyth, derives the answer to *cur deus homo*. Put briefly, the answer to the question is that God became man because that was the only way that sin could be dealt with for man's salvation, and God's end in the creation of man to be secured. Forsyth concurs with James Denney[11], that 'the rationale of the incarnation lies in the atonement.'[12] If the incarnation is to be seen rationally necessary and therefore credible, it must be looked at from the perspective of the atonement. Yet Denney does not agree with all that Forsyth wrote, primarily because Forsyth, to a greater extent than he, was able to appreciate elements of the new theology without being threatened. As Marvin Anderson suggests, 'Principal James Denney did not agree with all that Forsyth wrote, yet one senses his agreement with Forsyth in letters sent to W Robertson Nicoll on January 15 1898; Denney wrote of *The Holy Father and the Living Christ* (1897) that 'It is a book of real experience, a rediscovery of the Gospel, worth as much as most of the other little books put together'. Again in 1907 he wrote, 'The merit of Forsyth is that he returns to his New Testament, - I delivered unto you first of all that Christ died for our sins.'[13]

About the fact of the atonement, the Church, in Forsyth's view had always been very clear and explicit; of the written Gospels, nearly a fifth is devoted to the events of the last week of Christ's life. The history of the crucifixion was cherished and preached in great detail. Its saving power and significance formed the main burden of the gospel message from the very start. However, when we seek to discover how the atonement worked, we find the Church and the Bible not at all dogmatic or precise. The matter is left undefined. There are many theories, but none officially and exclusively adopted. We are free to speculate, provided we are faithful to the fact.

Another of P T Forsyth's contemporaries, R J Campell, the minister of one of the greatest non-conformist churches in London, City Temple (and the successor to Dr Joseph Parker), once said that 'The Cross of Calvary is the key to creation'[14] and when talking about the redemption of Jesus Christ he was able to say, 'My broken life is his, and the way of opportunity has opened before me because of the holiness of Christ, as well as his passion''[15] But R J Campbell is remembered not so much for these statements above, which could lie comfortably with both Denney and P T Forsyth, but rather for his many other controversial statements, such as 'We believe Christ is and was divine, but so are we. His mission was to make us realise our divinity and our oneness with God. And we are called to live the life that he lived.'[16] Campbell published his *New Theology* in 1907, where he stressed this divine immanence, rejected original sin and saw Christian revival as obtainable, only through social reform and moral action. The book stirred up so much antagonism towards Campbell's liberalism that he withdrew it from circulation. (At the end of this millennium is it conceivable to believe that a comparable volume would stir up similar responses today? Although the reaction to John Robinson and his *Honest to God* was quite astounding in the so-called liberal 1963.

Forsyth's years, were the years of Charles Haddon Spurgeon, who drew even more of a congregation than Dr Parker, to his Metropolitan Tabernacle The years also of *Lux Mundi[17]*, which was a controversial volume of Oxford essays under the editorship of Charles Gore (1853-1932), of Charles Darwin and *The Origin of Species* 1859, of dynamic religious revivals 1859 and 1904 and of the First World War.

In root form, the original meaning of atonement in the English language has been to signify the condition of being 'at one' after two parties had been estranged from one another. Soon a secondary meaning emerged - *Atonement* denoted the means, an act or a payment, through which harmony was restored. It occurs only once in the *Authorised Version of the New Testament (Romans 5:11)*, '…Jesus Christ, by whom we have now received the atonement.' where the Greek word *Katallage* is used elsewhere we have the use of reconciliation', eg (*l Cor 5:18f.*), 'God, who hath reconciled us to himself through Jesus Christ.' William Tyndale, when translating the New Testament into English, found the language of his day inadequate to express the richness of the Greek. Particularly baffling for Tyndale was this word *katallage*. His answer was to join together the simple words 'at' and 'one', which gives the word 'atonement'. This word atonement then passed into theological currency. Its etymology, therefore, provides us with the clue to its meaning - the bringing together of God and humanity, so that the two parties who were once separated by sin are now at one, through Christ's work on the cross. While William Tyndale in the sixteenth century chose to put together the word atonement, P T Forsyth at the beginning of the twentieth century brings together 'holy' and 'love'.

In the Old Testament, (*Authorised Version*) the phrase 'to make Atonement', frequently occurs in a ceremonial context. It denotes an action or series of actions by means of which guilt could be removed. At some time in Israel's history a *Day of Atonement (Lev 23: 26f)* began to be observed. Elaborate ceremonies were performed, and these were designed to expiate the sins of the whole nation. In a striking way the author of the *Epistle to the Hebrews (9:6f)* contrasts the 'once for all' character of Christ's atoning act with that of the Jewish high priest which had to be constantly repeated.

In revisiting P T Forsyth and the nineteenth and early twentieth century understanding of the doctrine of the atonement, we meet not only Forsyth himself but rather, we attempt to appreciate the intellectual atmosphere of his time; a period that was heavily influenced by the increasing tendency to emphasis the autonomy of the individual and the significance of inter-personal relationships. Our specific period of study begins some twenty years after the publication of Darwin's Origin of Species, 1859. P T Forsyth's dates are 1848-1921, the spirit of enquiry and unorthodoxy was prevalent, and, although evolution is popularly associated with science alone, yet ideas of development were permeating the fields of history, philosophy and theology. Truth thus came to be regarded not as something fixed and absolute, but rather as something in a state of constant growth, as fresh forms of knowledge seemed to rise above the horizon. This century also saw a profounder study of human psychology than had ever before been undertaken (Sigmund Freud was born in 1856 and Carl Gustaf Jung in 1875). This for Alan Sell 'made possible a new apologetic which no longer rely upon external evidences (which were being increasingly called into question with the growth of biblical criticism), but which would appeal to the religious man's spiritual experience.'[18] Now the question began to arise: How could atonement in the form of holy love and the Cross of Christ be viewed in the context of familiar human feelings and relationships? For some, the idea of the advance of human knowledge seemed difficult to reconcile with the orthodox idea of revelation as being, not the result of the discoveries of mankind, but the voluntary disclosure of God. Naturally the conception of development permeated theological perceptions. Much of this new found knowledge did seem to conflict with traditional biblical records; but this for the majority did not involve rejection; rather it led to a fresh examination of the Scriptures in the light which they brought, culminating in the quest for new insights into traditionally held doctrinal beliefs. P T Forsyth was no exception, neither was the doctrine of the atonement. And although P T Forsyth had rejected his earlier humanistic beliefs, he did not as Brown says in the *New Dictionary of Theology* 'forsake the tools of liberal higher criticism'.[19]

The final decades of the nineteenth century are marked by an effort to imbue the old orthodoxy with new confidence. Evolution was a leading *motif* amongst philosophers and theologians and the doctrine of biblical inerrancy, as it is now known, was frankly thrown overboard. By the close of the century the dogmatic stance of the Thirty-nine Articles was widely felt to be an anachronism. Adjustments had to be effected. A clergyman of the Church of England was now required simply to declare his belief in 'the doctrine of the Church of England, as therein set forth to be agreeable to the Word of God.' The question now was not whether such a course was permissible but where precisely it could be halted. Charles Gore (1853-1932),[20] the outstanding English theologian of the day, was himself in two minds. The Scriptures, he held, must be taken as the product of their own times and circumstances, resulting in the acceptance of inevitable human limitations as regard to their contents. However, the content of the creed remained and must remain the residuum of faith, apart from which Christianity ceases to be orthodox in form or even recognisable in substance. Gore devoted the final years of his life in defending the Christian faith, writing *Belief in God* (1922*), Belief in Christ* (1922), *The Holy Spirit and the Church* (1924). An interesting trilogy for the editor of *Lux Mundi*. The Broad Church had become increasingly more liberal with men like Hastings Rashdall (1858-1924) and his *Idea of Atonement* in (1919).

Forsyth's era is thus one of adjustment, slow, and at times painful and costly to some; adjustment to intellectual and social conditions of a kind which increasingly rendered the religious interpretation of life difficult in a way that it had never been before. But this interpretation for Forsyth was to be understood by looking to the Cross and what happened there - the work of the Cross, the holy love, the atonement was for him the key. C D F Moule says, of the atonement, 'Here was no overlooking of guilt or trifling with forgiveness; no external treatment of sin, but a radical, a drastic, a passionate and absolutely final acceptance of the terrible situation, and an absorption by the very God himself of the fatal disease so as to neutralise it effectively.'[21] This is true of P T Forsyth which could, perhaps, be interpreted as poetic understanding or the insight of faith, rather than a theological conclusion based on logical argument; but it is a conclusion, however, that does justice to the objective character of the atoning act. Here the Cross is no mere demonstration of God's love; it was a very costly act of 'self-propitiation', described throughout the years of these two millennia in language that is poetic, anthropomorphic and beautiful.

Forsyth can endorse only an objective view of the atonement. In Christ, he argues, God takes a part against Himself. His emphasis is not that God needs to be reconciled to man, rather man needs to be reconciled to God: God in the New Testament is always the subject of the verb 'to reconcile'. The atonement can only be objective in Forsyth's eyes; there is for him a powerful argument by the subjective school that the cross can induce penitence,[22] but this penitence is only made possible by the objective element in the atonement; that is, something effected in God, as well as by God.

J.K.Mozley was of the opinion that Forsyth emphasised the atonement at the expense of the incarnation and the resurrection. This is a criticism that Mozley levels against James Denney as well: 'Both Professor Denney and Forsyth seem to me to go wrong in their comparative depreciation of the incarnation except as the necessary presupposition of a true expiatory atonement. Incarnation without this latter does not necessarily drop to a level of a mystic doctrine of divine immanence, though I should admit that some of our Christian mysticsm, now so much in vogue, has dangerous inclinations in this direction.'[23] Neither Forsyth nor Denney wished to deny the place of the incarnation or the resurrection, but rather insisted on the centrality of the death of Christ, otherwise, as Alan Sell says, 'we land via neo-Hegelian immanentism in a mystico-metaphysical rather than a moral union of God with sinful men. There must be no sublimation of Christianity into ethical or spiritual principles, or into eternal facts, which absolve us from all obligation to a saviour who came in blood.'[24]

Forsyth worked against a background of confident liberalism, which was impatient with orthodox, conservative scholars and particularly critical of substitutionary atonement with its stress on sin, and the wrath of God. Forsyth's contention with the liberals was that he protested vigorously against human optimism. He took this optimism to be a betrayal of the New Testament emphasis on the death of Christ as an objective act of God. This objective act was for Forsyth best expressed in holy love and the Cross of Christ. Nevertheless, he agreed with many who criticised rigid orthodoxy that the idea of substitution had often been expressed in an excessively external way.

P T Forsyth urged a greater emphasis on the love of God, and on the demonstration of this love in practice. This is why he welcomed the works of Horace Bushnell (1802-1876)[25] and J McLeod Campbell (1800-1872),[26] who both stressed Jesus' identification with people in their need and despair. Although still welcoming, he feared that in reaction and response to their theories the essential truth of the objective view would be lost. For Forsyth it was not enough to appeal to the spirit of Jesus, or his spirit of obedience, or even the spirit in which he died: this took too simple a view of the New Testament and too superficial a view of the human situation. A theory was needed that took account of these, and also of the actual experience of Christians, in both sin and grace. Forsyth like Denney believed that 'The simplest preacher, and the most effective, is always the most theoretical. It is a theory, a tremendous theory that Christ's death is a death <u>for sin</u>. But unless the preacher can put some interpretation on the death - unless he can find a meaning in it which is full of appeal - why should he speak of it at all?'[27]

Sin, for Forsyth, is a breach of personal relationships, and not just an offence against an external law. Rather than speculating on the origin of sin, he expresses a view that human beings through their consciousness know themselves to be in a state of estrangement to God, of being wrong with God and in need of being reconciled to him. This sense of being wrong with God, under his displeasure, excluded from His fellowship, afraid to meet him, yet bound to meet him, is the sense of guilt. But there is more here than individual relationships; there is the social and organic aspect of sin, which involves the entire race and the entire created order in this breach of relationship. Forsyth can see this situation in no other way than that of humanity out of step with God and out of step with the very nature of life and the world itself; thus he is establishing for himself the biblical connection between sin and death. 'The wages of sin is death.'[28] The only answer was 'That death as punishment of sin was absorbed in Christ's sacrifice. Such was its atoning work that the judgement due to all mankind was absorbed ..'[29] Forsyth takes sin seriously, while he criticised many of his contemporaries who regarded sin as the result of ignorance now being outgrown. His wish was to recall theologians, but especially preachers, to a more biblical view of God's wrath and condemnation and to understand this view in relation to God's holy love. For those who identify with such feelings, to begin with the Cross seemed not only appropriate but also wholly necessary.

The cost to God was the giving up of his Son. This involved the whole of Jesus' life, which for Forsyth arrived at its climax in his death. Forsyth does not want to see the atoning work of Jesus and his culminating death as punishment, for while the innocent may suffer for the guilty, he can hardly be said to be punished for him. He has no room either for the scenario of an angry father being placated and pacified by a loving son. Nevertheless in so far as death is seen as the penalty appointed by God for sin, we must say that Jesus' sufferings were penal in nature. I will let Forsyth speak for himself; 'The sacrifice of Christ was a penal Sacrifice… The sacrifice of Christ, then, was penal not in the sense of God so punishing Christ that there is left us only religious enjoyment, but in this sense - there is a penalty and curse for sin; and Christ consented to enter that region. Christ entered voluntarily into the pain and horror, which is sin's penalty from God. Christ by the deep intimacy of his sympathy with men entered deeply into the blight and judgement which was entailed by man's sin and which must be entailed by man's sin if God is a holy and therefore a judging God'.[30]

Is there a contradiction here in as much as God appears to be on both sides at once? Forsyth was aware of this dilemma. He has no problem accepting that God, in his experience of saving, is both for us and against us: there is, for God the experience of judgement and grace: yet he sees another understandable contradiction 'The dereliction upon the Cross, the sense of love's desertion by love, was Christ's practical confession of the holy God's repulsion of sin... God made Him sin, treated Him as if he were sin; He did not view Him as sinful'.[31] It is here that Forsyth views God, treating His son as human sin and with His consent (Christ) judging human sin in Him and on Him. But although Christ took our sins upon Himself, yet He does not confess to those personal sins, that can only be done by the guilty, but He does confess on behalf of the human race - that is the Cross. 'There is a racial confession that can only be made by the holy; and there is a personal confession that can only be made by the guilty. The latter, I say, is a confession that Christ could never make… We alone, the guilty, can make that confession; but we cannot make it with Christian effect without the Cross and the confession there'.[32] The sin, therefore for Forsyth, is not to sin against the law but against the Cross, 'The sin of sin is not transgression but unfaith.'[33]

This, for Forsyth, was the kind of atonement, in theory, that people needed to hear; it would in his mind, provide the stimulus and power for Christian living. It was preachable, and in preaching it, it would make a difference in men's experience. He wished for a Church, that all its theologians were evangelists and all its evangelists theologians. But this message goes further than the Church when he says, ' The death of Christ is the central point of eternity as well as of human history.'[34] The apostles at the beginning of the first millennium never separated the act of reconciliation from 'the Cross and blood of Jesus Christ;'[35] neither does the subject of this paper.

P T Forsyth was a man of faith, a faith, not of intellectual assent, but of absolute wholehearted commitment to Christ. For him, life was to be lived in a state of forgiveness and gratitude to Christ. Christian perfection, for him, comes, not from awaiting certain gifts or graces, but from the assurance of salvation. This assurance is in itself the best guarantee of perfection and sanctification. This was what he taught his students - he continually reminded them that they were being trained for the ministry and not for intellectual gratification. 'Gentlemen, you are not here to graduate in the University of London. You may or may not do that. You are here to graduate in Christ and His ministry.'[36] Here Forsyth would be at one (excuse the phrase!) with Denney when he quotes Chalmers, who asks the question 'What could I do if God did not justify the ungodly?'[37] The earnest enquirer only asks this question. Such persons, thinks Denney, find the substitutionary theory simple and intelligible. Some, he fears, will still talk of St Paul as unintelligible, and contend that he presents Christianity in a way that does it injustice, so that the Gospel finds itself unacceptable to the 'thinking man'. But for those who do find Paul intelligible, he says: 'There are such people still, if not in theological classrooms, then in mission halls, at street corners, in lonely rooms. It is not historical scholarship that is wanted for the understanding of him, and neither is it the insight of genius: it is despair. Paul did not preach for scholars, or even for philosophers; he preached for sinners. He had no Gospel except for men whose mouths were stopped, and who were standing condemned at the bar of God.'[38] Yes Forsyth did find Paul intelligible. Again I quote what was said at the outset, 'I immersed myself in the logic of Hegel and corrected it by the theology of Paul.'[39]

P T Forsyth challenged modern theology to hold the incarnation and the atonement together. He was only willing to entertain a theological viewpoint that had practical implications for the believer and that would clearly demonstrate that the Church's Christ must always be He who is the 'Lamb of God that taketh away the sin of the world.' Sin, as he insists, is a terrible reality, but not a final reality. The ultimate is a love that submits to all that sin can do, yet does not deny itself, but loves the sinful through it all. Here is P T Forsyth, but at the same time Hastings Rashdall, for the liberal was claiming that the incarnation is Christ's own act while His death is brought about by others: 'The death was not His act, but the act of the Jewish priests, the Roman magistrate, and the Roman soldiers.[40] The natural conclusion for Rashdall in contrast to Forsyth is that Christ's death is less vital and less efficacious than his incarnation, although a necessary part of the whole incarnation or the self-revelation of God, 'the object of which was to make known God's nature and His will, to instruct men in the way of salvation, and to excite in them that love which would inspire sorrow for past sin and give the power to avoid sin in the future.''[41] This, says Rashdall, is the way in which the great fathers of the Church viewed the doctrine of the atonement, especially in the East. They did, indeed, teach that the death was a necessary part of the atoning or saving work of Christ. They never taught that it was the whole. P T Forsyth disagrees and holds this view to be a perversion and a distortion. 'When religion becomes perverted, to be a means of mere comfort and dense self-satisfaction, it becomes an integument so tough that even the grace of God cannot get through it, or a substance so flaccid that it cannot be handled.'[42]

The liberal school of Hastings Rashdall and R J Campbell at the beginning of this century believed that the substitutionary theory of the atonement to be crude, barbaric, immoral or subpersonal can be understood with some empathy at its close, while an idealistic view of mankind is today immediately dismissed. For Forsyth the atonement is not so much a concept that makes human beings better by meditating upon it, rather an action that offers life through the death of God's Son. The sacrificial imageries that these two thousand Christian years have accumulated can teach us so much about the way followers of Jesus viewed His death, but these images are not the atonement. P T Forsyth cannot substitute the work of God, the Father, in the death of Christ, his Son, with the process of history and Christian understanding and interpretation. The atonement, for him, remains as a single fact, in God's relationship to human beings, work was done that transformed 'darkness into light.' In this respect, the work was both penal and substitutionary, in that what was done was done for others. The Cross was the divine remedy for the fall of man and the sole hope of the human race. The writers of *Lux Mundi*(1889),[43] were suggesting that it was in the incarnation that one finds the atoning work of God in Christ. Here the notions of evolution and divine immanence were introduced. But this conception was reducing the cross to an almost accidental, though inseparable, accompaniment of the incarnation. This was criticised by Forsyth, for showing an imperfect appreciation of the place which the atonement had always held in Western theology, and even of the balance of the New Testament itself. The cross, after all, had been in every age the symbol of Christianity and as J M Creed said 'Unless the doctrine of the Incarnation is nailed to the Cross it tends to lose definition and to evaporate into a cosmic principle.'[44]

Forsyth was indeed influenced by the German modern-positive movement in theology and found scholars such as Reinhold Seeberg, Martin Schian and W Hermann[45] to be truly interested in bringing Christianity closer to the modem world, but at what price for the Christian Church? Forsyth attempted to appreciate these German theologians in his *Lyman Lectures,* in 1907, by drawing the contrast between the 'positive' and the 'liberal' preacher, 'The one begins with the world (as I say), the other with the Word.'[46] He welcomed these theologians sympathy with the orthodox conception of supernatural redemption rather than the liberal emphasis on subjectivism and religious experience. Yet was their influence on the theology of preachers helpful to the life of the Church is another matter; one that needs greater space than this short paper.

For Forsyth the mightiest moral action of all was the death of Christ, because it is in this act, for him, that we see God acting decisively and finally; the *tetelestai,*[47] that 'it is finished'. A M Hunter in *P T Forsyth, Per Crucem ad Lucem* finds him to be a theologian who is only interested in the business of God completing His work. It is not a matter of merely patching up a wound, but of grappling with the final facts of human nature, 'against which sentimental optimism is ever powerless....He deals with the facts of man's sin and guilt as he finds God's cure for it in a great Christ and a great Cross;'[48] hence Hunter's sub title to his book *Per Crucem ad Lucem,* 'Through Cross to Light'. It is here on the Cross that the work of reconciliation was completed. The work is done by God, towards mankind, 'When Christ did what he did it was not human nature doing it, it was God doing it. This is the great, absolutely unique and glorious thing. It is God in Christ reconciling. It was not human nature offering its very best to God. It was God offering his very best to man'.[49] It is here that Forsyth distinguishes between the Church and Civilisation. For him, civilisation, at its best represents the most that mankind can do with the world and with human nature, but the Church, 'centred upon Christ, His Cross, and His work, represents the best that God can do for them. The sacrifice of the Cross was not man in Christ pleasing God; it was God in Christ reconciling man, and in a certain sense reconciling Himself... It was not a heroic man dying for a beloved and honoured God... it was God dying for man."[50]

In conclusion Peter Taylor Forsyth does come to the Cross and the doctrine of the atonement saying that it is an act of God, that is of His holiness; that it is the only thing that can make any repentance or expiation of ours satisfactory to God; that it is not a stage in the evolution of mankind, but a revolutionary act which changed history for all eternity; and that our view of what Christ did must be the view that does most justice to the holiness of God and takes most profoundly and seriously the glorifying of His name. Forsyth can only be comfortable with a view of the atonement as an act of God; that the real objectivity of the atonement is not that it was made to God, but by God. The holy love demonstrates what God did, not what man was doing. This was not human nature offering its very best to God, rather the Cross is God offering His Son, His very best to man. He says, 'The prime doer in Christ's cross was God. Christ was God reconciling. He was God doing the very best for man, and not man doing his very best before God. The former is evangelical Christianity, the latter is humanist Christianity.'[51]

J K Mozley, although as noted earlier had reservations with Forsyth placing the atonement in a position to understand the incarnation, deals admiringly with P T Forsyth in his *Doctrine of the Atonement*, stating 'The student of this remarkable thinker feels that language is taken by force, and strained to its utmost capacity for the expression of the conceptions which raise themselves from the great deeps of a mind wherein the Christian has triumphed over the philosopher, and then served himself of his adversary's weapons. Systematic is not a word that one would naturally apply to Dr Forsyth; yet I know of no theologian of the day who has fewer loose ends to his thought. To adopt a phrase of his own he never attempts to set up in his theology a subsidiary centre, but at every point which he reaches in the gradual development of a position… one knows that there is a straight line back, as from any point on the circle's circumference to its centre, to that which is moral and therefore the only possible centre of the world - the Cross of Christ.'[52]   It is no wonder that at that Boston International Congregational Council in 1899, he suggested to the applauding audience that they should sing John Bowring's hymn, *In the Cross of Christ I glory...* [53]

Is then the atonement 'in reality, to be experienced, to be understood, and interpreted?'.[54] It is experience we encounter as we come to P T Forsyth and it was from this same experience that he articulated his message in his sermons, his lectures and his books. The reader cannot but relate to the author's warm heart, even if his style is both colourful in language and driving in tempo. It gives one an experience, as if standing underneath a waterfall with an eggcup, trying our best to catch some water, while so much new water keeps replacing what was in the cup originally.   Each of his sentences drives home his conviction that God through the Cross of Christ did reconcile mankind to Himself. I will conclude with Peter Taylor Forsyth; 'When Christ died at sin's hands, it meant that sin was death to the holiness of God, and both could not live in the same world. When He rose it meant that what was to live and rule in the world was the holy God....'[55]. Never is man so just with God as when his broken, holy heart calls just the judgement of God which he feels, but has not himself earned; and never could man be just with God, but through God's justification of Himself in the blood of Christ.'[56]

Peter Taylor Forsyth , a 'theologian for a new millennium' - not really, if Christian theology is to be something other than an instrument of evangelical Christianity but if theology is to serve the church's proclamation and mission, then here is a theologian and a Christian teacher that cannot but influence the preaching of the news that it is in the Cross of Christ that the sins of humanity are dealt with, once and for all and that it is this same Cross that fills the chasm between the holiness of God and the sinfulness of humanity. Preachers and professional theologians of this new millennium are well advised to quarry in the works of Forsyth for not only will their theological perceptions be challenged, but also their hearts *could be warmed.*

Notes:

[1]   P T Forsyth, *The Cruciality of the Cross*, Hodder & Stoughton, London, 1910, p 9.

[2]   P T Forsyth, *The Work Of Christ*, Hodder & Stoughton, London, 1910, p xvi.

[3]   Forsyth was to retain many of the ideas that he obtained from Maurice although as Williams Lee Bradley, (*P T Forsyth, his life and his works*, Independent Press, London, 1952, p.97) would have us believe, 'it is probable more correct to think of Maurice's lasting influence as inspirational rather than intellectual.'

[4]   Ibid.

[5]   Ibid, p xviii.

[6]   Thomas Hywel Hughes, *The Atonement. Modern Theories of the doctrine,* Allen & Unwin, London, 1949, p xi.

[7]   Ibid, p xi.

[8]   Ibid.

[9]   Ibid, p xii.

[10] P T.Forsyth, *The Work of Christ.* op cit, p 22.

[11] James Denney, 1856-1917, was a contemporary of Forsyth and Principal of the United Free Church College, Glasgow. Denney wrote, *The Christian Doctrine of Reconciliation*, which were the *Cunningham Lectures* for 1917.

[12] James Denney, *The Christian Doctrine of Reconciliation*, Hodder & Stoughton, London, 1919 p 71.

[13] Marvin Anderson, *P T Forsyth, Prophet of the Cross*, Evangelical Quarterly, Vol.XLVII No.3, pp 151-152.

[14] R J Campbell, *City Temple Sermons* Hodder & Stoughton, London, 1903 p 12.

[15] Ibid, p 71.

[16] *Daily Mail,* January 11th 1907.

[17] *Lux Mundi*: *Studies in the Religion of Incarnation*, Charles Gore (ed), 1889.

[18] Allan P F Sell, *Theology in turmoil,* reprinted, Eugene or Wipf and Stock 1998.

[19] R Brown, *New Dictionary of Theology P T Forsyte* , IVP 1988, p260.

[20] Charles Gore, *The New Theology and Old Religion*, John Murray, London, 1907.

[21] C D F Moule, *The Sacrifice of Christ* , Hodder & Stoughton, London, 1956, p 28.

[22] Possibly the most distinguished member of the subjective school was Hastings Rashdall (1858-1924), an Oxford philosopher who became Dean of Carlisle. His moral view of the atonement and his abhorrence with the theory of substitution is clearly defined in his work, The Idea of Atonement in Christian Theology, London, 1919.

[23] op cit, p 212.

[24] A P F Sell, *Theology in Turmoil* op cit, p 216.

[25] Harold Bushnell is regarded as the father of American Liberal Theology and of the Social Gospel movement.

[26] John McLeod Campbell, The Nature of the Atonement, 1860. Deposed from the ministry of the Church of Scotland in 1830 because he taught that Jesus died to save the whole of mankind, he influenced Forsyth not because of his universalist teaching on the Cross, rather because he stressed that the Cross and not the incarnation lies at the heart of the biblical view of the atonement.

27 James Denney, *The Death of Christ*, Hodder & Stoughton, London, 1902, p 86.

28 *Romans 6: 23.*

29 P T Forsyth, *The Work of Christ*, op cit,, p 156.

30 op cit, p 146.

31 Ibid, p 150.

32 Ibid, p 151.

33 Ibid, p 151.

34 Ibid, p 154.

35 Ibid.

36 P T Forsyth, *The Work of Christ* op cit, p xix.

37 James Denney *The Christian Doctrine of Reconciliation*, Hodder & Stoughton, London, 1917, p 80.

38 Ibid, p 180.

39 P T Forsyth, *The Work of Christ* op cit, xvi.

40 Hastings Rashdall, *The Idea of Atonement in Christian Theology*, MacMillan & Co, London, 1919, p 441.

41 Ibid, p 443.

42 P T Forsyth, *The Work of Christ* op cit, p 162

43 *Lux Mundi: A series of Studies in the Religion of the Incarnation*, 1889. This was a controversial volume of Oxford Essays under the editorship of Charles Gore (1853-1932).

44 J M Creed, *Mysterium Christi*, p 129, taken from Frances Young's *Sacrifice and the work of Christ.*

45 Additional reading on the German Modern-Positive Movement during Forsyth's time can be found in *P T Forsyth, The Modern-Positive Movement in Theology* by Gerald Birney Smith, American Journal of Theology, Vol.XIII, pp 92-99, Chicago, 1909.

46 P T Forsyth, *Positive Preaching and the Modern Mind*, Hodder & Stoughton, London, 1907, p 249.

47 *John 19: 30.*

48 A M Hunter, *P T Forsyth - per Crucem ad Lucem*, SCM, 1974, p 7.

49 P T Forsyth, The Work of Christ, Hodder & Stoughton, London, 1910, p 24.

50 Ibid, p 25.

51 P T Forsyth, *The Cruciality of the Cross*, Hodder & Stoughton, London, 1910, p 27.

52 J K Mozley, *The Doctrine of the Atonement*, Duckworth & Co., London, 1915, p 182.

53 John Bowring 1792-1872
In the Cross of Christ I glory,
Towering o'er the wrecks of time:
All the light of sacred story
Gathers round its head sublime.

54 T H Hughes, *The Atonement*, George Allen & Unwin, London, 1949, p xi.

55 P T Forsyth, *The Cruciality of the Cross*, op cit, p 213.

56 Ibid, p 214.

5.

The Work of Christ in the Thought of P T Forsyth

Kenosis and Plerosis Revisited

Richard L Floyd

To talk of 'the work of Christ' in the thought of P T Forsyth is not to refer to merely a section of his systematic theology but to point to the heart of his theology. Forsyth's entire theological project looks to the Cross of Christ as the decisive act of the Holy God. It mattered little what subject Forsyth approached in his writings, be it marriage, the arts, war and peace, he always returned again and again to the Cross as his fixed point, his north star, his magnetic north. He used the navigational image himself: 'The church must always adjust its compass at the Cross.'[1]

The term 'the Cross' functions as theological shorthand for Forsyth, as it did for Paul, to mean the whole dramatic activity of Christ culminating at Calvary and vindicated by Easter. 'I desire to keep in view the Cross, the organic crisis of Christ's whole life, earthly and eternal, as God's one kerugma, as the burthen, key, consummation and purpose of Christ's whole person and mission…[2]

Thus, the Cross for Forsyth is never merely an emblem of who God is; it is something God does, an act of the holy God. The Cross is constitutive for salvation rather than illustrative of it. It is the instrument that puts into effect God's holy love rather than a symbol that only demonstrates God's love. Christ's death on the Cross is nothing less than God acting:

> He (Christ) was God, therefore, and His death was God in action. He was not simply the witness of God's grace, He was its fact, its incarnation. His death was not merely a seal to His work; it was His consummate work. It gathered up His whole person. It was more than a confirmatory pledge; it was the effective sacrament of the gracious God, with His real presence at its core. Something was done there once for all, and the subject doer of it was God. The real acting person in the Cross was God.[3]

We can see that Forsyth's theology focuses on God as a personality, as one who acts, who is best understood not for who he is but rather for what he does.

And in the same way Forsyth's Christology focuses on what Christ does rather than who Christ is; his person is known in his work, which is the work of God. Soteriology controls Christology. It is only Christ in his Cross that does justice to New Testament Christianity; his teachings alone do not make him an object of faith and worthy of worship. Forsyth insists that:

> Faith is an attitude we can take only to God. God is the only correlate of faith, if we use words with any conscience. Faith in Christ involves the Godhead of Christ. Faith in Christ, in the positive Christian sense, means much more than a relation to God to which Christ supremely helps us. It is a communion possible not <u>through,</u> but only <u>in</u> Christ and Him crucified. <u>It means that to be in Christ is to be in God. It means that the experience that the action of Christ with us is God's action, that Christ does for us and in us what holy God alone can do, and that meeting with Christ we meet with God</u>.[4]

So in Forsyth's theology a two-act Christology replaces a two-nature Christology, with an act from the divine side and a corresponding one from the human side. The divine <u>kenosis,</u> or self-emptying, coincides with the plerosis, or self-fulfilment, of Christ.

But if Forsyth holds to a kenotic theory, it is a kenotic theory with a difference. It is construed in moral rather than in metaphysical language; it is dramatic and active rather than static, in keeping with its object, the free God who acts in the man Jesus Christ. The term *kenosis* is derived from the Greek *heuton ekenosen*, 'he emptied himself,' of *Philippians 2:7.* As a substantive it is used, in the technical sense, of the Christological theory which sets out' to show how the Second Person of the Trinity could so enter into human life as that there resulted the genuinely human experience which is described by the evangelists.' (HR Macintosh, *New Bible Dictionary;*[5] See also N T Wright, *The Climax of the Covenant,*[6] for a comprehensive review of the history of the interpretation of *Philippians 2.)*

In the late nineteenth century, kenotic theories of the atonement were popular among German Lutherans (ie, Gottried Thomasius, W F Gess, F H R von Frank) and with some British Anglicans, notably Charles Gore who gave the Bampton Lectures at Oxford in 1889. Kenotic views of incarnation or atonement put forth the idea in one way or another that, in Christ, God relinquished some aspect of his divinity.

The kenotic approach was criticised for a number of reasons: that it was pantheistic, blurring the line between God and humanity; that it undermined the doctrine of divine immutability; that it jeopardised the Trinity, for a humanised Son empty of divine attributes could be no part of the Trinitarian life; that it failed to recognise the proper relationship between divine existence, divine attributes and divine essence when it claimed the former can be separated from the latter; and, finally, that the kenotic Christ is neither God nor man and, therefore, doesn't solve the problem it sets out to solve. The popularity of the kenotic approach was already waning by Forsyth's day. This he no doubt knew, as he knew the criticisms and difficulties. 'Many difficulties arise readily in one's own mind,' he wrote, 'It is a choice of difficulties.'[7] He takes pains in places to separate himself from some of the more vulnerable of the kenoticist's views.

Nevertheless, he does not shy away from the kenotic language as long as it is in his distinctive moral vocabulary. Although Forsyth's full treatment of kenosis will wait until 1909 with *The Person and Place of Jesus Christ*, we see a kenotic emphasis already by 1895 in a sermon on *Philippians 2:5-8* entitled *'The Divine Self-Emptying'* (later to appear in the anthology *God the Holy Father*). In that earlier treatment Forsyth already has in outline the two-act Christology, which will be spelled out in the kenosis/plerosis scheme of *The Person and Place of Jesus Christ*. Where the critics of kenotic theories worry about loss of divinity, Forsyth wants to view kenosis as constitutive of Christ's divinity. He understands Christ's self-emptying as the very act which makes him Lord. It is only <u>because</u> of his Godhead that Christ can empty himself and in so doing he fulfils his Godhead. So in this case limitation is understood as a power rather than a defect:

> Well, notice here that Christ's emptying of Himself is not regarded as the loss of His true Godhead, but the condition of it. Godhead is what we worship. Christ's emptying of Himself has placed him at the centre of human worship. Therefore He is of Godhead. We worship Him as the crucified— through the Cross, not in spite of the Cross.[8]

One of the traditional objections to a kenotic theory is that if the divine nature is given up how can the subsequent human act be an act of God and therefore a saving act, since only God can save? But Forsyth's view of kenosis doesn't involve the loss of divinity so much as its self-retraction or self-reduction. This is language about a free personality who chooses to act and is known by his acts, rather than language about a deity known by his attributes.

From Kant, Forsyth acquired a metaphysical agnosticism; this keeps him away from using the language of two natures to understand how the human Jesus relates to his Godhead. Rather than thinking about Christ in the language of two natures, Forsyth wants more active categories. He refers at times to 'two modes of being' and elsewhere to 'two moral movements':

> Let us cease speaking of a nature as if it were an entity; of two natures as two independent entities; and let us think and speak of two modes of being, like quantitative and qualitative, or physical and moral. Instead of speaking of certain attributes as renounced may we not speak of a new mode of their being? The Son, by an act of love's omnipotence, set aside the style of God, and took the style of a servant, the mental manner of a man, and the mode of moral action that marks human nature.[9]

This 'setting aside' is the language one would use of a personal subject, and this is what Forsyth presses for, a move away from the terms of entities and their substance to the terms of personalities and their freely chosen moral acts. So:

> As the union of wills we have in Christ, therefore, the union of two moral movements or directions, and not merely their confluence, their mutual living involution, and not simply their inert conjunction. Much that may seem obscure would vanish if we could but cease to think in terms of material substance or force, however fine, and learn to think in terms of personal subjects and their kind in union; if our minds gave up handling quantities in these high matters and took up kinds. It is the long and engrained habit of thinking in masses or entities that makes so unfamiliar and dark the higher habit of thinking in acts.[10]

Forsyth believes that construing the act of God in Christ in dramatic and moral terms is truer to the witness of the New Testament than the metaphysical language of Greek Philosophy and the Fathers of the early centuries. It is also truer, he is convinced, to the Christian experience of an atoning saving Christ There is a decidedly experiential dimension to Forsyth's understanding of Christian authority: 'It is the evangelical experience of every saved soul that is the real foundation of Christological belief anywhere. For Christ was not the epiphany of an idea, nor the epitome of a race, nor the incarnation, the precipitate, of a metaphysic—whatever metaphysic he may imply.'[11]

Kenosis is then a moral necessity for the God who is holy love. The holiness of God requires the divine intervention of the atoning Cross against human sin. For Forsyth God's holiness is his defining attribute, God's very nature. He writes:

> The holy law is not the creation of God but His nature, and it cannot be treated as less than inviolate and eternal, it cannot be denied or simply annulled unless He seems false to Himself. If a play on words be permitted is such a connection, the self-denial of Christ was there because God could not deny himself.[12]

Again we can see how Forsyth's understanding of God in moral rather than in metaphysical terms leads him to the logic of the Cross. Human sin requires a real atonement. For Forsyth the wrath of God is not some arbitrary anger, but the response of the holy God to the very antithesis of holiness, which is sin. Sin could be defined for Forsyth as the denial of holy love. So divine holiness reacts to human sin with wrath and judgement. Forsyth's theology takes sin and evil with utmost seriousness. God cannot tolerate sin. It threatens his very being:

> God is fundamentally affected by sin. He is stung to
> the core. It does not simply try Him. It challenges
> His whole place in the moral world. It puts Him on
> His trial as God. It is, in its nature, an assault on His
> life. Its vital object is to unseat Him. It has no part
> whatever in His purpose. It hates and kills Him.[13]

So God is not just love, but holy love at war with sin. Liberal
theology knows only a benign mercy that overlooks sin
without overcoming it. That is why it can do without an
atoning Cross.

But a theology that takes God's holiness seriously must also
take sin and evil seriously and realise that they are at war. God
must not only forgive sin, but also destroy it by atonement.
During the First World War, Forsyth wrote these words to
describe the holiness of God and the power of His holy Cross:

> The great Word of the Gospel is not God is love. That
> is too stationary, too little energetic. It produces a
> religion unable to cope with crises. But the Word is
> this—Love is omnipotent for ever because it is holy.
> That is the voice of Christ—raised from the midst of
> time, and its chaos, and its convulsions, yet coming
> from the depths of eternity, where the Son dwells in the
> bosom of the Father, the Son to whom all power is
> given in heaven and on earth because He overcame the
> world in a Cross holier than love itself, more tragic,
> more solemn, more dynamic than all earth's wars. The
> key to history is the historic Christ above history and in
> command of it, and there is no other.[14]

The phrase 'the historic Christ above history' points to
Forsyth's high Christology. If Christ truly shares in the
Godhead he cannot have been created or arrived in time, but

must have been God from before the beginning. The idea of a pre-existent Christ is, of course, seen here and there in the New Testament, most notably in *John 1* and in *Colossians 1:15f.* Forsyth's Christology requires such a pre-existent Christ if the atoning Cross is to truly be an act of the God who in the beginning created the heavens and the earth. Against the claim of 'the history of religions school' that such passages reflect Gnostic influences, Forsyth argues that the earthly career of Christ requires that he has always been part of the Godhead.

An important passage for Forsyth is *Matthew 11:27*: 'All things have been handed over to me by my Father; and no one knows the Son except the Father, and no one knows the Father except the Son and anyone to whom the Son chooses to reveal him.'[15] He cited this text against liberal critics to show that it was not just in the Gospel of John but also in the Synoptics that a high Christology was present. He argues that pre-existence is not some add-on to the Gospel, but an intrinsic feature of the Christ who is God. The Gospel requires a pre-existent Christ, and Christian experience confirms it. For example, he suggests that Paul's affirmation of the pre-existence of Christ came from his experience, that Paul 'worked back from the faith that all things were made for Christ to the conviction that, as the end was in the beginning, all things were made by Christ; and by a Christ as personal as the Christ who was their goal.'[16]

So Christ's kenosis is not just an act in time but an act that was established from beyond time:

> Christ's earthly humiliation had to have its foundation laid in heaven, and to be viewed but as the working out of a renunciation before the world was.'[17] 'His emergence on earth was at is were the

swelling in of heaven. His sacrifice began before He came into the world, and his Cross was that of a lamb slain before the world's foundation. There was a Calvary above which was the mother of it all.[18]

What does the kenosis involve? What is given up? Forsyth speaks of the self-reduction of God's attributes rather than their destruction; they go from being actual to potential. It is not so much limitation as concentration. They are drawn in. He says that divine attributes such as omniscience are not destroyed but are reduced from the actual to the potential. 'They are only concentrated. The self-reduction, or self-retraction, of God might be a better phrase than the self-emptying.'[19]

Forsyth gives a series of examples of how a personality might freely choose to limit himself - a wise vizier to a foolish young sultan who voluntarily takes a cup of poison meant for his master and dies a prolonged and debilitating death; a musical genius in Russia who knowingly chooses to dedicate himself to political associations that cause him to be deported to a life in Siberia where he can never play the violin again; a university student brilliant in philosophical pursuits who, upon the death of his father, gives up his career to take over the leadership of the family business.[20] In each case a conscious choice, motivated by love, is made which limits the personality. In each case, something precious is lost, but more is gained, and love is the motivation of each choice.

In Christ's case the free obedient act of the Cross is not just love, but holy love concentrated at one point. Forsyth argues that since holy love is the supreme category of the Almighty, and the object for which his omnipotence exists, how could his omnipotence be imperilled by its own supreme act? 'The freedom that limits itself to create freedom is true omnipotence, as the love that can humble itself to save is truly

Almighty.'[21] Far from imperilling the Godhead of Christ, the kenosis of incarnation culminating in the Cross is the most powerful act of Godhead, even more powerful than the creation of the world:

> To appear and act as Redeemer, to be born, suffer, and die, was a mightier act of Godhead than lay in all creation, preservation, and blessing of the world. It was only in the exercise of a perfect divine fullness (and therefore power) that Christ could empty and humble himself to the servant he became. As the humiliation grew so grew the exaltation of the power and person that achieved it. It was an act of such might that it was bound to break through the servant form, and take at last for all men's worship the lordly name.[22]

So it is fitting that 'at the name of Jesus every knee should bend, in heaven and on earth, and under the earth, and every tongue confess the Jesus Christ is Lord, to the glory of God the Father.' (*Philippians 2:10,11 NRSV*) Here in praise and confession are represented the whole of creation according to the cosmology of the day.

So kenosis leads to plerosis, self-emptying to self-fulfilment, and not just at the final vindication but as a process throughout the life of Christ. Kenosis by itself is inadequate, Forsyth says:

> What we have chiefly in view is the sort of uniqueness in the man Jesus which is required for the final and personal gift of Godhead in him. Now for such a purpose a Christ merely kenotic is inadequate... We have examined the kenotic or self-emptying theories of such an act, and we have found them either more helpful or less. But whether we

take a kenotic theory or not, we must have some doctrine of God's self-divestment, or His reduction to our human case. Yet, if we go no farther than that, it only carries us half-way, it only leads us to the spectacle of a humbled God, and not to the experience of a redeeming and royal God. For redemption we need something more positive. It is a defect in kenotic theories, however sound, that they turn only on one side of the experience of Christ, viz., his descent and humiliation. It is a defect because that renunciatory element is negative after all; and to dwell on it, as modern views of Christ do, is to end in a Christian ethic somewhat weak, and tending to ascetic and self-occupied piety.[23]

If kenosis by itself is inadequate, what must be the corresponding plerosis? The question that Forsyth wants to address in his two-act Christology is how is the humanity of Jesus related to his Godhead. Forsyth want to take seriously both the historic Christ and his Godhead. He turns aside the liberal view that Christ is the apex of the spiritual evolution that emerges into a divine height in humanity, the divine blossom of the race, or its 'heaven-kissing hill.'[24] No, the historic Christ comes to save humanity and not to exhibit humanity's salvation. 'The King makes the Kingdom, and not the Kingdom the King.'[25] It is an invasion not an evolution. 'Man does not simply unfold to God but God descends and enters man.'[26]

It is not that divinity and humanity share in being, rather they meet in action. There are two movements, God to man and man to God.

> God and man meet in humanity, not as two entities or natures that coexist, but as two movements in mutual interplay, mutual struggle and reciprocal communion.

On the one hand we have an initiative, creative, productive action, clear and sure, on the part of the eternal and absolute God; on the other we have the seeking, receptive, appropriative action of groping, erring, growing man. God finds a man who did not find Him, man finds a God who did find Him.[27] (The capital 'h' on the last word is either a misprint or, more likely, Forsyth's subtle way of saying that God finds man only in Christ.)

Thus Christ embodies these two movements in which God and humanity meet. Forsyth says that in Christ we have two things: we have the action of the Godhead concentrated through one hypostasis (or mode of being) within it, and we have the growing moral appropriation by man's soul moving God-ward of that action as its own. This is the two-act Christology, which is the heart of Forsyth's project. It has God entering our world: 'We have that divine Son, by whose agency the world of souls was made, not now creating another soul, but himself becoming such a soul.'[28] And he enters it to bring man to God as Christ acts in his humanity to be obedient to the will of the Father. Christ never ceases to be what he has always been, but grows in consciousness of his divinity through the unfolding moral crisis, which he enters in the world.

> ...the history of Christ's growth is then a history, by gradual moral conquest, of the mode of being from which, by a tremendous moral act, he came. It is reconquest. He learned the taste of an acquired divinity who had eternally known it as a possession. He won by duty what was his own by right.[29]

So Christ in his humanity shares the human reality of growth. Human life does not begin as a finished article. 'It begins with certain possibilities, with a destiny engrained in the protoplast;

but it only passes from a destiny into a perfection through a career.'[30] Christ grows by moral struggle. He is tempted, but without sin. Again and again he must freely choose the way to go. Throughout his life he grows in his consciousness of what he was, although not in Godhead itself, which he always had. Here Forsyth is able to speak of a progressive incarnation, although in very qualified language:

> We may speak of a progressive incarnation within his life, if we give it a kenotic basis. He grew in the grace in which he always was, and in the knowledge of it. As his personal history enlarged and ripened by every experience, and as he was always found equal to each moral crisis, the latent Godhead became more and more mighty as his life's interior, and asserted itself with the more power as the personality grew in depth and scope. Every step he victoriously took into the dark and hostile land was an ascending movement also of the Godhead which was its base. This ascent into Hell went on, from His temptation to His tomb, in gathering power. Alongside his growing humiliation to the conditions of evil moved his growing exaltation to holy power. Alongside the Kenosis and its negations there went a corresponding Plerosis, without which the Kenosis is a one-sided idea.[31]

Kenosis and plerosis together constitute two movements of a single act of God. The more Christ laid down his personal life the more he gained his divine soul. 'He lives out a moral plerosis by the very completeness of his kenosis; and he achieves the plerosis in resurrection and ascension.'[32]

The moral struggle that Christ was involved in was the struggle to be obedient to the Father's will. It was the struggle to become a servant. What does Christ's becoming a servant mean? It means that he took on a state of subjugation in which he was called upon to render obedience. What Christ becomes by his kenosis is a servant, and it is the free moral act involved in his obedience to the Father's will that is decisive for his Lordship. It is not his suffering, but his obedience, that makes him Lord. Forsyth rejects the idea that what is satisfied in the atonement is God's wounded honour or God's justice:

> We have further left behind that the satisfaction of Christ was made either to God's wounded honour or to His punitive justice. And we see with growing and united clearness that it was made by obedience rather than suffering. There is a vast difference between suffering as a condition of Atonement and suffering as the thing of positive worth in it, what gives it its value.[33]

But although Christ takes on full humanity, there is a limit. He remains without sin, as he must for only the sinless one can accomplish the work of the Holy God against sin. Forsyth counters the argument that this somehow makes Christ less than human. He argues that Christ was indeed tempted in every way that humans are, and that his struggles were real. 'Because Christ was true man he could be truly tempted; because he was true God he could not truly sin; but he was not less true man for that.'[34] Forsyth suggests that kenosis involved the limitation of Christ's knowledge of the impossibility of sinning. He put aside his omniscience, so that he didn't know. But if he didn't know, it was because he chose not to know. This makes more sense of his human struggles as depicted in the Gospels than the docetic Christ whose exertions are a charade. Clearly Christ's struggles must persuade us that he took the possibility of sin seriously. In the Garden of Gethsemane Christ agonises over whether the Cross is truly the Father's will. Forsyth says that he chose not to know that for him sinning was impossible, and in doing so, shared the full human experience of temptation:

> ...to his own experience the moral conflict was entirely real, because his self-emptying included an oblivion of that impossibility of sin. As consciousness arose he was unwittingly protected from those deflections incident to inexperience which would have damaged his moral judgement and development when maturity came. And this was only possible if he had, to begin with, a unique, central, and powerful relation to the being of God apart from his own earthly decisions. So that his growth was growth in what he was, and not simply to what he might be. It was not acquiring what he had not, but appropriating and realising what he had. It was coming to his own unique self. I have already said that I am alive to the criticism to which such a position has been exposed, in that it seems to take him out of a real moral conflict like our own. And the answer, you have noted, is threefold. First, that our redeemer must save us by his difference from us, however the salvation get home by his parity with us. He saves because he is God and not man. Second, the reality of his conflict is secured by his kenotic ignorance of his inability to sin. And third, his unique relationship to God was a relation to a free God and not to a mechanical or physical fate, or to an invincible bias to good.[35]

For Forsyth the death of Christ is really a sacrifice, but it is not a sacrifice made to God as much as a sacrifice made by God:

> Atonement to God must be made, and it was only possible from God.'[36]

Christ became sin for us, and took the penalty for that sin on himself. So the Cross is penal but God doesn't punish Christ. The atonement is penal but it is not penitential. The punishment of sin fell on Christ's personality, to his consciousness, but not to his conscience. There was no self-accusation in it, since he remained sinless. Christ never felt that God was punishing him:

'It was the consequence of sin, though not of His sin.[37]

In the sacrifice of the Cross, Christ is both priest and victim 'The priest, in his grace, becomes the victim, and completes his confession of God's holiness by meeting its acting as judgement. To forgive sin he must bear sin.'[38] This makes for a priestly Christ, a priestly religion and a priestly Church.[39] Forsyth believed that:

New Testament Christianity is a priestly religion or it is nothing. It gathers around a priestly Cross on earth and a Great High Priest Eternal in the heavens. It also means the equal priesthood of each believer. But it means much more. That by itself is ruinous individualism. It means the collective priesthood of the Church as one. The greatest function of the Church in full communion with Him is priestly. It is to confess, to sacrifice, to intercede for the whole human race in Him.[40]

That is where the act of God in Christ becomes contemporary, in the priestly ministry of the whole Church of Jesus Christ, where soteriology informs theology, and the kenotic Christ creates the servant Church in each succeeding generation.

How would we assess Forsyth's kenosis/plerosis proposal? Its purpose is twofold: (i) to safeguard the full humanity of Christ against a docetic view, and (ii) to assert against liberal theology the full participation of Christ in the Godhead. I think it succeeds on both counts. He depicts a fully human Christ as one engaged in a mighty moral struggle, freely acting finally in obedience to the Father's will at the expense of his own life. The human struggle is not passed over lightly, yet the whole action is seen as an act of God.

Doctrine is the conceptual redefinition of the biblical narrative. Has Forsyth done justice to the biblical narrative? Here, too, Forsyth has been successful for he has successfully kept scripture clearly in view throughout. He deals with both the high Christology of John and the Epistles, and the human Jesus of the Synoptics, the one who went through the full experience of the passion. Donald MacKinnon wrote that 'the realities of Gethsemane refuse to allow him (Forsyth) to neglect the extent to which the passion was suffused by a kind of terrible uncertainty.'[41] Forsyth captures that 'terrible uncertainty' and the powerful moral drama that is the passion.

There is great rhetorical power to Forsyth's theology as he addresses issue after issue returning always to the Cross as the centre. *In The Person and Place of Jesus Christ* he offers a highly nuanced theological interpretation that tries to make sense of the meaning of the Cross. His kenotic Christology attempts to explain the mystery of the incarnation and the inner workings of the atonement without using the metaphysical language of which he was so suspicious. Both Donald MacKinnon and Colin Gunton have criticised Forsyth for eschewing metaphysical language, particularly ontological language, and for his too easy dismissal of the truths of Chalcedon. I have to agree in part with Colin Gunton's charge that Forsyth imported a metaphysic through the back door after all, when you talk about 'modes of being' you are pretty close to metaphysics if not already there. Gunton is right when he says: 'Forsyth's kenotic theory of the incarnation is essentially an attempt to make logical sense of the incarnation conceived as something that really happened in human history. It thus belies his proclaimed lack of interest in metaphysical theories.'[42]

Yet, having acknowledged the charge, let me say that I think Forsyth's attempt to articulate a Christology outside the usual metaphysical framework is part of what gives his writings such rhetorical punch and dramatic power. He is a good theologian, but he never stops being a preacher, which may account for his continued popularity with preachers. Looking backward he reminds one at times of Luther in his freedom to talk about an experience of one person of the Trinity happening to another. In other respects he anticipates the various canonical and narrative approaches that are associated with the 'Yale theology' of Hans Frei, George Lindbeck and their students. Like them (and like Karl Barth) Forsyth's theology is thoroughly exegetical and takes the final form of the canon as the decisive text. Like them he doesn't eschew historical criticism, but recognises that it is 'a good servant but a dangerous master.' Yet, unlike at least some interpretations of the Yale School, he insists that the Gospel is more than a cultural linguistic narrative, which sets norms for a community, the Church. For Forsyth it is also God's truth for the whole world. In this he remains decidedly evangelical, and his hermeneutic has an important experiential dimension. But this is not just any experience! Forsyth would have understood 'experience' more along the lines of Jonathan Edwards' view of Christian experience than that of those today for whom individual or group experience is authoritative. He would have had little use for the idea of 're-imagining' God in the light of our own experience. 'See to the Gospel,' he said, 'and experience will take care of itself.' With that admonition in our ears I will end with a benediction in Forsyth's own words:

And now may he who so emptied himself that he was filled with all the fullness of God dwell fully in us; may he raise, rule, and perfect us in all holiness; to the end that, bowing before him with every knee both in heaven and upon earth, and ever more calling Him Holy, Holy, Holy Lord, we may be, in Him, to the praise and glory of the Father's Grace Who made us acceptable in the Eternal Son, world without end. Amen.[43]

Notes:

1   Untitled article by P T Forsyth in *The Atonement in Modern Religious Thought*, Whittaker, New York, 1901, p 62.

2   P T Forsyth, *The Preaching of Jesus and the Gospel of Christ*, New Creation Publications, Blackwood, South Australia, 1987, p 83.

3   P T Forsyth, *Positive Preaching and the Modern Mind*, Independent Press, London, p 358.

4   P T Forsyth, *The Person and Place of Jesus Christ*, Independent Press, London, 1948, p 6 with emphasis added by the writer of the article.

5   H R Macintosh, *New Bible Dictionary.*

6   N T Wright, *The Climax of the Covenant: Christ and the law in Pauline Theology*, Fortress Press, Minneapolis, 1993.

7   P T Forsyth, *The Person and Place of Jesus Christ* op cit, p 294.

8   P T Forsyth, *God the Holy Father*, Independent Press, London, 1957 p 32

9   P T Forsyth, *The Person and Place of Jesus Christ* op cit, p 307

10   Ibid, p 346.

11   Ibid, p 9.

12   P T Forsyth in *The Atonement in Modern Religious Thought* op cit, p 70.

13   P T Forsyth, *Positive Preaching and the Modern Mind*, Independent Press, London, p 366.

14   P T Foryth, *The Justification of God* p 227.

15   P T Forsyth, *The Person and Place of Jesus Christ*, op cit, p 81.

16   Ibid, p 269.

17   Ibid, p 270.

18   Ibid, p 271.

19   Ibid, p 308.

20   Ibid, pp 296-298.

21   Ibid, p 314.

22   Ibid, p 315.

23   Ibid, pp 328-329.

24   Ibid, p 33.

25   Ibid, p 334.

26   Ibid, p 334.

27   Ibid, p 336.

28   Ibid, p338.

29   Ibid, p308.

30   Ibid, p 345.

31   Ibid, p 349.

32   Ibid, p 300.

33   P T Forsyth in *The Atonement in Modern Religious Thought* op cit, p 67.

34   P T Forsyth, *The Person and Place of Jesus Christ*, op cit, p 302.

35   Ibid, p 342.

36   P T Forsyth, Positive Preaching and the Modern mind, op cit, p 365.

37   P T Forsyth in *The Atonement in Modern Religious Thought* op cit, p 85.

38   P T Forsyth, Positive Preaching and the Modern Mind, op cit, p 362.
39   See Richard L Floyd, *The Cross and the Church: The Soteriology and Ecclesiology of P T Forsyth*, in *Andover Newton RReview* 3, 1992.
40   P T Forsyth, *The Person and Place of Jesus Christ* op cit, p 12.
41   Trevor Hart(ed), *Justice the True and Only Mercy*, T & T Clark, Edinburgh, 1995 p 108.
42   See Colin Gunton, *Yesterday and Today: a study of continuities in Christology,* Eerdmanns, Grand Rapids, 1983, pp 168-173.
43   P T Forsyth, The Person and Place of Jesus Christ, op cit, p 357.

6.

P T Forsyth's Doctrine of the Church

David Cornick

'Dr Forsyth is a real prophet. It is a pity that he wishes to stand before us as a theologian also; for in this latter role he can hardly be termed a great success. The two are not easily combined, and in Dr Forsyth the prophet comes first, the theologian is a poor second'.[1]

Thus did Harold Hamilton welcome Forsyth's *The Church and the Sacraments* in the *Journal of Theological Studies* in 1917. However the editor allowed him four pages, and then as now, four pages indicates a work of significance - 'a challenging, penetrating, fascinating book, sparkling with epigram, pointed antithesis and plays upon words, and replete with those over-statements which are quite allowable in a prophet who wish a dull-witted people to see his point, but which the careful theologian must avoid above all things' He could have said the same of Luther - and that comparison should not be dismissed out of hand. A theologian is not just a technician of the faith. As Luther once remarked, 'Not understanding, reading or speculating, but living nay dying and being damned, make a man a theologian'.

What annoyed and perplexed Hamilton in equal measure was Forsyth's method, or what he perceived (wrongly) to be his lack of it. It is hard not to sympathise with his protests about imprecision - 'Church' is a slippery term in theological discourse, and Forsyth's style does nothing to help his reader hold it firmly. However, such complaints, although just, are really tangential. It is true, as Hamilton protested, that the apparatus of scholarship is completely absent - no footnotes, no references, no labelling of patristic tibia and fibula. But that was not arrogance, as Hamilton assumed. It was rather a different way of doing theology. Forsyth was a theological prose poet, a pulpit theologian. His reading was profound and multi-lingual, but lightly worn. His language cut through academic convention with flashes of rhetorical lightening, distracting the unwary from the ruthless Reformed logic that undergirds all his thought. Here was prophetic theology rather than theological prophecy. Such texts require a different kind of reading to that accorded to precise, scholarly dissections of patristic writings.

However, Hamilton grasped and grasped well that this was a topical book, a prophetic book for troubled times. As the Free Churches toyed with federalism, Forsyth strove to provide them with an ecclesiological rationale. In an age of intellectual crisis, Forsyth sought to replace the authority of an inerrant Bible with the objective authority of the gospel behind and within the gospels. To a denomination floating on the waves of liberal subjectivism, blown every which way by the winds of the 'New Theology', Forsyth offered a strange, radically Biblical alternative.   With backhanded generosity Hamilton noted that it was, 'an immense advance on the views usually associated with Nonconformist theology…. He has some harsh things to say of the Church of England (who, indeed, has not?); but then he has very much harder things to say of the Free Churches; the Roman Church, perhaps gets off the easiest. All of which goes to show that those whom he loves most he chastens most, which is as it should be'.

Those whom he loved most - his students and fellow ministers - 'Certainly the dearest men to me there are', the people of Shipley and Hackney, Cheetham Hill and Clarendon Park, Leicester and Emmanuel, Cambridge, with whom he had broken open the Word and forged a theology.[2]   The Principal of Hackney might long have jettisoned the liberalism of his Shipley days, but the social reality of Yorkshire and London and Manchester lived with him always. 'Do not take my arm and lead me away to the dwellings of pound-a-weeks and the nothing-a-weeks and tell me if I want realities to consider there', the Chairman of the Union told his hearers in 1905,

'Long ago I was there and worked there, and considered there, and have been considering ever since'.[3] If ever there was a theologian who crafted his theology from the stuff of pastoral reality, it was P T Forsyth. These were the people he loved. And it is these Congregationalists whom he chastises most, for he loved them most, and knew what they might be and ought to be but in his eyes were failing to be.

Forsyth's doctrine of the Church was the product of a specific history. If we are to understand it aright, we must place it in its context of Edwardian England, Congregationalism's silver age. Politically Congregationalism was far from a spent force. The Passive Resistance movement occasioned by Balfour's 1902 Education Act re-lit stirring, if anachronistic, flames in Congregationalist hearts and the unexpected 1906 landslide Liberal victory showed that there was life in the old alliance of nonconformity and Liberalism despite the miseries of 1886. Statistically membership continued to rise - there were 11.08% more Congregationalists in England in 1914 than in 1900, and the pulpit giants still commanded eager followings and an attentive press.[4]

Theologically liberalism was in an almost unchallenged ascendancy. As late Victorian Christians struggled with the philosophical legacy of the Enlightenment, the growth of the physical sciences, the development of evolutionary theory and the rise of scientific history, liberal Protestantism seemed to offer the most legitimate and useful method of religious discourse. It created an intellectual climate which sought continuities rather than discontinuities and which was wary of the supernatural and the unique. The publication of Harnack's *What is Christianity?* in 1901 confirmed the suspicion of many lesser minds that the uniqueness of Christianity lay solely in Jesus' teaching about the fatherhood of God and the brotherhood of man. That translated into pulpit rhetoric as an optimistic Unitarianism which found God in human experience, exalted human relationships, ignored the Cross and looked for the dawning of the kingdom at the hands of socialism. That is a caricature, but only just a caricature, of the most notorious work of Congregational liberalism, R J Campbell's *'The New Theology'* (1907) which occasioned a furious controversy within the denomination in which Forsyth was leading protagonist.

In the wake of the 'New Theology' controversy, the Reformed conception of the Church became a subject of serious discussion by nonconformist theologians. In his spring address as Chairman of the Union in 1909 J D Jones of Bournemouth chose as his subject 'Catholic Independency' and explored the nature of a Reformed Catholicism, in which freedom and authority might be property balanced. He also clearly repudiated liberalism, protesting against its 'exaggerated and excessive subjectivism'.[5] As Congregationalism considered its own structures and its response to the growing movement for unity amongst the Free Churches, the doctrines of the Church and ministry received new attention. In 1910 the Baptist leader J H Shakespeare propounded the idea of United Free Church of England, an idea which had the unlikely gestation of a speech by Hensley Henson to the 1910 Congregational Union autumn meeting.[6] In 1912 the Free Church Council committed itself to a thorough Free Church Inquiry, investigating their resources and potential for mission, and tentatively exploring possible forms of Unity, including the concept of federation.[7]

It was that mixture of hope and failure, new possibilities and diverse theologies, which led Forsyth to turn his attention to ecclesiology. Much of what he wrote was not new to him, although it clearly was to some of his reviewers. His discovery that the victory of liberalism '... has been disappointing on the whole … It is a spent movement'[8] is impossible to date accurately, but certainly took place before 1893, and his writings from then on are a fugue on a few dominant themes - the holiness of God, the reality of sin, the centrality of the Cross, the significance of grace, the place and person of Jesus Christ, and the nature of the Church.

During this period his prophet's ear was acute. In 1905 whilst membership figures still continued to climb, he lamented Congregationalism's seeming inability to retain the best minds of the age, particularly women, and put his finger on the gentle leakage to Anglicanism, which he ascribed to a failure of authority in his own denomination.[9] During his Lyman Beecher lectures at Yale two years later he lamented the triviality of the Free Churches. 'The minister's study becomes more an office than an oratory. Committees suck away the breath of power.   Socialities become the only welcome sacraments. The tea meeting draws people together as the communion table does not'.[10]

To a world made wise by the misery of war, such realities were only too obvious. Forsyth lamented the loss of influence of the Free Churches with 'the leaders of public affairs'. The days had gone when the decision of provincial town councils passed first through the deacons' meetings of the Free Churches. The climate of the age had changed. It was no longer a man's life in the Congregational chapel - 'The Christianity of the men has ebbed, and left the godliness of the women more conspicuous…. The men have retired though the women have not (though too many of them have) … We do not appeal to the strong men who have insight and decision…'[11] The working class movement was set to make the political running, and from its deliberations the voice of nonconformity was significantly absent.

The identification of the symptoms of the disease was accompanied by a theological diagnosis of the problem that was breathtakingly original in a climate of liberal orthodoxy. If Barth's Commentary on Romans was a response to a world in crisis, so too were the works of Forsyth's mature ecclesiology, *Faith, Freedom and the Future* (1912) and *The Church and the Sacraments* (1917). In 1912 he considered the Church to be in crisis 'comparable only to that through which it went in its collision with Gnosticism in the second and third centuries - a far deeper crisis than the Reformation was'.[12] Christianity and Western civilisation were so inextricably blended that many 'do not know where to take their stand - on the core of the Word or the best of the World'. Liberal Christianity had been 'busy erasing difference, tracing continuity, and reducing collision' in comparative religion, philanthropic endeavour and political science. Small wonder Congregationalism was in danger of being mistaken as a club for the creedless rather than part of the one, holy, catholic Church.[13] By 1917 the enormity of war had changed his historical focus. 'We have found out Germany;' he wrote with the sadness and seriousness of one who loved Germany dearly and who owed an incalculable debt to the German theological tradition, 'And we have rediscovered Satan'.[14] The crisis now facing the Church was analogous to that which confronted Augustine when he wrote '*The City of God amid the sack of Rome*'. As the world confronted the heart of darkness, as the facile optimism of liberalism withered and died amidst the blood of the trenches, the vastness of the moral and theological agenda before the Churches became appallingly clear. In general the response was woefully banal, but here at last was one theologian willing and able to answer the implicit questions of Wilfred Owen, Siegfried Sassoon and the countless numbers of the sorrowing and maimed.

He was able to do so because, like Luther, he was a theologian of the Cross. His debt to Luther is considerable, although rarely acknowledged. What Forsyth valued especially about Luther was his method, not his conclusions - 'We have to repeat Luther's method, in another place and climate, but with the same gospel'.[15] Luther never wrote extensively about the Church. Forsyth does, and part of his greatness as an ecclesiologist lies in his synthesis of a fundamentally Lutheran theology of the Cross, the Anabaptist and therefore Independent understanding of freedom, and a high Calvinist perception of Church order.

Rarely has there been such a penetrating and power study of the nature of Congregationalism as *Faith, Freedom and the Future*, that 'brilliant and prophetic book' as Daniel Jenkins termed it in 1954.[16] As he wrestled with the specific genius of Independency, the relationship between Word and Spirit, authority and freedom, Calvinism and Anabaptism, fused in the crucible of post-Reformation English politics, Forsyth applied what he consider to be Luther's methodology to the nature of the Church. It was an intensely moral method. Luther did not 'just tumble into his contemporary world with a vehement iteration of New Testament themes' and throw the gospel at the world 'in a Low Church way'. Rather, he allowed the gospel to 'g[e]t to his moral case', to the dilemmas of the generations before which had made him what he was and then to act on him experientially. In such a way the old gospel answers fitted the new questions. Using that method Forsyth reminded Independency first, that it was 'a really Church of the Holy Spirit'; second, that it was built solely on 'repentance toward God and faith in Jesus Christ': third, its freedom was a product of that redemptive foundation and that alone; fourth, that its first 'social service' was due 'to the great apostolic Church of the Spirit' (shades of Luther's *On the Papacy in Rome* of 1520) 'and especially to the uniting of all the Churches', and finally 'that it must exercise the true Church's effect on public affairs for the sake of the Kingdom of God'. [17]

It was the 'hell-harrowing, heaven-scaling Cross of Christ'[18] which was the sole source of the Church. In an implicit rebuke to Anglican incarnationalists like Gore, Forsyth emphasised that the ground of the Church was not Christ's teaching and character but 'His Office and Work. His atoning Cross and Resurrection… His redemption from moral death to eternal life'. The Church's one foundation 'is not simply Christ, but Christ crucified' for there God's love took on the for it must take when confronted with human sin. Far from being a human organisation for the like-minded, the Church is 'a new creation of God in the Holy Spirit', a spiritual organism composed of all those who are in Christ'.[19] That gospel word spoken in the Cross was universal and final for Forsyth, so the Church has a claim on every soul. It is 'the only society with a fulcrum outside the world; and therefore the only one which can move the world as whole life.' He was a thoughtful and fearless exclusivist - 'A Gospel which is not exclusivist will never include the world because will never master it.'[20]

This was the foundation of his clarion call to the Free Churches to rediscover their true identity and gain a proper sense of perspective. They should stop regarding the epistle of the Ephesians 'as a piece of theological poetry, not to say rhapsody'[21] and begin to take it seriously as a divine charter. It is hard to imagine any ecclesiology more at variance with an ecclesiastical culture that shied away from creeds, busied itself in the good works of institutional Church and sought in the realm of good Liberal Caesers.

The Church was composed of those who were in Christ by faith through the Holy Spirit. Church unity therefore already was - 'It was created by Christ's Cross, and then by His Holy

Spirit individualising it. We never realise our true individuality but in communion'.[22] Unity, catholicity, was therefore a spiritual necessity. As A M Hunter has shown, Forsyth was a penetrating New Testament scholar. His analysis of the use of **ekklesia** in the New Testament was far in advance of his time.[23] His New Testament studies revealed what other later confirmed, that **ekklesia** (local Churches) are outcrops of the one great **ekklesia**, or as Forsyth memorably put it, 'What the Apostles planted was not Churches but stations of the Church. What the Gospel created was not a crowd of Churches but the one Church in various places. What we have everywhere is the one Church of Christ put down here and there, looking out in Corinth, Ephesus or Thessalonica. People did not go to a meeting which was on its way to become a Church; they went to the Church at a certain place of meeting. Wherever you went it did not matter, you went **to the one Church**'.[24] Independent shibboleths were set to tumble. The 'clotted individualism' of Congregationalism, its atomistic exaltation of the local, was un-Scriptural. It would not do. But here, in Scripture, was a theological undergirding for the new Free Church ecumenical enterprise - 'To the one God, the one Gospel, the one Christ, there can but answer the one Church'.[25] Images and similes of the relationship between the Great Church and the local flow from his pen with poetic intensity - an expression, an outcrop, 'as England to her counties', an ambassador's house abroad which 'is all England if need and crisis bring all England to that spot'.[26]

Union was Unity taking effect, and although Forsyth's eyes were primarily on possible developments within the Free Churches, he acknowledged that 'the treatment means to be Great Church'.[27] What he had to say about the method of unity and the nature of polity was therefore of wider ecumenical import. The two were closely related. Forsyth sought federation: he believed it to be the objective correlative of the 'inner unity' of the gospel, which already existed. True unity subsisted in the gospel, not in politics. It was precisely because the Holy Spirit was a federalist producing a community of communities in Christ that the mission of the Free Churches was 'to stand for the Christian right and reality of the federal idea of Church Unity and Catholicity'. All monopolies, apart from the Church's monopoly on the gospel, were to be eschewed.

True succession for Forsyth, as for most people in his tradition, was evangelical. It was a clever, if quirky, argument that the successor of the original apostolate was the New Testament, not the episcopate. It was not that he objected to episcopacy as a polity, he simply refused to accept it as a source of disunity. What would we think of a writer who excluded Switzerland and America from the family of states because they lacked monarchs? 'No bishop, no church' was exactly analogous.[28] The basis for Church unity was not polity, but faith, and he therefore encouraged the Free Churches in their work of producing a common credal statement.

The Church rested on the solid, objective foundation of God's holy grace in Christ's Cross, on redemption, the new creation. That 'Gospel of moral Redemption' is its sole source and unity.[29] Sacramentarian and pneumatic models of unity, for example Catholicism and Quakerism, will therefore always be inadequate, for the gospel is the gift of the Spirit and the sacraments the Word enacted.

Such an act of divine grace demanded an active response - 'It is an act which draws on the whole life - on the whole man in action, the whole race at last answering the whole God. It is an act of final self-commitment to Christ'.[30] Faith followed by worship. Never one to avoid commercial imagery, he had after all spent half his life as the suburban minister of a suburban people. Forsyth stated bluntly that 'The greatest product of the Church is not brotherly love but divine worship'.[31]   As a minister he had shown gentle anxiety about liturgy and sought improvement wherever possible.[32]   If worship and confession of the holy love of God was the primary task of the Church, the second was the creation of holiness.

Forsyth had not been Ritschl's pupil for nothing. Ritschl's fondness for speaking of Christianity as an ellipse with the two foci of Jesus who reveals God's love to us and the Church whose goal is the transformation of human society into the kingdom of God lies behind Forsyth's telling analysis of the relationship between Church and society.[33]   Forsyth, predictably, collapsed the two foci into one pivotal point, the Cross. The Cross not only reveals God's love; it also creates the kingdom.   He moves with sure-footed, lucid precision as he unpacks the multivalent beauty of the image 'kingdom' - present and future, come and coming, relation of kingship, society of such relations, spiritual entity, historic reality, but above all Christ's 'New Covenant', the kingdom as relation. What then is the relationship between Christ's two foundations, the kingdom and the Church?

The Church is 'the family hearth' of the children of God - a happy image at once relational and domestic, yet suggestive of heat, power and coming and going. The kingdom is wider than the Church, for the 'luminous penumbra' of God's work reaches far beyond the family hearth. The Church is kingdom relations made into a society of God's kingdom. God's moral rule, opens eyes to the reality of the kingdom of evil.   'It is the grand International, if our eyes could see it, since it gauges the whole moral situation of man and has no illusions'.[34]   It is the key to human history, and the power of the key is given to the Church. That is the moral basis for the Church's relationship to society. That is why the Church is missionary, apostolic, sent.

'I seek a City', he told the Congregational Union in 1905, 'and a city which has foundations. And this holy city has two foundations - first, Christ's final satisfaction of the holiness of God; second, His final destruction of the kingdom of the unholy. These are two aspects, upwards and downwards, of His one act'. The Cross revealed the true moral organisation of society. 'Christ came… to make Christian nations, and thus change society into the Kingdom of God'.[35] The Church was called to be the moral guide of society. And that brought him back to the genius of Independency, the mother of democracy and liberty. Congregationalism's freedom, as he never tired of saying, was founded freedom, founded on the authority of the gospel whose very nature was to create freedom.[36] True freedom is not anarchy, but freedom in Christ for Christ and the kingdom. Therefore only a free Church in a free state can be the moral guide of society. The Ephesian Church was Christ's, not Constantine's.

Prophets are rarely honoured in their homelands, and it is frequently said that his contemporaries ignored Forsyth. That is an odd judgement on a career which in its maturity encompassed the pastorates of Clarendon Park, Leicester and Emmanuel, Cambridge, twenty yeas as a theological college Principal, including a period as Dean of the Faculty of Theology of London University, and occupancy of the chair of the Congregational Union. He may not have been understood. The Young Turks of the Union may well have written him off as a conservative old man. Those of different theological persuasions may have criticised the stresses of his theology, but few doubted that here was a theologian of genuine stature.

That stature has increased with the passage of time, not least because he is now seen to have anticipated the neo-orthodox movement which has played such a significant part in theology since the days of Barth. Scholarly attention has naturally focused primarily on his theology of the atonement. His ecclesiology has received comparatively little attention. The Free Church federal movement, which glowed with promise and inspired *The Church and the Sacraments,* delivered little, and the history of twentieth century ecumenism preferred the corporatist route, both in the creation of the Church of South India and the formation of the United Reformed Church. The relationship between the inner and outer forms of the Church has retained a higher profile in ecumenical discussion that he might have expected. The nature of episcopacy remains problematic. If the rhetoric of the early decades of the century can be laid to one side though it is clear that Forsyth's perceptions of the relationship between Scripture and community in the earliest years of the Church provide guidelines for genuine conversation about the nature of succession and authority.

That is the value of Forsyth's ecclesiology for the Church on the brink of the third millennium. No Reformed theologian of a past age would expect to speak directly to another. Forsyth would expect us to treat him as he treated Luther. He would expect us to internalise the gospel and let it speak to our condition. What he can, and must be, is the most stimulating of theological conversation partners. As Stephen Sykes has pointed out, we are still 'perceptibly embroiled' in many of the difficulties which Forsyth identified.[37] In some ways his work is still fresh and prophetic. The dilemmas of Church order and the nature of establishment are as perplexing now as then. The quest for authority is still a serious theological problem, the more so in the light of post-modernism. Forsyth is still asking the right questions. What of his answers?

Forsyth's ecclesiology is rooted in the Reformed tradition. The most frequent quoted sources in his corpus are St Paul, Luther and Calvin - in that order.[38] That tradition has always struggled to gain a voice in English ecclesiological discussion. It is not without significance that it is a German scholar who has noted that Forsyth's ecclesiology is profoundly Lutheran.[39]   In other words, his accent maybe too Germanic for the English tradition which gives greater weight to the incarnation than Forsyth is willing to allow. The primacy of revelation ad redemption and the lack of any systematic doctrine of creation in his work opens him to the criticism that he ignores the created order. It is here, at the point where the doctrines of redemption and creation meet, that Forsyth has been gently taken to task by two Anglican admirers, Dan Hardy and Stephen Sykes. Hardy, who interestingly pairs Forsyth with Bonhoeffer (note the Lutheran link), argues that his lack of interest in creation results in an inadequate conception of human sociality upon which he might have built his ecclesiology.[40]   Sykes perceives 'a challengeable negativity about creation, which makes the construal of the life of an actual, historical Church puzzling and frankly implausible'[41]   Those are substantial criticisms, and they reflect on Forsyth's usefulness as a theologian for our times. Can a theologian as committedly exclusivist as Forsyth speak to our pluralist world? Can an ecclesiology which seems so blatantly Christocentric, at the expense of what Sykes terms 'legitimate trinitarianism' provide a sensible basis for contemporary Church life?

Forsyth was not, in the strict modern understanding of the word, a systematic theologian. He never wrote at length on the doctrine of creation. However, as Colin Gunton has shown, that does not mean that he lacks an awareness of the theological significance of creation. Even when his focus was elsewhere he had intuitive peripheral vision. For Forsyth, salvation was not simply a moral transaction divorced from physical reality. The whole of creation is included in the process of redemption and the justification of God is simultaneously the justification of the whole world.[42] Hints of the same perception can be seen in his treatment of the kingdom, in what he calls 'redemptive evolution', which begins with nature 'or God over us', continues with grace 'or God with us' and ends with glory 'or God in us'. And so often he repeated by re-phrasing.   The movement is richly trinitarian, beginning with the revelation of the Father and his power, passing by way of the revelation of the Son and his love to the Spirit and his holiness - 'But these three are one. The revelation of the Father remains in that of his Son. And the Father and the Son remain within the revelation of the Holy Spirit, where the kingdom covers all and pervades all'.[43]

Any conversation we are to have with Forsyth must continue to draw out that implicit relationship between creation and redemption.   It must also bring to the fore the trinitarian dynamics which are there, but which are sometimes masked by the proper concerns of a theologian of crisis to let the gospel speak to the heart of darkness. If such a conversation happens, we may yet find that he helps us to be the Church in a perplexingly pluralist world. If we attend to him, he will never let us forsake the ground of our being, and the basis of our authority, which can never be anything other than the Cross of Christ.

Notes

1   Harold Hamilton, review of *The Church and the Sacraments* in *Journal of Religious Studies,* 19 October 1917, pp 91-94.

2   P T Forsyth, *The Grace of the Gospel as the Moral Authority of the Church* in *The Church, the Gospel and Society*, London, 1962, pp 71-127, a reprint of a talk given in Leeds in 1905 when Forsyth was Chairman of the Congregational Union, p 99.

3   op cit, p 94.

4   For statistics see Robert Currie, Alan Gilbert and Lee Horsley, *Churches and Churchgoers*, Oxford, 1977.

5   Alan Argent, *The Pilot on the Bridge: John Daniel Jones (1865-1942)* in *Journal of the United Reformed Church History Society*, Vol 5 no 10, June 1977, pp 592-622; J W Grant, *Free Churchmanship in England*, London, nd, pp 206ff.

6   David Thompson, *The Unity of the Church in Twentieth Century England: Pleasing Dream or Common Calling*, in R W Swanson (ed) *Unity and Diversity in the Church* (Studies in Church History 32), Oxford, 1966, pp 507-31.

7   J K Jordan, *Free Church Unity, History of the Free Church Council Movement 1896-1941*, London, 1956, pp 127-129.

8   D G Miller, *P T Forsyth the Man* in Donald G Miller, Browne Barr and Robert Paul, *P T Forsyth, the Man, the Preacher's Theologian, Prophet for the Twentieth Century: a contemporary assessment*, Pittsburgh, 1981, pp 1-31.

9   P T Forsyth, op cit p 72.

10 P T Forsyth, *Positive Preaching and the Modern Mind*, London, 1907, p 117.

11 P T Forsyth, *The Church and the Sacraments*, London, 1917, pp 22-24.

12 P T Forsyth, *Faith, Freedom and the Future,* London, 1912, p 241.

13 P T Forsyth, *The Church and the Sacraments*, London, 1917, p 31.

14 op cit, p 37.

15 P T Forsyth, *Faith, Freedom and the Future*, op cit, p 188.

16 Daniel Jenkins, *Congregationalism, a re-statement*, London, 1954, p 48.

17 P T Forsyth, *Faith, Freedom and the Future*, op cit, pp 186-90.

18 P T Forsyth, '*A holy church the moral guide of society*' in *The Church, the Gospel and Society*, London, 1962, pp 5-64, at p 21.

19 P T Forsyth, *The Church and the Sacraments*, London, 1917 pp 33-34.

20 op cit, pp 7 and 18.

21 op cit, . p 123.

22 op cit, p 44.

23 A M Hunter, *P T Forsyth: per crucem ad lucem*, London, 1974, pp 31-44.

24 P T Forsyth, *The Church and the Sacraments*, London, 1917, pp 68-69.

25 op cit, pp 44 and 62.

26 op cit, p 66.

27 op cit, p xv.

28 op cit, pp 47 - 48.

29 op cit, p 60.

30 op cit, p 61.

31   op cit, p 25.

32   Clyde Binfield, *P T Forsyth as a Congregational Minister* in Trevor Hart (ed) *Justice the True and Only Mercy,* Edinburgh, 1995, pp 168-196, 183-187.

33   P T Forsyth, *The Church and the Sacraments*, London, 1917, pp 99-92.

34   op cit, pp 94-97.

35   P T Forsyth, *A Holy Church, the Moral Guide of Society*, p 13.

36   P T Forsyth, *Faith, Freedom and the Future*, pp 289-90.

37   Stephen Sykes, *P T Forsyth on the Church* in Trevor Hart (ed) *Justice the True and Only Mercy.* Edinburgh, 1995, pp 1-5, at p 15.

38   Robert Benedetto, *P T Forsyth: Bibliography and Index*, Westport and London, 1993.

39   Christoph Schwobel, *The Creature of the Word; recovering the ecclesiology of the Reformers'* in Colin Gunton and Daniel Hardy (eds) *On being the Church: Essays on Christian Community*, Edinburgh, 1989, pp 110-156, at p 125.

40   Daniel W Hardy, *Created and Redeemed Sociality*, in Colin Gunton and Daniel Hardy op cit, pp 21-48, 39-40.

41   Sykes, op cit, p 14.

42   Colin Gunton, *The Real Redemptive: Forsyth on Freedom and Authority*, in Hart (ed) *Justice the True and Only Mercy.* Edinburgh, 1995, p 51.

43   P T Forsyth, *The Church and the Sacraments*, p 100.

7.

P T Forsyth on Ministry

A Model for our Time?

David R Peel

I sat under P T Forsyth for the best part of three academic years, his eyes peering down at me and his stern look suggesting disapproval of my undergraduate activities. The location was 527 Finchley Road, London, where I was in the hostel while an undergraduate reading chemistry, but, more to the point, where Forsyth arguably had been at the zenith of his ministry. Portraits often tell us as much about the painter as the subject, but the one which hung on the wall above the table where I dined during 1968-71 left me with the impression of Forsyth as a firm no-nonsense father-figure who had a clear idea about what constituted a proper undergraduate life. You learn a lot about my days in the hostel at New College by hearing me confess that the great principal-preacher of an earlier era did not get the dubious pleasure of having me as his number one fan. It came as no surprise much later on to discover that at the heart of Forsyth's theology lay an unwavering awareness of the yawning chasm between the holiness of God and the sinfulness of human beings, and his firm conviction that at the centre of human existence there lies a basic issue which can only be settled by 'the grace of God in historic, moral, mystic action... upon racial guilt' in the Cross of Jesus Christ.[1] Somehow the painting of an unsmiling, sombre and threatening Forsyth matched the preacher who thundered that it will not do to believe that 'All you need is love'[2] to address the waywardness of humanity - unless of course the love in question is the holy love of God revealed at Calvary.

I owe a lot to this period of my life. While in London I met my wife; midway through my chemistry studies I discerned a call to Christian ministry; and through the influence of Charles Duthie, the then Principal of New College, I started to read theology - when, of course, I should really have been honing up my knowledge on topics like thermodynamics, reaction kinetics and eutectics! The writings of Pierre Teilhard de

Chardin started developing connections between my background in science and my Christian faith, while the sermons and essays of Paul Tillich gave me a basic approach to the theological task from which I have hardly ever wavered. But no one at New College suggested that I read Forsyth. Each year the College awarded the winner of the P T Forsyth prize with a complete set of Forsyth's works - or at least those still kept in print by Independent Press largely for the American market. The honoured recipients found it a dubious privilege to receive a stack of books by a theologian from long ago. This was the era of *Honest of God*, the *Secular City* and 'the Death of God', when P T Forsyth's distinctive version of 'the tradition of great theology',[3] with the Christ at the centre, was the very kind of orthodoxy which *avant-garde* liberal theology was hell-bent on overcoming.

During my preparation for ministry at Northern College, Manchester, the work of P T Forsyth was not mentioned in a single theological course I attended at the University. Tony Burnham, to his credit, in College courses extolled the virtues of Forsyth as a model for a young preacher to revere, but it seems odd that I was not required to read *Positive Preaching and the Modern Mind*, a reward that I was directed to by an American Methodist! No one in the student body at Manchester was reading Forsyth but, on reflection, it has to be said that there was not much theology of any kind being read. Primary attention was being paid to changing society, or revamping crumbling Victorian Church buildings, or, recently imported from the United States of America, non-directive counselling as a model for pastoral care. Working hard at developing a faith to live by and preach in ministry did not appear to be the all-consuming activity it perhaps should have been. A typical example of the way in which Forsyth's words come back to haunt us in more recent times is found in this salutory observation:

> It has been the vice of our college system in past
> years that the men (*sic*) it sent out were often but
> autodidacts after all. They had to pick up or make
> their own theology. What they have done in the
> circumstances is wonderful. But what have the
> Churches not lost? And what a hunger exists for a
> theology among preachers. They feel its need.[4]

During my preparation for ministry, therefore, it appeared
that, while Forsyth may have been 'A Nineteenth-Century
Prophet' (Lovell Cocks)[5], or, in 1914, 'A Theologian for the
Hour' (Kellogg),[6] his contribution to contemporary
theological thought was going to be minimal.

P T Forsyth: Theologian for the 21st Century?

Now, over a quarter of a century on and after being stimulated
and challenged by Forsyth's thought, I suspect the same
verdict will be announced on the impact that his theology will
likely have on the Church as the twenty-first century beckons.
In several ways his theology seems dated or inadequate.
Allow me to suggest six of them:

First, Forsyth offends those attitudes and speech which have
been fundamentally influenced by the insights of feminism.
The offence is more deep-seated than the fact that, along with
all writers in the English language until quite recently, Forsyth
does not use inclusive language. Nor can Forsyth be faulted
for failing to see that God is beyond gender characterizations.
He can assert, for example, that 'God himself (*sic*) is more
than a man' and that 'The Divine is part womanly'.[6] Forsyth
will not accept that God can be imaged after the likes of either
man or woman.

'Against all forms of anthropocentrism, Forsyth's theology is contemptuous', asserts Colin Gunton, since 'the deity in whom he believes is glorious in his transcendent self-sufficiency'.[7]   So what is the basis of objection? It is that Forsyth invariably associates 'the heroic features of faith' stereotypically with male strength, power and assertiveness and that what he considers distortions of true faith are linked by him to the 'feminine'.[8] Bewailing the lack of men in the Congregational Churches of 1917 he applauds those Churches' women in a backhanded way:

> It is not so much that we have now more female Christianity, but that we have less male. The Christianity of the men has ebbed, and left the godliness of the women more conspicuous. It is realised much has always been due to them.[9]

Given what was happening in Western Europe at the time it was hardly surprising that the Churches were down in their male membership figures. We have a right to ask, though, what constitutes 'female Christianity' and 'the Christianity of men'? Forsyth's answer was clear - the former is a religion of 'the heart and the temperament' with a proponderance towards sentimentality, the latter 'a faith for the mind, the conscience, and the will'.[10] You will find few better examples of sexual stereotyping in Christian theology. It reflects an impaired understanding both of people and the make up of Christian Churches.

Secondly, Forsyth's theology does not have the benefit of recent work in biblical studies and, as a result, his use of the Bible in framing his theology appears to be at best overconfident and at worst naive. He made the radical observation for his time that the Bible is not the authoritative norm for all Christian thought and practice; rather, he argued, the Bible is the authoritative source of that norm. It is the Gospel which 'was there before the Bible', and 'created the Bible', that is normative.[11] Years before neo-orthodoxy was to take a similar line, Forsyth therefore argued that Christianity is directly rooted in the Word, or better the event to which an encounter with the Word gives rise - 'the personal cruciality of the Cross',[12] and hence it is ultimately grounded in the Bible insofar as the Bible is the *source* of the apostolic witness to that Word. Of course, given his very unsystematic way of doing theology, there are times when one can be led to think that he conceives the Bible's authority for theology in a quite different way. For example, in *Lectures on the Church and Sacraments*, he describes 'the minister's charter' as 'the New Testament . . . the precipitate of the apostolic preaching at first hand', since the New Testament is 'the legatee' of the 'unique authority' of the apostles.[13] More usually however Forsyth avoids making either the Bible or the New Testament authoritative in any way other than as a source for a yet higher authority. Earlier in the same book we find the following:

> We must go back to the Bible. The Christian back to the Bible; the scholar with all his (*sic*) splendid modern equipment back to the Bible... It is now back to that which makes the Bible the Bible. Back to that which is... within and beyond the Bible. Back to the Gospel of our moral redemption through faith in the pure grace and mercy of God in Christ crucified. That is the most certain thing in Christianity.[14]

The Bible therefore plays a fundamental role in Forsyth's theology, but he could never be accused of bibliolatry; nevertheless, his confidence in scholarship's ability to delineate a clear and unified account of 'the apostolic preaching' or 'the Gospel of our moral redemption' today looks decidedly utopian. As Ernst Kasemann has powerfully argued, the New Testament displays 'many different versions of the Christian proclamation', and one has to draw the obvious conclusion that both the Christian Church in its polity and practice and also the very gospel itself were plural phenomena in the early days of their existence.[15] And further problems for Forsyth's way of using the Bible emerge when one takes into account the way in which exegetes today accept that the different standpoints of the readers invite multiple readings of the same text. There is no easy route to underpinning Christian thought and practice with biblical warrants when the challenging conclusion is drawn that 'all that can possibly be meant by 'biblical interpretation' is not any single way of interpreting the biblical writings, but only a plurality of such ways, only some of which either are or need to be orientated by the question or questions to which the biblical writings themselves intend to give answer'.[16] Of course, many New Testament scholars argue for a greater unity in the early Christian witness of faith recorded by the New Testament, while others press the claim that the proper meaning of a text is that intended by the original author. But this wide divergence of opinion in the world of biblical studies only adds to the problem of delivering positive outcomes from a 'back to the Bible' strategy.

Thirdly, Forsyth's gift to illuminate and obscure in the self-same paragraph is borne by a style of writing, which delights in the contrast of 'either/or', rather than tenaciously exploring the subtleties of 'both/and'. It might be argued that this is the legitimate exploitation of the preacher's art, but it can lead people to conclude that Forsyth has not seen the whole picture. Allow me to give an example of one such false antithesis. At the very core of his theology rests his broad methodological decision to advocate 'revelation' over and against 'reason'. As we have seen, he eschews anthropocentrism in Christianity and theology. His starting point is the reconciliation of the human race with God, which is proclaimed in the Christian revelation: 'The test and trial of all is the grace of God in Jesus Christ, and in Him as crucified'. And lest we have not got the message he immediately adds: 'Everything is imperishable which is inseparable from that'.[17] He was attacking a liberal approach to theological thinking which, while laudable in its apologetic attempt to speak to the age, had seriously reduced the content of the gospel to what, he believed, underpinned rather than challenged that age. That liberal approach began with the human mind rather than the 'positive' theology which starts with the revealed Word.

> ... by liberalism I mean the theology that begins with some rational canon of life or nature to which Christianity has to be cut down or enlarged (as the case may be); while by a modern positivity I mean a theology which begins with God's gift of a super-logical revelation in Christ's historic person and Cross, whose object was not to adjust a contradiction but to resolve a crisis and save a situation of the human soul.[18]

But, we must ask, how can one grasp the 'super-logical' revelation in a way which bypasses the cultural conditionedness and relativity of all understanding? Every witness to Jesus has occurred in a particular context and has been interpreted through that particular context's cultural lens. There is, as David Pailin has pointed out, 'a reciprocal relationship between revelatory insights and existing thought'.[19] While Forsyth can readily accept that 'the old faith' will need to be expressed in 'a new theology' by each generation in the Church, he is quick to point out that this will involve 're-interpretation' rather than 'revision'.[20] This reflects a belief that, while the form in which the gospel is expressed may alter, its content is fixed. But where is there a point in Christian history that provides us with a firm awareness of the gospel's content free of a contextually conditioned form? There is none, and the problem for Christian theologians the first Easter onwards has been 'how to distinguish between a proper apprehension of the reality of God revealed in Jesus as the Christ and an attractive, but basically fictitious, cultural invention'.[21] Both in principle and in practice, reason *and* revelation are alike anthropocentrically conditioned. We cannot avoid starting with ourselves; all we can hope to do is to avoid the inevitable relativity of all thought slipping into a vicious relativism by attending to the checks and balances which emerge through the mutuality of inter-cultural enquiry, conversation and debate.

Fourthly, one of the most challenging aspects of Forsyth's thinking is his clear belief that the Christian gospel is the sole means by which the world will be brought to its proper goal. He argues that

> ... what society radically needs is *salvation;* and it is salvation that the Church offers to all. The Church alone has this secret - the Church, the greatest product of man's (*sic*) past, and the only trustee of his future... the Church is the only society with a fulcrum outside the world; and therefore the only one that can move the world as a whole.[22]

Forsyth's exclusivist tones were matched by an unshakeable conviction that was evangelical in style and missionary in approach. His was the age in which large numbers of Christians began working 'to evangelize the world in this generation',[23] although he was not as confident as most of them were about the outcome; but it was also a time in which people's encounters with non-Christian faiths and ideologies were largely oblivious to the sincerity and insights of those who belonged to them. While there are still many who follow the exclusivist stance of insisting that there is no salvation outside the Christian confession of Christ as the Redeemer, many others no longer can support such a contention. First hand encounter with non-Christians in our multi-racial society has left them with a deep appreciation of religions other than Christianity. They find it difficult to believe that there is no salvific value in them. Rather than accept an *exclusivist* attitude of Christianity towards other religions, they want to be more affirming of those religions. This may involve people in continuing to affirm that the Christ event *constitutes* the possibility of salvation, but making the added claim that the work of Christ can be seen 'anonymously' in the other great world faiths;[24] or it can involve people arguing that the Christ event is *representative* rather than constitutive of the possibility of salvation;[25] or it might mean that people travel across the theological Rubicon to a *pluralist* view which sees all the world faiths as different but, in some degree, legitimate means of offering salvation.[26] However, whichever position such people adopt it will be opposed to statements like this: 'It is only by Christ's holy work, translated into the holy society of the Churches, that Society at large can be converted into the holy Kingdom of God'.[27] This accounts for a further reason why many contemporary people will consider Forsyth's theology inadequate.

A fifth source of inadequacy in Forsyth's theology is highlighted by those who perceive its agenda to be parochial when set in a global context. The problem which is the starting point for his theology is human sin, and for Forsyth it is sin which causes the offence of which the human race is guilty before God. However, as Raymond Fung has observed, the primary problem which besets the inhabitants of the Two-Third's World is not that they are sinners but rather that they are repeatedly and systematically being sinned against by a global economic and political system which maintains them in grinding poverty and merciless dependency.[28]   Their problems are not self-inflicted but imposed by others; they are political rather than personal, social and not simply individual. From the perspective of the underside of history, therefore, Forsyth's prescriptions for human ills will appear to be merely palliative; he will be dismissed as naive, since few today can seriously subscribe to the view that the simple and straightforward way to establish justice and equality in society is to work on changing the lives of individuals. And yet this was the Forsyth's strategy: 'Set that right in every man by what sets right also the race, and right views and right relations will follow as the night the day'.[29]   Robert Paul acknowledges that 'Forsyth was perhaps too optimistic at this point'.[30] It's always tempting in a Western sitting room to wax eloquently about the world becoming a better place, as more and more people turn from their personal sin through their encounter 'with the event which has seen the destruction by God in Christ of sin's guilt and sin's distrust, and sin's blocking of the sky'.[31] But, as Reinhold Niebuhr has taught us, sin is a most complex phenomenon, and it is found in its most virulent form in social, economic and political manifestations which prove to be somewhat immune from the kind of individualistic strategies typically advanced by Western theology.[32]

Following Forsyth, Colin Gunton, though, insists that 'the Church's being, acts and words... fulfil its responsibility to society' when they are directed to the basis of 'all human social life... in redemption'. This leads him to conclude: 'The primary task is not to organise the world, but to be within it as a particular way of being human, a living reminder of the true basis and end of human life'.[33] But, we may ask, is the basis of 'all human life' found 'in redemption' *alone*? Is there not a further dimension, one that flows out from Jesus' injunction that we love our neighbour as ourself - as well as loving God with all our heart and mind? Isn't the theme of 'emancipation' also to be brought into view if we are to give an adequate account of God's liberating work? If that liberating work involves the 'emancipation' of people as well as their 'redemption', then it is legitimate to conclude that 'the Christian community' is here to do something more than 'remind the state that political and moral programmes are secondary to and dependent upon redemption'. In obedience to the One whose liberating work encompasses *both* 'redemption' *and* 'emancipation', the Church, rather, ought to be engaged in social and political activity to establish 'political and moral programmes' that become the context in which 'the creative transformation of relationships' does take place.[34]

The underlying criticism of the overt emphasis found in Western theology upon a classical redemption-centred view of God's liberating work leads to our sixth and concluding reason for believing that Forsyth is likely to continue as a marginal figure in contemporary theological developments. Many will see his work (like that of Barth *et al*) as 'a self-critical moment in the history of liberal theology' rather than liberal theology's obituary.[35] Whatever may have been the mistakes of liberal theology, the argument runs, we must not attempt to go behind so much as go on from liberalism. And nowhere is this approach more in evidence than in consideration of the work of Christ.

Paul Fiddes, for example, raises an old issue: 'How can a particular event in the past have an effect upon our experience of salvation today?'.[36] And he concludes that Forsyth's theology does not provide a satisfactory answer to this question.[37] But, as Trevor Hart tries to show, Forsyth may in fact manage to hold together both objective and subjective dimensions in his doctrine of the saving work of Christ:

> Forsyth... because he sees atonement primarily not as a matter of either the status or the experience of individual persons, but an adjustment of the cosmic order of things which thereby inevitably has universal implications... presents both aspects under the one rubric of the self-realization of the Holy: first, in the order of reality, and secondarily, as that 'reorganisation of the universe' works itself out in actuality and history.[38]

Be that as it may, the liberal suspicion of Forsyth's emphasis on the heart of theology residing in an objective atonement will not be easily overcome.

David Pailin has argued that 'the images of the divine and of the divine-human relationship suggested by some models of the atonement... are so fundamentally misleading that they impede rather than enliven faith's self-understanding'.[39] Like many others, Pailin objects to accounts of the work of Christ which pre-suppose images of God that are 'pre-Christian (or sub-Christian)', and which take their leave from some of the worst rather than best features of human beings - 'hostility, anger, offence, injured dignity' rather than 'sorrow, pity, loving concern and patient hope'.[40] Instead, Pailin insists that 'Christian believers and theologians should take radically seriously the insight into the divine nature presented by the life and death of Jesus, and not distort it by interpreting it in terms of sub-Christian views of God'.[41] Of course, that is precisely what Forsyth would argue he has done, and, against Pailin's favoured idea of the Christian understanding of God as 'a father who runs forward to welcome home a son who has come to his senses',[42] he would no doubt assert his understanding of the Holy One who, when the law of the divine moral order is broken, expects restitution to meet the requirement of the divine life:

> God... could not waive his moral order, but must honour it, for the guilt of humanity is no mere matter of private and personal affront, but rather of a public justice, a public truth, in which God must safeguard not his own honour or his own feelings, but truth itself.[43]

However sophisticated the interplay between God's holiness and love may be in Forsyth's treatment of the work of Christ, the priority which he places on the holiness of God is an understandable reaction to a liberalism which cuts down Christian love to the size of human kindliness; but it, perhaps, does not do justice to an understanding of love rooted in what is involved in the laying down of one's life for one's friends. It is easy, therefore, to see why Pailin might argue that Forsyth is tied to a vision of God constructed after the manner of a cosmic moralist rather than his preferred Whiteheadian 'brief Galilean vision' of God as operating 'in quietness... by love'.[44] And perhaps Forsyth's theology is so 'perilously like the old orthodoxy' against which liberal theology originally rose up that many contemporary people are, like those of Forsyth's day, 'not going to be dragged from the sunlit air of simple faith in the love of God' to become committed to a view from which they had thought they escaped.[45]

There are good reasons, therefore, to believe that the theology of P T Forsyth is not going to be formative for shaping our theology at the dawn of a new millenium. This does not mean however that we do not have important things to learn from Forsyth. It is in his writings on the nature and function of Christian ministry, I believe, that some of those insights occur.

A Sacramental View of Christian Ministry

Forsyth's thinking on Christian ministry can be mapped out by considering his opposition to the sacerdotal and hierarchical understanding displayed in Roman Catholic and Anglican polity and practice, as well as his deep unease about the perception of Christian ministry which he found operative in the Congregational Churches of his day. As is often the case we discover what a person is for by observing what that person is against.

Forsyth delineated two principle forms of Christianity. He saw them as being rooted in quite different understandings of God's grace. The Catholic form is essentially sacramental, while the Protestant is evangelical. They are not compatible:

> The Catholic and the Evangelical ideas of faith are incompatible, because each claims to be absolute. The priest of the sacraments has no room for the minister of the Gospel; the ministry of the Word has no place for the vicarious priest.[46]

In the Catholic view, grace is 'the infusion of the divine essence into our souls'.[47] Forsyth says that, for Catholics, it is akin to 'a sort of antiseptic influence made to pervade the spiritual system like new blood'.[48] By contrast the Protestant view understands grace as 'an act and way of God's treatment of us'.[49] It involves God's merciful action upon the human will:

> In a word, for Catholicism grace is magic, for Evangelicalism it is mercy. The grace of Evangelicalism is Christ, the Gospel, the Word. The faith that answers that is living faith in a living person directly in converse with the soul.[50]

For Forsyth, therefore, grace is not God's gift of a magical, subliminal power but the merciful activity of God operating on the will of sinful human beings. In the Catholic view the common access to grace was *via* participation in the sacraments; so, Forsyth argued, those authorized to administer the sacraments in effect become the means by which people have access to grace. For an advocate of an evangelical understanding like Forsyth, however, grace is conveyed in the 'hearing' of the gospel as the Word is preached and the sacraments are administered. The believer therefore has access to God without needing recourse to a priest; so for an evangelical the Church is 'the priesthood of all believers'. The result is that the sacerdotal emphasis in Christian ministry becomes greatly qualified:

> The true inwardness of the Reformation was the rejection of priest and mass. And it was a rejection caused by a return to the Bible and the rediscovery of the Gospel. What dislodged the priest was the Gospel. It was the faith that made every Christian man his (*sic*) own priest in Jesus Christ.[51]

The 'sacrificing priesthood' is replaced by Forsyth with the minister of the Word.[52]

Forsyth's objection to sacerdotal views of ministry was matched by his opposition to the monarchical episcopal system he saw in the Roman Catholic and Anglican Churches. He described both 'episcopacy and the priesthood' 'as mere historic growths'.[53] They were not of the *esse* of the Church. This did not mean, however, that Forsyth denied that there is a sacerdotal emphasis in ministry, or that episcopacy is 'a good polity among others'.[54] He could say, for example, that he had 'no objection to Episcopacy in itself' and confess that he could do his work 'happily under a bishop, and feel honoured under the episcopate of many'.[55] His argument was with a system which had linked together the priestly and administrative functions of leadership in an order of ministry that had become a constitutive dimension of the Church.

In the first century, Forsyth argues, the episcopate as we have come to know it was not a feature of ecclesiastical life. 'Such an idea did not dominate the whole period of the undivided Church'.[56] To insist upon episcopacy as a pre-condition for Christian unity, therefore, seemed to Forsyth tantamount to unChurching 'all the Christian communities of the New Testament'.[57] What ought to be the basis of unity is the gospel preserved in the apostolic preaching found in the New Testament and proclaimed faithfully by Christians today. The true apostolic succession, therefore, is not found in an order of ministry:

> The Apostolic succession has no meaning except as the Evangelical succession. It does not mean, at the one extreme, a historic line of valid ordinations unbroken from the Apostles to the last curate. Nor, at the other end, does it mean merely cultivating the spirit of the Apostles, or their precepts for sanctification. But it is the succession of those who experience and preach the Apostolic Gospel of a regenerating redemption.[58]

Equally objectionable for Forsyth was the style of leadership that the bishops exercised. He could find no warrant for the monarchical approach which had emerged in the Patristic period:

> The original constitution of the Church, whatever it was, was not monarchical. It was corporative until Cyprianism; and until the black (*sic*) years when first Constantine and then Charlemagne made it a State Church, and turned its officers into civil servants and its government to a bureaucracy.[59]

And, not surprisingly, Forsyth saw the dangers of an alliance between Church and state, which could lead to the Church's ministry being under state control. He believed that the 'spiritual necessity' in the Reformation would one day require the Establishment of the Church of England if the Reformation was ever to be considered complete: 'The battle with the world for a free Gospel can only be won by a free Church; and a free Church is the inevitable effect of a free Gospel, of the freedom of the spiritual power'.[60]

All of this would have fallen upon welcome ears in Congregationalist circles, but an equal focus of Forsyth's attack was the ministerial practice of his denomination's Churches. He was one Congregationalist theologian who recognized the way in which the doctrine of the priesthood of all believers had been so diluted that it had become synonymous with a view of ministry which does justice neither to Church members nor to ordained ministers. It was being used as a licence to authorize anyone to do anything in the Church - irrespective of ability and sometimes without due preparation. As a result, Forsyth pointed out how the standard of leadership had declined. If it was true that 'the Church will be what its ministry makes it' then it followed, for Forsyth, that the Church needed a renewed vision about ministry if it was to regain its health and strength.[61] He is caustic about the way in which Churches view their ministers:

> There are those who look on the minister simply as one of the members of the Church - the talking or the presiding member. They think anything else spoils him as a brother (*sic*). They believe a Church could go on without a minister, only not so well, with less decency and order.[62]

While ministers must have colluded to some extent in this lowering of their stature, it is the Church members who are reminded of the task ministers are called to perform and of the esteem that they should have in the Church.

> ... let the religious public at least have some consideration for its ministry, which it irritates and debases by trivial ethics, and the impatient demand for short sermons and long 'socials'. Let it respect the dignity of the ministry. Let it cease to degrade the ministry into a competitor for public notice, a caterer for public comfort, and a mere waiter upon social convenience or religious decency. Let it make greater demands on the pulpit for power, and grasp, and range, and penetration, and reality. Let it encourage the ministry to do more justice to the mighty *matter* of the Bible and its brethren, and not only to its beauty, its charm, its sentiment, or its precepts. Let it come in aid to protect the pulpit from that curse of petty sentiment which grows upon the Church, which rolls up from the pew into the pulpit, and from the pulpit rolls down upon the pew in a warm and soaking mist.[63]

It was Forsyth's belief that the Churches of his day were desperately in need of rediscovering their roots in the gospel. He called for 'a reformation of faith, belief, and thought to make the Churches adequate to the nation, the world, and the age, a bracing up and a coupling up of our Churches, and a renovated theology as the expression of the Church's rich and corporate life'.[64] And ministers were to be a fundamental means by which that reformation came about. They are to take on a sacramental function at the heart of the Church's life; they are called by God and set apart by the Church to *convey*, and not merely declare, the grace of God:

> In the sacrament of the Word the ministers are themselves the living elements in Christ's hands - broken and poured out in soul, even unto death; so that they may not only witness to Christ, or symbolise Him, but by the sacrament of personality actually convey Him crucified and risen.[65]

Or Forsyth in a more personal vein can say of his calling:

> How solemn our place is! It is a sacramental place. We have not simply to state our case, we have to convey our Christ and to convey Him effectually. We are sacramental elements, broken often, in the Lord's hands, as He dispenses His grace though us.[66]

A 'higher' view of ministry is difficult to imagine.

In Forsyth's analysis of the work of ministers he turns our attention to four primary functions. First, ministers are preachers. In *Positive Preaching and the Modern Mind,* Forsyth presents a treatment of preaching which is full of tremendous insight as well as practical help. The book starts with the claim that 'with its preaching Christianity stands or falls'.[67] This, in turn, points to the crucial role of the preacher in the life of the Church. Preaching demands 'complete immersion in the Bible', so it follows that 'the ideal ministry is in real touch with the Bible, constant and supreme touch with the Bible'.[68] Forsyth, of course, sees God's saving work in the Easter event as the kernal of the preached message: 'This Christ is the message that makes the preacher'.[69] But, as well as being devoted to biblical reading and study, there is also a need for 'deliberate prayer', since without this ministers 'easily become dilettanti not in theology only but in soul, religious amateurs instead of spiritual masters, mere seekers, and experimenters instead of experts of the Gospel and adepts of faith'.[70] The minister's second function is pastoral work. This is a continuation of the preaching function in that it is not merely a matter of the minister extending concern and kindliness to people; rather, it is the way the minister takes Christ to people 'not for humane objects only, but for the sake of the Kingdom of God'.[71] Ministers are sacramental in their pastoral endeavour as they become subjects of grace through which the gospel of grace works. The third function of the minister is more priestly than it is prophetic. The minister's conduct of public worship, and especially the leading of a congregation in prayer, is an important part of a minister's responsibilities. When carrying it out the minister is more sacerdotal than sacramental. This prompts Forsyth to make the following observations:

> As priest, the ministry offers to God the Church's soul, as prophet it offers to it the salvation of God. In the minister's one person, the human spirit speaks to God, and the Holy Spirit speaks to men. No wonder he (*sic*) is often rent asunder.[72]

But, as our earlier discussion suggested, Forsyth argues that ultimately the minister 'is sacramental... more than sacerdotal', since the minister

> ... is chiefly what he (*sic*) is for God. And for God he (*sic*) is agent of His Christ, the vehicle of His Word. And it is only God's Word to us that makes possible our Word to God.[73]

Fourthly, the minister has social and philanthropic functions outside the Church in the wider community and society. Forsyth was so suspicious of any social gospel strategy that he tended to think that this function was already receiving enough attention by ministers at the time - or, more truly, far too much attention, to the detriment of the other functions. The more that ministers involve themselves in these matters, the less time there is for the preaching, teaching and the liturgical side of ministry. Forsyth also makes the telling point that such a ministerial strategy 'takes work away from the laity'.[74]

Forsyth, therefore, offers us a theology of ministry in which the minister of word and sacraments is essential for the *bene esse* of the Church. There is a clear role for a body of people who are set apart in the Church for the purposes of leadership, particularly through the media of preaching and teaching. Such people are to be carefully selected for their office and rigorously prepared to undertake it. Forsyth's view of ministry was demanding. How else, he observed, can we get the heart back into the Church? 'If the ministers do not rise to the level of ministry it is for the Church to see that they are better selected and trained'.[75] With its emphasis upon preaching and teaching one suspects that Forsyth's view of ministers imposed high theological demands upon them. It was certainly an educated ministry that he was aiming to produce:

> ... to be true at once to the Gospel and to the age the ministry must be an educated one. I mean as a whole. And by educated I do not mean learned, and I do mean more than merely trained ... trained in the wisdom and knowledge which is the stored precipitate of past ages of earnest Christian experience.[76]

In modern terms we might say that Forsyth's minister is required to be a practical theologian who enables the whole Church to be aware and confident of the faith it holds. Speaking about preachers needing to be rooted and grounded in theology, Forsyth remarks that

> ... it needs much skill in the treatment of truth to grasp with the right hand the marrow of the Gospel and manipulate with the other the civilization of the time, to stand with one foot on the earth and the other in the infinite sea. Do not think this trained mind, this due knowledge, is a luxury of the literates. It is a necessity for the whole Church... .[77]

While not part of an order, ministers are set apart, among other things, to maintain the order of the Church. They are accountable to the demands which the gospel places upon them rather than the wishes of the congregation. Not out to impress people and have people take notice of them, ministers are pneumatics rather than charismatics. They convince by 'the power of the word, the inner nature of the Gospel, the intelligent demonstration of the spirit'.[78] Ministry 'is not a matter of mental or miraculous gifts', as the out-and-out charismatic would have us believe; rather, it is rooted in 'the gifts of faith, hope and love in the Gospel'.[79]

The Relevance of P T Forsyth's Model of Ministry for Today

It has been my experience in recent years that the ordinands who have read P T Forsyth on ministry have found in his model of ministry thinking that is as relevant at the end of the century as it was ar its start. This is partly because Forsyth's outline of the crisis facing the Church is more obviously real to us than it was in his day; in that sense, Forsyth was a prophet who largely went unheaded. What my students see very clearly is a contemporary Church which has lost touch with its roots in the gospel, that does not possess a credible account of that gospel to share with others, and which has largely lost its confidence to be the Church in today's society. They regard themselves as future ministers of the Church charged with developing fresh patterns of leadership that will enable the Church to be reformed anew. And for a number of reasons the 'model of ministry' provided by Forsyth resonates with their ideas and convictions about ministry.

First, Forsyth presents to us a 'job' which it is worth committing one's life to doing. Looked at realistically, the ministry of Word and Sacraments is awesome in its demands and impossible in the expectations. The temptation, therefore, is to cut it down to a series of tasks that are manageable and assessable by human criteria. So it is possible to draw up job descriptions and person specifications for the ideal minister, but in the process the cutting edge of the calling can become lost as patterns of ministry are made to fit congregational expectations rather than the demands of the gospel. The spiritual gets secularized and contact with the sacramental is lost. Forsyth's reminder that the minister is directly in the service of the gospel and only indirectly in the service of the Church is salutory: 'A man (*sic*) is an ideal minister not by his success with the public but by his stewardship of the word, by his adequacy and fidelity to Him that called him'.[80] Far too much emphasis perhaps has been placed in recent years upon models of ministry which owe their content and shape to secular professions and their theories. So, for example, Christian patterns of leadership have been re-written in the light of management theory, pastoral care has been reconstructed in the light of non-directive counselling ideas, and mission has been re-shaped by insights from the social sciences. While secular disciplines have a great deal to teach us, there is the obvious danger that they become a powerful means by which the essentially sacramental nature of ministry is lost as ministry comes to resemble a series of activities which are formally little different to their secular counterparts. Forsyth's sacramental emphasis provides us with an outlook on ministry which sees it as a means of grace rather than a conglomeration of secular 'works'. And that is the kind of ministry to which the ordinand feels called - even if it is 'awesome in its demands and impossible in its expectations' when judged by human criteria.

Secondly, Forsyth presents us with a model of ministry against which we can assess contemporary ministerial practice. My observation of ministers at work suggests that there are models of ministry on display which come nowhere near the understanding set by Forsyth. Admittedly, ministers are forced into such styles of ministry due to the pressure of the circumstances in which they are called to work. Those who serve in multi-Church pastorates or some ecumenical contexts often have little time to do anything but manage decline. The practice of spreading ever fewer ministers over the Churches was not devised out of a clear mission strategy; it has seemingly been adopted to prolong a chaplaincy model of ministry. But ministers themselves must share some of the blame for colluding in such developments. A close inspection of ministers at work suggests that some of the emphases on display, for example, are management of an organisation, community work, counselling, social work and administration. It is frightening how many ministers have rationalized away as unimportant the emphasis upon the Word so typical of Forsyth's ideal minister. Let me firmly state that my argument has nothing at all against management, community work, counselling, social work and administration; quite the reverse in so far as any local Church will be enriched if it can pursue excellence in each field. What I'm concerned about is that ministers build up their congregations in the Christian faith so that such activities become the means rather than the end of discipleship. On their own they will never deliver what the Church needs, although it can be freely admitted that management, community work, counselling, social work and administration are what many ministers seem to focus their ministry on, wittingly or not.

In 1899 Forsyth proclaimed, 'What the Church needs as the condition of reformation is a regeneration of the idea of faith'.[81]   But why faith?   Why not an emphasis on management, community work, counselling, social work and administration? Forsyth's answer is clear:

> The mystery and the power of Christianity is faith - understood not merely as a religious sympathy or affection, but as direct, personal communion with Christ, based on forgiveness of sins direct from Him to the conscience... Believe in the Lord Jesus Christ, and thou shalt be saved - not in the Church, not in the sacraments, not in the priesthood.[82]

And, we might add, not in ministry focussed on management, community work, counselling, social work and administration! Forsyth goes on to add: 'All these have their great worth as exhibitions and energies of the Church, not as conditions between Christ and the Lord', since 'they are not objects of faith'.[83]

Today, it can be argued, the Church is in even greater need of a reformation based on 'a regeneration of the idea of faith'. There is clear evidence that many Church members lack a disposition of faith - a disposition to think, feel and do the things of God. This will only be cultivated in a Church which makes worship central, takes the Bible seriously and gathers in Church Meeting to discern the mind of Christ rather than decide on a show of hands what the members want to do. Forsyth's model of ministry is precisely what the Church needs to enable those things to happen. The attraction of the New Age movement and events such as Hillsborough, Dunblane and the death of Diana, Princess of Wales also suggest that there are large numbers of British people who have deep religious questions, profound voids at the heart of their lives and an untapped spiritual dimension. Neither the

Church nor its ministry serve them well when the accent is placed on 'religious sympathy or affection' rather than inviting 'direct, personal communion with Christ'; while Churches delude themselves into thinking that they have attended to their task if they are well managed and well-versed in the arts of personal therapy and social involvement.

Thirdly, Forsyth's view of ministry is so designed that one of its primary aims is to set the Church free for its own tasks of ministry and mission. The model is one of leadership by enablement. What a minister does in preaching, teaching or pastoral work is 'to equip the saints for the work of ministry' (*Ephesians 4:12*).   Forsyth argued that Christ ordained a ministry but that the Church ordains ministers; and the latter is done to provide leadership for the former. He is adamant that the task of the minister is to build up the Church and make it effective for mission. Through preaching, prayer, teaching and pastoral work the minister enables the Church to be the Church. Forsyth is clear that 'it is the Church that is the great missionary to humanity, and not apostles, prophets, and agents here and there'. So it follows that for a preacher 'to act on the world he (*sic*) must, as a rule, do it through his (*sic*) Church'.[84] Forsyth adds that

> ... the minister's first duty is to his Church. He must make it a Church that acts on the world - through him indeed, but also otherwise. He is to act at its head, and not in its stead.[85]

At this point, Forsyth's model of ministry helpfully steers a middle course between the Scylla of social gospel approaches and the Charybdis of quietism. He is opposed equally to patterns of ministry that so focus on outreach that they underplay their role in building up the faith of the Church members, and to those which focus upon building up faith at the expense of the Church's activity in and on the world.

Given the importance that Forsyth attaches to the role of
ministers in enabling the faith development of Church
members it is hardly surprising that, fourthly, he reminds us of
the need in the Church for an ordained ministry which is
rigorously prepared for its important task. This is an
opportune reminder to Churches, which, due to declining
memberships, are facing a reduction in the numbers of
available ministers, due either to a recruitment shortage or
financial necessity - or a combination of both. They are
tempted to plug the gaps left by devising new patterns of
ministry which require less qualifications, lower levels of
preparation and more modest responsibilities. In the clamour
to have ecclesiastical leadership functions covered in the
absence of stipendiary ministers, it is understandably tempting
to rob the Churches of some of their best lay-leaders, make
them part-time, non-stipendiary ministers and thus solve a
deployment crisis in almost a financially neutral way. Where
this has been done there is some evidence that it has been at
the price of devaluing stipendiary ministry in people's
perception and practice - as well as undermining the
importance of lay ministry.

Be that as it may, Forsyth's insistence that an educated
ministry is essential for the well-being of the Church cannot
be underscored enough at a time when congregations are apt
to hallow their buildings rather than their ministers. In
Forsyth's day it appears that people had more noble reasons to
be cutting down on ministry:

> The condition of the ministry requires the attention of
> the Church quite as truly as the condition of the poor
> does. To provide a ministry equal to its own work is
> at least as much a concern of the Church as to
> provide work or play for the people. A Church that
> was keenly interested in technical or elementary

education to the neglect of an education for its own ministry, elementary in the Bible and technical in theology, would be dying out as a Church.[86]

And, one is prompted to say, there is evidence of that happening. What Forsyth was pleading for was the provision, at the heart of the Church's life, of leaders who were rooted in prayer, bible and theology. Preparation for such a ministry in the nature of the case focusses upon the theological basis for the life and witness of the Church. And, today, when the intellectual challenges to Christianity are even greater than in Forsyth's day, the need for theologically articulate ministers (to enable the Church as a whole to become theologically credible) is even greater. What important standards this man set:

> No man is entitled to discuss theology in public who has not studied theology. It is like any other weighty subject. Still more is this requisite if he sets to challenge and reform theology. He ought to be a trained theologian.[87]

To hear a URC Synod laugh loudly when a senior URC minister publically confessed with pride that he had not read a theological book since leaving college made me wonder who is to be most pitied, the minister or the members of his Synod. There are few things more needed today than ministers who, steeped in theology themselves, can lead the Churches to have a faith to share that arrests the heart and mind of contemporary people.

Fifthly, Forsyth's insistence that success or failure in both the Church and ministry should be set by standards that emanate from the gospel is salutary. The ethos of the Church Growth Movement in recent times has pandered to the worldly spirit of assessing value in quantitative rather than qualitative terms. The falsity is propagated that the faithfulness of a Church and its obedience to Christ is measured by the numerical size of a congregation. And yet history shows that it has been when the Church has been strongest in worldly terms that the seeds of its demise have been sown. The saplings of faithlessness and disobedience have sprouted forth heralded by the Church's triumphal hymn of praise. Forsyth yet again has a word in season:

> There is hardly a Church that has not suffered from its success. And when I say suffered I mean it has suffered in its power of witnessing the Gospel. It has gained comfort, affluence, and influence, but it has lost its prophetic soul, it has fallen from its apostolic insight and succession... Indeed, in organising themselves the Churches have often organised themselves in the world.[88]

Equal caution must be extended to judging the performance of a minister by similar criteria. And this needs to be borne in mind as the Church moves in to the era of ministerial appraisal. Forsyth warns about 'producing a race of religious leaders with a general way and breezy charity, who would lead only as they spared and indulged their followers, and told them what fine fellows they are; whose speech was of rights far more than of duty; who would sacrifice society to their class or sect, and who were so full of the wrongs these endure that they had no word against the sins they cherish, or the wrongs they inflict'.[89] Such ministers may be popular, but they are neither faithful nor obedient. Forsyth acknowledges that 'if a rebuking and demanding Church must be an unpopular Church, then the Church must accept its unpopularity'.[90] A corollary is that first rate ministers may receive bad reviews!

Finally, Forsyth's tremendous insight is again apparent when he tries to anchor the minister's life and work in prayer and spirituality. Minister's generally do not fail because of a lack of training in professional skills. The causes of failure go much deeper since the temptations in ministry cannot be overcome by the minister's own resources. Forsyth observed that the minister

> ... is a dealer in words; and it is very hard to keep them full of the Spirit, and yet to keep himself their master. He (*sic*) is a popular leader; and it is hard to lead the people without being led by the people to yield to them. The winning of souls, or the leading of souls, often costs the soul.[91]

Earlier he had argued that 'the life which has religion for a profession is the most dangerous of all' since it is attractive of 'so many temptations to unreality' particularly concerning 'the deepening of the spiritual life'.[92] And, yet, an ongoing 'deepening of the spiritual life' is essential if ministry is to be successful and effective, faithful and obedient. No one is going to be a sacrament through which God graciously meets people if they have lost touch with God in their own spiritual life.

> A preacher whose chief power is not in studious prayer is, to that extent, a man who does not know his [*sic*] business. A stringent ethic would say he was in danger of becoming a quack. That of prayer *is* the minister's business.[93]

It is sad that, until relatively recently, very little was done in the preparation of ministers in the Free Church tradition to help them develop patterns of personal spiritual devotion which would sustain them in the demands of ministry. But it is the congregation, which ultimately suffers when ministers find it impossible to say their prayers.

Conclusion

The argument of this paper has been that while there are some rather obvious reasons why Forsyth's theology will not be conducive to many as they study theology today, his understanding of ministry is as appropriate a basic model now as it was at the turn of the century. But, even at this point, certain reservations begin to emerge when we remember that Forsyth's context was rather different to ours. So, without in any way wanting to compromise my admiration for Forsyth's high view of ministry, I will end by pointing to four areas which will need to be addressed if Forsyth's insight is to benefit the contemporary Church.

First, the Church he saw emerging so clearly is now very much the Church we see around us today. Almost a century of decline has beset the Free Churches since the prophetic voice of Forsyth asked the Congregational Churches to engage in a root and branch self-examination. He was very confident that the right kind of ministers could turn round the situation. But many a faithful minister has not been able to neutralize the acids of twentieth-century secularism. The Church's recent story is littered with faithful ministers who *have* been obedient. What resilience they have shown as their noble efforts have brought little evident reward! However prophetic Forsyth was, he could hardly have anticipated a society which can seem so apathetic. Cunliffe-Jones points to the need to attend to the apologetic dimension of Christian ministry rather more thoroughly than did Forsyth:

> However ultimate our Gospel, we have to let it make contact with a work-a-day world. The trouble is not that we are faced with a world so intransigently opposed to the Gospel that by no stretch of imagination can we suppose them to be reconciled. Rather are we dealing with a world whose habits have never been saturated in the Gospel.[94]

We have to work out anew in our time what it means to say: 'The ultimate problem of human life has been met and mastered in Jesus Christ'.[95] That will demand as much patient listening to the stories of contemporary people as preaching to them. The latter cannot be done adequately without the former having taken place.

Secondly, the nature of society has changed since Forsyth's day. Any worthy contemporary model of ministry will need to reflect that we live in a world that is multi-racial, a society in which equal opportunities are a basic right, a community which is ideologically suspicious of people in authority, and a period when class and hierarchies are not as prominent. In Forsyth's day the Congregational minister walked down the High Street and his (invariably!) fellow citizens acknowledged an important figure; today most people do not know the URC minister in that kind of way. In an age when Christianity has to earn its place in society, the minister is likely to be by-passed as a focus of ridicule rather than someone to be revered as was the case at the turn of the century.

Thirdly, styles of leadership differ from those in Forsyth's day. Any model of ministry which does not reflect the contemporary accepted norms of good leadership will be deemed inadequate. Just as the relationship between teacher and student, parent and child, employer and employee, has changed, so has that between minister and Church member. Forsyth's model of ministry hardly does justice to the mutuality of relationship, the participatory endeavour and collaborative spirit expected in modern forms of leadership. It is significant, for example, that Forsyth hardly ever discusses the relationship between ministers and other Church leaders, eg. deacons or elders. His minister seems to work 'on' the Church in lonely isolation from the rest of the Church members; the lay/ordained distinction is so clear that at times it appears to be a complete separation.

Then, fourthly and finally, we should recognize that far more is asked of today's ministers than in Forsyth's day. By and large, the absence of quality lay-leadership, a symptom of Church decline, has added to the burden. In addition the Churches have become increasingly bureaucratic as they have adopted more participatory structures and encouraged further lay-involvement. Ecumenical activity has also added a further series of meetings to attend and activities to plan; while the advent of the photocopier and information technology means that the quantity of administration asked of ministers has grown beyond imagination since Forsyth's day. It is difficult to envisage how the modern minister has time to tackle the essential work of ministry; often they don't, for that very reason!

It is to Forsyth that we can turn for as challenging account of that 'essential work' as is available anywhere in theological writing. And until we re-invent ministry on the basis of his model the Church will not have the leadership it needs and deserves.

Notes:

1,2   P T Forsyth, *Lectures on the Church and the Sacraments* Longmans, Green and Co, London 1917, p 122.

3   'All you need is love' is the title of a famous Beatles' song popular with people of that era - and many still today.

4   H Cunliffe-Jones, 'P T Forsyth: Reactionary or Prophet?', *Congregational Quarterly*, 27 (October 1950), p 354.

5   '*The Ideal Ministry*' in John Huxtable (ed.), *Revelation Old and New: Sermons and Addresses*, Independent Press Ltd, London, 1962, p 109.

6   The title of a BBC broadcast by H F Lovell Cocks on 20 July 1948, the script of which is in the Lovell Cocks papers in Dr Williams' Library, London.

7   Edwin H Kellogg wrote an article entitled 'A Theologian for the Hours: Peter Taylor Forsyth'. It can be found in the Bulletin of Western Theological Seminary 6 (April 1914), pp 204-233. [The information concerning the above work and that mentioned at n 5 above is taken from the P T Forsyth bibliography prepared by Leslie McCurdy for Trevor Hart (ed.), *Justice the True and Only Mercy - Essays on the Life and Theology of Peter Taylor Forsyth*, T & T Clarke Ltd, Edinburgh 1995, pp 256-330.]

8   Quoted by Clyde Binfield, '*P T Forsyth as Congregational Minister*', found in Trevor Hart (ed), *Justice the True and Only Mercy: Essays on the Life and Theology of Peter Taylor Forsyth, op cit,* p 172.

9 '   The Real as the Redemptive: Forsyth on Authority and Freedom' in Trevor Hart (ed.), *Justice the True and Only Mercy: Essays on the Life and Theology of Peter Taylor Forsyth,*op cit, p 55.

10   P T Forsyth, *Rome, Reform and Reaction: Four Lectures on the Religious Situation*, Hodder and Stoughton, London, 1899, p 14.

11   P T Forsyth, *Lectures on the Church and the Sacraments,* op cit, p 19.

12   P T Forsyth, *Positive Preaching and the Modern Mind*, Seventh Impression, Independent Press Ltd, London, 1964, p 10.

13   John Huxtable (ed.), *Revelation Old and New: Sermons and Addresses*, op cit, p 104.

14   P T Forsyth, *Lectures on the Church and the Sacraments,* op cit, p 129.

15   Ibid, p 69.

16 '   The Canon of the New Testament and the Unity of Church' in *Essays on New Testament Themes*, SCM Press, London, 1964, p 96.

17   Schubert M Ogden, *Doing Theology Today*, Trinity Press International, Valley Forge, Pennsylvania, 1996, p 44.

18   P T Forsyth, *Lectures on the Church and the Sacraments,* op cit, p 15.

19   *The Anthropological Character of Theology: Conditioning Theological Understanding,*: Cambridge University Press, Cambridge 1990, p 136.

20   P T Forsyth, *Lectures on the Church and the Sacraments,* op cit, p 143.

21   John Huxtable (ed.), *Revelation Old and New: Sermons and Addresses*, op cit, p 108.

22   David Pailin, *The Anthropological Character of Theology: Conditioning*

Theological Understanding, op cit, p 138.

[23] P T Forsyth, *Lectures on the Church and the Sacraments,* op cit, pp 4 -5.

[24] The title of a missionary programme of the time.

[25] See the work of Karl Rahner in *Theological Investigations* Vol 5, Darton, Longman & Todd, London, 1966 and Vols 6, 1969, 14, 1976 and 16, 1979 for a sophisticated treatment of the 'inclusivist' position.

[26] For a sustained defence of 'pluralistic inclusivism' (as distinguished from Rahner's '*monistic* inclusivism') see Schubert M Ogden, *Is There Only One True Religion or Are There Many?*, Southern Methodist University Press, Dallas, 1992.

[27] See John Hick and Paul F Knitter (eds), *The Myth of Christian Uniqueness*, SCM Press, London, 1987.

[28] P T Forsyth, 'A Holy Church the Moral Guide of Society', in *The Congregational Year Book*, 1906, p 33.

[29] I owe my understanding of the distinction between being a sinner and being 'sinned against' to Raymond Fung's series of letters on evangelism published some time ago by the World Council of Churches.

[30] P T Forsyth, *Positive Preaching and the Modern Mind,* op cit, p 40.

[31] Robert S Paul, 'P T Forsyth: Prophet for the Twentieth Century' in Donald G Miller, Browne Barr and Robert S Paul,
P T Forsyth: The Man, The Preachers' Theologian, Prophet for the 20th Century: A Contemporary Assessment: The Pickwick Press, Pittsburg, Pennsylvania 1981, p 51.

[32] P T Forsyth, *Positive Preaching and the Modern Mind,* op cit,., p 40.

[33] See Reinhold Niebuhr, *Moral Man and Immoral Society*, Charles Scribner's Sons, New York, 1932.

[34] Colin E Gunton, *The Actuality of Atonement: A Study of Metaphor, Rationality and the Christian Tradition*, T & T Clark, Edinburgh, 1988, p 193.

[35] Ibid,

[36] See Schubert M Ogden, 'Truth, Truthfulness, and Secularity. A Critique of Theological Liberalism', *Christianity and Crisis*, xxxi, 5 (April 5, 1971), p 56.

[37] Paul Fiddes, *Past Event and Present Salvation: The Christian Idea of Atonement*, Darton, Longman and Todd, London, 1989, p ix.

[38] Ibid, pp 105-106.

[39] ' Morality, Atonement and the Death of Jesus: The Crucial Focus of Forsyth's Theology' in Trevor A Hart, (ed) *Justice the True and Only Mercy: Essays on the Life and Theology of Peter Taylor Forsyth,* op cit,., p 30.

[40] ' *The Doctrine of Atonement. (2) Does it Rest on a Misunderstanding?'* Epworth Review* 18:3, September 1991, p 71.

[41] Ibid, p 75.

[42] Ibid, pp 76-77.

[43] Ibid, p 76.

[44] ' Morality, Atonement and the Death of Jesus: The Crucial Focus of Forsyth's Theology', op cit,., pp 27-28.

[45] ' The Doctrine of Atonement (2) Does it Rest on a Misunderstanding?', op cit,., p 77, n 7.

46 H Cunliffe-Jones, '*P T Forsyth: Reactionary or Prophet?* op cit,., p 353.

47 P T Forsyth, *Rome, Reform and Reaction: Four Lectures on the Religious Situation* op cit, p 140.

48 P T Forsyth, *Lectures on the Church and the Sacraments,* op cit, p 37

49 P T Forsyth, *Rome, Reform and Reaction: Four Lectures on the Religious Situation* op cit, p 56.

50 Ibid, p 47.

51 Ibid,

52 Ibid, p 59.

53 P T Forsyth, *Lectures on the Church and the Sacraments,* op cit, p 100.

54 P T Forsyth, *Rome, Reform and Reaction: Four Lectures on the Religious Situation* op cit, p 86.

55 Ib., p 97.

56 P T Forsyth, *Lectures on the Church and the Sacraments,* op cit, p 42.

57 Ibid,

58 Ibid,

59 Ibid, p 102.

60 Ibid, p 72.

61 P T Forsyth, *Rome, Reform and Reaction: Four Lectures on the Religious Situation,* op cit, pp 23-24.

62 P T Forsyth, *Lectures on the Church and the Sacraments,* op cit, p 121.

63 Ibid, p 123.

64 P T Forsyth, *Positive Preaching and the Modern Mind,* op cit, p 100.

65 P T Forsyth, *Lectures on the Church and the Sacraments,* op cit, p 104.

66 Ibid, p 131.

67 John Huxtable (ed.), *Revelation Old and New: Sermons and Addresses*, op cit, p 121.

68 P T Forsyth, *Rome, Reform and Reaction: Four Lectures on the Religious Situation* op cit, p 1.

69 John Huxtable (ed.), *Revelation Old and New: Sermons and Addresses*, op cit, pp 102, 113.

70 P T Forsyth, *Positive Preaching and the Modern Mind,* op cit, p 49.

71 John Huxtable (ed.), *Revelation Old and New: Sermons and Addresses*, op cit, p 106.

72 P T Forsyth, *Lectures on the Church and the Sacraments,* op cit, p 135.

73 Ibid, p 136

74 Ibid, p 136.

75 Ibid,

76 Ibid, p 121.

77 John Huxtable (ed.), *Revelation Old and New: Sermons and Addresses*, op cit, p 109.

78 Ibid,

79 Ibid, p 112.

80 Ibid, p 111.

81 Ibid, p 93.

82 P T Forsyth, *Rome, Reform and Reaction: Four Lectures on the Religious*

*Situation,*op cit, p 5.

83   Ibid, p 92-93.

84   Ibid, p 93.

85   p 52.

86   Ibid,

87   John Huxtable (ed.), *Revelation Old and New: Sermons and Addresses,* op cit, p 96.

88   P T Forsyth, *Positive Preaching and the Modern Mind,* op cit, p 69.

89   P T Forsyth, *Lectures on the Church and the Sacraments,* op cit, p 66.

90   Ibid, p 12.

91   Ibid,

92   Ibid, p 131.

93   Ibid, p 130.

94   Ibid,

95   ' *P T Forsyth: Reactionary or Prophet?*', op cit,., p 355.

96   Ibid,

8.

Forsyth on Gospel and Society

A Matter of Principle

by Anna Robbins

It is reported that Albrecht Ritschl once gave the following advice to Adolf von Harnack: 'Never mind about the politics - get on with writing the books that will change the way people think. In the long term, that is what will be of decisive importance.'[1] Unlike so many of his contemporaries, who worked to guarantee the future of Christianity in political and social expression, Peter Taylor Forsyth sought instead to use the power of word and pen to challenge the theological basis of the social Christianity which surrounded him. Through his work, he presented a visionary and prophetic Gospel challenge to Church and society, which would surpass in power and duration any activist politic pursued in his time.[2] The advent of the First World War could have caused him to gloat in his foresight and assessment, as religious sentimentality and zeal for utopian Christianity began to fade. But Forsyth pressed on in his quest to assert a positive theology of the Cross of Christ as the moral crisis and centre of a new humanity in the Kingdom of God. The relative lack of attention gained by his work in his lifetime notwithstanding, Forsyth's theology has been re-awakened by those who have been re-awakened by him to a faith of full redemption, moral renewal, and prophetic challenge.

Analysis of Forsyth's ethics in general, and social ethics in particular, has been sporadic at best.[3] I seek to offer at least some correction to the oversight, as Forsyth's theology is, at its very heart, ethical. His interpretation of gospel and society spills over into nearly every aspect of his theology,[4] and to attempt to understand Forsyth without grasping first the nature of the tumultuous social situation that surrounded him, is to neglect a pivotal aspect of his scholarly and pastoral motivation. I will attempt first to outline some key influences in the development of popular Christian social thought at the turn of the century, introduce Forsyth's thought as it countered much of what may be termed 'social gospel'[5] and examine its theological method. I hope then to offer an assessment of what is yet recoverable, applicable, and challenging to the church today, on the verge of a new millennium, with its ethical confusions and moral ambiguities crying out for renewed clarity and prophetic intervention.

The social situation confronting the Churches, which so distressed Forsyth, represented a changing tide in socio-political thought, with evolutionary science making a significant impact on philosophies of progress which were finding expression in trade unionism, Marxism, and liberal Protestant theology. In popular theological circles, these developments placed new stress on immanentism, incarnation, idealism, fraternity, and unity, which were, in turn, manifested in the Churches. They found expression in new building programmes which added recreational and social meeting facilities to sanctuaries, in the development of social organisations of all types and for all ages, and in a sort of preaching that spoke little of the traditional doctrinal themes of sin and authority but much about love, sympathy, and brotherhood.[6] Thus, the Churches sought to meet the social needs emerging from the fact of rapidly increasing urbanisation, which contributed, among other problems, to the alienation of an entire class of workers and the marginalisation of the poor in society.

Hugh Price Hughes, the Welsh Methodist, offers an early example of the adoption of an ethic of sympathy in his introduction to a book of sermons. Making reference to Herbert Spencer's evolutionary ethics,[7] and criticising their basis of authority, Hughes agrees, nonetheless, that what Spencer discovered about ethics was already known by Christians through Jesus Christ, whose very atonement was described as 'the kindness and philanthropy of God.[8] Hughes attempts to Christianise Spencer's conclusions, baptising his assertions and raising them to a higher theological level. The reinterpretation of Christian doctrine and ethics in the light of the optimism of the age is unmistakably evident in Hughes' description of his reason for publishing his sermons. 'The main object of this book,' he writes, 'is to describe and illustrate in various ways that Fraternal Love which Mr Spencer calls Sympathy; which is the reflection of the Philanthropy of God as moonlight is the reflection of sunlight, and which is destined to fill this earth with a gentle and peaceful radiance until the morning breaks and the shadows flee for ever.'[9]

For Spencer, and later for the social gospel, ethics was, quite simply, the order of nature. 'Here then,' Spencer wrote, 'we have to enter on the consideration of moral phenomena as phenomena of evolution.... If the entire visible universe has been evolved... if one and all conform to the laws of evolution; then the necessary implication is that those phenomena of conduct in these highest creatures, with which Morality is concerned, also conform.'[10] Conversant with the ethics of Aristotle, Spencer understood virtue in a utilitarian manner, with moral beings 'not being classed as such because of an intrinsic community of character,' but 'classed as such because of something extrinsic...they are united by their common relationship to ...[their] result, while they are not united by their inner natures'.[11]

In accordance with such naturalistic assumptions, Spencer and others like him further reinterpreted social contract ideas in light of evolutionary science.[12] The views presented were widely adopted by advocates of social Christianity, though in varied and modified forms. As Spencer argued, and many agreed, the well-being of society was necessary for the well-being and further evolution of humanity, though Spencer's view had a rather individualistic basis: 'As fast as the social state establishes itself, the preservation of the society becomes a means of preserving its units. Living together arose because, on the average, it proved more advantageous than living apart.... Hence, social self-preservation becomes a proximate aim taking precedence of the ultimate aim, individual self-preservation.'[13] In general terms, social gospel interpreters of Spencer affirmed his evolutionary ethical discoveries as confirmations of the Christian faith emphasis on the growth of the earthly Kingdom of God, and its accompanied social improvement as inevitable consequence. They were reluctant, however, to adopt his individualism and negative basis for society's improvement,[14] preferring instead the idealism of T H Green[15] and others who espoused a critical Kantianism, seasoned with more than a sprinkling of the utilitarianism of J Bentham and J S Mill.[16] The marriage of evolutionary ethics with Protestant liberalism and Hegelian materialism had obvious formative influences on social Christianity on both sides of the Atlantic.

No discussion of the philosophical and theological influences on social thought at the time of Forsyth could fail to mention F D Maurice, whose ideas were widely drawn upon by social thinkers from across the theological spectrum. Forsyth's indebtedness to Maurice has been widely noted, as has been the influence Maurice had on the development of Christian socialism. Maurice has been described as a Platonist and an idealist, who embraced socialism as the preferred programme for social change.[17] He 'distrusted democracy and feared political action of any sort as an instrument of Christian moral idealism,'[18] displaying an attitude which would echo later in Forsyth's work. As one of the earliest leading voices for Christian socialism, Maurice focused on the universal and inclusivist nature of the Kingdom of God,[19] an idea that found expression, to varying degrees, in Forsyth and the social gospel alike. The influence of Maurice on the development of social thought in the period is unmistakable. As a direct result of his contribution, the role of the Church in society could not be avoided. 'No longer could thoughtful Christians be content to ignore the human aspect of the Industrial Revolution... from now on churchmen increasingly were to find themselves at one with the worker in his struggle for a better place in society both economically and politically.'[20]

This limited introduction to a complex but fascinating intellectual ethos demonstrates that various combinations and expressions of socio-ethical ideas were well entrenched in Christian social thought, and were finding practical expression in the churches, by the time Forsyth emerged to address the issues they raised and the problems they posed. Not content to adopt such approaches uncritically, his general reaction to the situation, and contrasting tone, is encapsulated well in the following words:

> We do not sympathise with our Saviour, we worship Him. The Gospel is not a humanity but an authority, and the only one, which guarantees the human fraternity of the world. We must give ourselves with all our might to recover for our Churches the faith which joys more in the experience of redeeming grace than in all the victories of reform.... A social Gospel will only turn our Churches into clubs and our religion into hearty bustle, unless it flow from a new reality of faith among us. And that again can only flow from a new grasp of Christ's grace which may bewilder orthodox and liberal alike, Churchman and Humanist. It will seem great and good to those alone who live in their Bible, but only breathe in the free and moving world.[21]

Let us, then, turn to the elements of Forsyth's thought which led him to reach such conclusions about a social movement which was sweeping the Church, but which he refused to embrace.[22]

In *Socialism, the Church and the Poor*, Forsyth explained explicitly his concern for the state of Christianity as a result of the permeation of Socialism, the social gospel ideas. He identified the problem in this way:

> The social side of the Church is one that at the present moment receives an absorbing amount of attention. There are thousands and thousands of people who believe they are Christians, and who are yet little concerned about either the truth of Christianity or its experience, in comparison with their interest in the social work, or the social genius, of the Church. It need hardly be said that were that type to become dominant, it would mean the demise of Christianity, and of the Church by consequence.[23]

The social error, as Forsyth saw it, was not rooted simply in the Church's preoccupation with the needs of the workers and the poor, but rather the 'peril of the hour' was 'a religious subjectiveness' which was 'gliding down into a religious decadence for want of an objective authority on which to climb.'[24] Forsyth supported Church involvement in certain public activities, but on a very different basis from those who sought progress for humanity through a mere anthropocentric feeling of good will. He repudiated this expression of utopian idealism at every opportunity, out of concern for the potential power of the real social influence of the Church, which he felt was being denied. He suggested that simple religious sentiment 'robs us of spiritual power. That loss robs us of moral strength. And that lack again deprives us of social insight and public weight. The politics of pity destroys the politics of real power…'[25]

Forsyth aligned himself immediately and without reservation with those who claimed that the social gospel would not only water-down Christian belief, but would lead to large numbers abandoning their faith and the Church. These concerns were sufficiently widespread to warrant reaction from one of social gospel's most famous exponents, the American Walter Rauschenbusch, who dismissed falling numbers as growing pains.[26]

It cannot be said that Forsyth had no pastoral concern for the issues at hand. Like many theologians who met pastoral crises which proved pivotal to their careers, he was involved in issues of social concern within his pastorate.[27] But, unlike many theologians, he experienced firsthand the matter of poverty and social crisis from meagre beginnings and squalid student days.[28] Yet, Forsyth refused to allow mere sympathy for such difficulties to dictate theological method, arguing that 'Society is past saving by the philanthropists... it is in our morals and not our miseries that we confront the greatest realities of the world. It is an age's moral poverty that faces us...'[29] For Forsyth, it was precisely a pastoral, theological, and moral matter that faced the Church. He did not question the fact of the new social concern but its very premise, which he firmly believed was based on a flawed theological foundation. Forsyth benefitted greatly from his time at Gottingen,[30] but did not retain all of the Ritschlian liberalism[31] which instructed him there, as did so many of his contemporaries, including many social gospel leaders, who embraced it uncritically for the duration of their lives. Forsyth pushed against the current.

Forsyth recognised early the dangers of certain evolutionary assumptions in the socio-ethical practice of the church. While not opposed to the theory in toto, he had serious reservations about its value to the Church as a basis for social activity. He questioned especially its ready adoption by ethicists and social activists, preferring to maintain a Ritschlian separation of religion and science. His reservations focused on evolution's anthropocentric starting point, lack of teleological meaning, and emergence of utility as the interpretative paradigm for human existence. Forsyth believed evolutionary theory to be merely descriptive, and asserted that the concerns of the Church, and indeed humanity, have more to do with searching for explanation than mere description. 'Explanation has far more to do with purpose than cause or method,' he wrote. '*How* man was made does not tell us *why* he was made, and cannot.'[32]

Such a comment points to Forsyth's concern that evolutionary ethics could lead the Church into a social doctrine that was empty and meaningless. He saw the outcome beginning to manifest itself in Church and society, and warned: 'The progressive spirit is morally hollow, and fatal as well, if it encourage in an age the pride and insolence which not only go before a fall but produce it.'[33] The social spirit concerned Forsyth when, as he observed, 'Religious zeal and even unction are found to co-exist with moral stupidity and vulgarity. These are fruits we see only too palpably around us. And they are much due to the extent to which evolution has unconsciously become a theology, and has ceased to be a scientific hypothesis.'[34] Again, Forsyth's preferred Ritschlian dualism is apparent, but he had real reasons for wanting to prevent evolutionary assumptions from infiltrating the social ethic, and indeed the wider theology, of the Church.

One area in which this became evident was in his unreserved rejection of simple, sympathetic, fraternally motivated, human progress. Washington Gladden, the father of the social gospel movement, understood society to be united in an inclusive brotherhood of moral good will, based on the universal Fatherhood of God over all creation.[35] Undermining the significance of the atonement in creating a new humanity - something which Forsyth emphasised - Gladden argued, 'The work of redemption is just bringing man back to his real self.'[36] The social gospel constructed a new understanding of the Kingdom of God, derived from liberal presuppositions and socio-ethical application of evolutionary doctrine. Rauschenbusch spelled out his method quite clearly as one which sought to reinterpret doctrine in the light of evolution, rather than interpret evolution in the light of Christian doctrine. He wrote:

> The spread of evolutionary ideas is another mark of modern religious thought. There is no denying that this has unsettled the ecclesiastical system of thought, much as the growth of the tree roots will burst solid masonry. But it has prepared us for understanding the idea of a Reign of God toward which all creation is moving. Translate the evolutionary theories into religious faith, and you have the doctrine of the Kingdom of God. This combination with scientific evolutionary thought has freed the Kingdom ideal of its catastrophic setting and its background of demonism, and so adapted it to the climate of the modern world.[37]

Rauschenbusch echoes J S Seeley, one of social Christianity's earliest advocates, who concluded in his classic work on the humanity of Christ, 'It may, therefore, be affirmed that Christ's Kingdom is a true brotherhood founded in devotion and self-sacrifice.'[38] Forsyth advocated a notion of brotherhood, but one quite unlike the soft, enthusiastic, materialistic one that grew out of Hegelian idealism, and which embraced and peddled the premises of evolution and progress. Like many social Christians, Forsyth acknowledged the essence of Christianity as 'brotherhood', but he understood this to be a 'brotherhood of faith', not a mere 'natural fraternity.' The premise upon which 'brotherhood' was founded, he argued, was not sympathy, but 'son-ship.' 'Christianity did not come to reveal man's natural brotherhood, but to create a spiritual,' wrote Forsyth:

> Some form of brotherhood is not the principle of Christianity, but only one of its expressions. And it should be clear that any social programme to which Christianity may seem to point more than to another always has for its postulate the Christian faith and Christian love, distinctly and positively understood... A Christian socialism always begins there, and is only workable on the supposition that men are changed men. The Sermon on the Mount presupposes such men as the Cross alone can make. And it is this Cross, not the Sermon on the Mount, that is fundamental Christianity.[39]

Forsyth thus strongly repudiated any notion of the Kingdom of God that emerged from an anthropocentric notion of goodwill or compassionate fraternity. He saw it as 'one of the most serious perversions in current Christianity, that a Church is not more than a congenial brotherhood or sympathetic group instead of a household of faith.' In practice, he saw that such belief would mean 'a fatal transfer of the centre of gravity from an objective gospel to a subjective piety; from a faith filled with God to a religion preoccupied with man, from Evangelical Theism to a Christianised Humanism where no Church can live.'[40] It becomes evident that Forsyth was not content to leave social Christianity unchallenged on what he considered the error of constructing a theology from below. Whereas social gospel advocates were seeking actively to interpret theology from the perspective of current thought, human need, and social tendencies, Forsyth argued for a theology from above. The underlying notion in social Christianity seemed to be 'that the first object of a faith is to include men or promote action, rather than to confess and glorify God,' he wrote. 'Faith is urged to extend its power rather than to establish it, to further the evolution of Humanity rather than to own, honour, and guard in practice the one revelation God has given of the way in which alone mankind must reach its divine destiny. This is anthropocentric religion rather than theocentric.'[41] Therefore, in Forsyth's view, Christianity had to be interpreted from the objectivity of the Cross, and not the subjectivity of human social systems, no matter how adequate they may be as tools for societal organisation. For that reason, he insisted that 'Christianity is not bound up with any particular scheme, dream, or programme of social order. Its essence is redemption as forgiveness or eternal life, and the Kingdom of God flowing from these. And the eternal life can be led under almost any form of society.'[42]

Another concern expressed by Forsyth was that evolution provided no teleological explanation of human life. Instead, it simply 'registers a method of past procedure.' Forsyth lamented, 'it has no world goal. It has no teleology on a cosmic scale. There is nothing that gives us to know the problem set us as living souls in the world, far less to find ourselves in that problem.' He continued, 'It does not explain the world, it only marshals it. It is an organiser and not an interpreter. It sets up the type in lines and pages, but it cannot read the book or open its seal. It follows its grammar, but not its logic; and it does not discern its spirit. It is not revelation but illumination. Knowledge of the world is one thing and that can be expressed in science; but the explanation of the world is another thing, and it has to do with destiny.'[43] Many social gospellers who welcomed and developed social application of evolutionary theory did not sufficiently

question its basis, as did Forsyth. In fact, although Rauschenbusch would most likely agree with the words of many of Forsyth's conclusions, he would probably reject his critical method of eliminating an evolutionary element in the foundation of Christian ethics, whereby Forsyth offers, 'an individualist teleology, or a eudaemonism, can no longer be maintained. The world does not exist for the happiness of its several units. It is there for man only as a member of society, and for his happiness as a lover of the Kingdom of God.'[44] Both Rauschenbusch and Forsyth wanted a social ethic whose scope embraced society as a whole; both would want the Kingdom of God to provide the motif for the racial solidarity of humanity; but the historian could not see past the ethic of sympathy and philanthropy, into the theologian's moral crisis of the Cross of Christ.

Forsyth's astute observation that evolutionary doctrine submerged humanity in an inevitable tide of progress, leading to a loss of humility and a gain of futility, is prophetic. He seems to have glimpsed the relativistic future for ethics when evolutionary doctrine substitutes process for moral effort. When this happens, he asserted:

We lose the moral vigour, which resists a majority, the public, or the priest; and the moral sympathy, which helps to its feet... the struggling right. We learn to distrust truth itself. It is all relative only, something in the making, and something, which we can make. And it is all over with truth when man feels himself its creator. His truth is not worth martyrdom then, for it is too changing to be an object of faith; and it is hardly worth propagandism for it will change ere he can convert an audience, to say nothing of a generation. Reality gives way under our feet, and standards vanish like stars falling from heaven.[45]

Forsyth continues to explain that under such misconceptions as evolution provides, morality ceases to be an objective centre of religion, exercised in humility. 'Man becomes his own maker, and he has a moral fool for his product. Goodness, by becoming but one contributer to the struggle for existence, ceases to be goodness and becomes a mere utility...Thought along these false lines, therefore, destroys its own conditions; it commits suicide, and man evolves over an abyss.'[46]

Forsyth saw the need for a spiritual, teleological, objective, gospel truth upon which to base a Christian social ethic, one that would be sufficient to weather change, and which was not wed too closely to the breezy spirit of the age. Where the social gospel sought to make Christianity relevant by reinterpreting its doctrines in the light of modern thought and discovery, Forsyth was careful to interpret society in the light of the gospel. Cautious about many developments which were taking place, Forsyth queried, 'Must the newest be the truest?'[47] He was especially hesitant about the method employed by social Christianity to use the Church to achieve its goals. Forsyth attempted to reverse that inclination as he refuted the tactics of certain trade unions. 'You say everything, even Christ and his Church, must be made to serve the great social ideal. I say everything, every social ideal, must be made to serve Jesus Christ, His Cross, His Gospel, His meaning of the Kingdom of God,' he explained. 'You have one gospel, I have another. Yours is ideal Humanity with Christ as its champion and servant. Mine is the Kingdom of God with Humanity as His witness and servant.'[48] Forsyth makes his method very clear when he states, 'Your social ideals are not the principles of my religion, but they are among its fruits.'[49] Social action may be a part of the Christian life, but not its premise. In the muddy world of evolutionary and liberal social ethics, Forsyth saw that through the Cross, indeed, through the Gospel, God 'gives us the fixed point at which we can make stand against the torrent of civilisation, and bring our hurried evolution to its moral senses.'[50] When we learn to face the moral situation with courage, he argued, 'we find that the re-organisation of society is a small matter compared with the re-organisation of the soul.'[51]

It is here that the heart of Forsyth's positive method of social ethics is most clearly revealed. He was intent on persuading Christians to base their social work on a foundation, which was solid and lasting, and yet relevant to the needs of the day. Anyone familiar with Forsyth's work might readily see how the Cross, as the centre of theology, would stand as the foundation of a socio-ethical system. The great decisive moral act of God in Christ could never be substituted or replicated by human effort. 'Earnestness of ethical enthusiasm can never do the work of faith in grace... We lose the element of evangelical ethic in the atoning Cross which keeps sentiment as strong as it is sweet and as permanent as it is fine. There is no kindness like the moral tenderness of those who are forgiven much.'[52] Forsyth's portrayal of the atonement treated human sin and God's glory much more seriously than the optimism demanded by the social gospel.

Forsyth's social ethic contrasts clearly with the social gospel emphasis on the immanence of God, and portrayal of the Kingdom of God as a mere spiritual expression of an evolutionary human process. While he understood the teleology of the Kingdom to involve a gradual process of growth toward a revealed goal, Forsyth's version of idealism managed to strike a successful balance between the immanence and transcendence of God, and anticipated many conclusions of moral theology following a generation or more later. Although an analysis of Forsyth's eschatology stretches beyond the scope of this paper, it is important to note that he shared a great deal with social Christianity, as he perceived the scope of Christ's work to involve the whole of the human race in an effective, if not actualised, manner. In this respect he did not break with contemporary thought, which emphasised a realised eschatology over one which looked forward to some sort of catastrophic consummation. His moral realism and its interpretation of the Kingdom and brotherhood of faith were founded on an understanding of the universality of the work of Christ, which was constantly moving toward its potential fulfilment in gradual process. Though holding a great deal in common with his contemporaries in this regard, his portrayal of the Kingdom's accomplishment rings a deeper, richer note than so many other approaches which preferred to highlight the love of humanity rather than the holy love of God.[53] Forsyth consistently maintained that the universality of the Kingdom, its inclusive scope, and its gradual manifestation in society, and as society, could only be asserted on the basis of one principle: the holy love of God revealed in the great moral act of the Cross of Christ. In this sense, the Kingdom has come, the deed of reconciliation and atonement accomplished once and for all. He summed up its relevance for Church and society in this way:

> It is the nature and faith of this Kingdom - the faith and not simply the ideal of a Kingdom, which is actually set up in the Cross - that makes Christianity universal. It is universal, not empirically, not yet actually, but potentially in its nature, genius, and destiny. It cannot but be missionary. We believe in the world because we believe in its goal, and we believe in its goal because we believe supremely in its God, and consult His Glory more even than the happiness of men. And we believe in God because of His Christ, His Cross, His victory, and His Gospel.[54]

Moral principle, based upon moral act, provided the foundation for Forsyth's understanding of society in the light of the gospel. The precepts of Jesus, of which many social Christians were particularly fond, found only a secondary place in Forsyth's moral theology.[55] Only upon the all-encompassing principle of the Cross did Forsyth envision the possibility of building gradually a society which was truly lasting and truly loving. Only upon this perennial principle could a social ethic be built which restored objectivity and authority to every practical activity of the Church.

Having considered the social context which Forsyth addressed, and outlined some of the premises of his own social argument, it is now for us to determine whether, and to what degree, his observations are relevant today to a Church facing a socio-ethical crisis of millennial proportions. We find ourselves beginning yet another generation removed in time from the thought of a man who challenged, inspired, changed, and strengthened the mind and soul of many who turned to him for insight. Has everything that needs saying about Forsyth and his moral theology been said? After all, how can a man who lived and wrote a century ago have anything helpful to say to a society which has faced more change in the past fifty years than it has throughout the history of civilisation? The conclusion of this paper will reveal the firmly held contention that, despite his inability to foretell all things, Forsyth's very method of approaching social ethics renders him perpetually relevant. Despite some apprehension which this author experiences over certain aspects of Forsyth's eschatology, weak ability to apply his theology to his situation, and his often confusing use of the terms 'Church,' 'kingdom,' and 'society,' the fact cannot be avoided that Forsyth's method grasped the foundational importance of perennial principles in social ethics. His portrayal of their significance, as prior to any theology of praxis, is one reason why his work stands as a particularly helpful signpost in the confusing traffic of social ethics today, and will continue to do so for generations to come.

At first glance, Forsyth's preoccupation with the ethical fallout from the proliferation of evolutionary theory may seem irrelevant and quite simply outdated. But consider the following quotation taken from a recent national newspaper: 'Darwin is everywhere these days, his fortunes waxing while the century of Freud and Marx wanes. As a generation of pundits become sceptical of childhood trauma and socialist visions of human perfectibility, ideas about innate and inherited characteristics surge up to take their place.'[56] While the author has obviously missed the connection between evolutionary theory and the emergence of utopian politics, her statement about the continuing interest in Darwin, and evolution, reflects a reality which has permeated our culture, society, and ethics in almost imperceptible ways, as the distinction between good and evil has become almost invisible. The erasure of this distinction was one which Forsyth foresaw, as he was uniquely poised in his day to witness the effects of such theology on society and ethics, as it was beginning to have significant impact on the Church. In *Positive Preaching and the Modern Mind* Forsyth indicated three weaknesses he perceived in the Church, and I believe his ethical method clearly addresses their modern expressions in significant ways. He stated that the Church suffered from complacency, uncertainty, and triviality,[57] and it is my suggestion that, in general terms, the Church suffers from these three things more than ever, especially with respect to its treatment of social ethics. I would further suggest that the tenacity of these problems relate directly to the Church's neglect of those aspects of social ethics about which Forsyth was so concerned and attempted to address in helpful ways. His insight diagnosed an illness which has gone on to infect the moral theology of the Church, and which remains untreated in many quarters still today, finding expression in its complacent, uncertain, and trivial treatment of ethics in general, and social ethics in particular.

Evidence of the Church's complacency is revealed insofar as it has succumbed to the self-satisfaction which plagues humanity as a whole, as evolutionary theory has instructed us that nothing is impossible for the human race. A lack of humility, which Forsyth's method counters, means that society becomes preoccupied with artificial intelligence, cloning, and building colonies on the moon, rather than seeking to meet the basic needs of those who comprise the scope of the Cross's redemption. And then, even on these complex, technological issues, which affect society at the core of its being, the Church stands remarkably silent. When the Church does become involved in social issues, it seems to be with a divisive self-assurance that each one, or each group, knows what is best to be done. The pride, which Forsyth observed in expressions of the social gospel, remains at the fore. His remedy for such complacency rests in his concept of God's love as holy, and the note of judgement that holiness sounds in our salvation. Throughout his work, he 'maintained that there can be no philosophy of ethics apart from some theory of judgement, and it was his convinced opinion that the Christian Evangelical view alone adequately met the case.'[58]

Forsyth was equally prophetic in his diagnosis of the sense of uncertainty in the Church, and this is especially so with respect to contemporary social ethics. Forsyth believed that uncertainty was multiplied when theology was neglected, and Ronald Preston would agree that recent ecumenical social ethics suffers from confusion as a result of the lack of input sought from theologians and other similarly-trained members of the Church.[59] Forsyth blamed the ethos of the day for negative attitudes toward theological leadership, as he stated adamantly: 'I repeat, the Christian theologian is the champion of the Christian laity, the pleader and justifier of general Christian experience. If he is repudiated, it is by a laity victimised by something feebler than the Gospel, or by an age that demands a biographical Christ for its interest instead of an evangelical Christ for its salvation.'[60] Not only the Church, but culture as a whole, has slid into the very relativism about which Forsyth warned, predicting that it would emerge when evolutionary science replaced religious truth in the hearts and minds of society. In fact, it has come to indwell the heart of society, so that certainty has become an outdated term for all but the most dogmatic, or those who wish to retreat into a Christian narrative framework.[61]

Forsyth wanted to make abundantly clear the essential need for a basis of authority which rested outside of oneself and even one's own experience. 'In other words, it is important that the believer should be able to say 'I am certain', but it is no less essential that he should be able to pass beyond this and say 'It is certain'.'[62] The authority of certainty lay beyond faith experience, and it further challenges the problem of ethical relativity: 'The real ground of our certitude, therefore, is the nature of the thing of which we are sure, rather than the nature of the experience in which we are sure,'[63] Forsyth asserted. This kind of objectivity, provided by Forsyth's understanding of Gospel authority, is capable of grounding theology in a confident centre, whence constructive conversation and dialogue in social ethics may take place with those within and without the Christian faith.

The problem of triviality, observed by Forsyth, is yet with the Church, and, as he argued, is corrected by putting theology in its rightful place over religious feeling. Forsyth dreaded the day when emphasis on the 'Spirit' of Christ would overshadow the fact of his Cross. This is a judgement which ought to draw attention from across the theological spectrum, as Christians of various stripes become engaged in political activities in the name of the 'Spirit' of Christ, and yet who appear to have little theological basis for their endeavours. This applies equally to those from one extreme, who base an entire socio-ethical programme on a handful of Christian precepts, with little evident connection to the Gospel principle,[64] as it does to those from another, whose liberation programme differs little in kind from the utopian basis of the social gospel.[65] In such situations, 'we can see where they have arrived, but since we cannot make out the route by which they have travelled, their conclusions are offered for acceptance only on their own authority.' [66] Forsyth's tenacious clinging to the Gospel principle saves his ethics from this criticism, and his proposal of a certain, holy, just, authority as found in that principle may yet save the Church from the same. As he clearly stated, the principle of the Gospel 'is the central foundation of Christian ethics.'[67] It is the same principle that was rediscovered by the Reformers, that Forsyth would argue is still relevant today, for 'their principle and method are organic to Christian history, and perennial.'[68] The task, then, of theology, in relation to all activities of the Church, 'is to repeat this Apostolic Gospel for its own age, but not to change or adapt it.'[69] The Gospel is creative, not static, and, after the task of evangelism, discipleship and mission, Forsyth placed the role of the Church to 'become the moral guide of society, and translate her holy Gospel into large social ethics closely relevant to the time.'[70]

Translating the gospel into a programme of social ethics was not something at which Forsyth seemed particularly adept. His own attempt to make practical suggestions built on his theology did not reveal his prophetic edge. In *The Church, the Gospel and Society*, he makes what he admits are merely suggestions for application, and they seem surprisingly inadequate even for his day. One example is his call for the economic system to continually increase production, as a way for the economic needs of everyone to be met. Today, it is evident that sustainable development is the only kind of production which fragile creation can support. The attitudes which lead to constantly increasing production are seen to be grounded more in greed and pride of human sin than in any sort of Christian social ethic. Part of his weakness at this point was the lack of connection forged between principle and precept. Preferring to emphasise the aspect of principle, Forsyth was quick to assert that 'Jesus had no interest in social ethics in our modern and economic sense of the phrase. His kingdom of God was ethical, but it was not economic. He had no programme for it - only a principle and a power.'[71] It is perhaps a result of his emphasis on the principle of the Gospel that Forsyth struggled to build a bridge of relevant application. Moreover, he could not see beyond the notion of process, insisting that the kingdom was growing in positive power as history progressed. He wrote, 'Indeed, it is actually a holier Church today than in the first century. And its Gospel is doing more to moralise society and to rear a Christian wisdom for the age.'[72] Anyone at all familiar with the present moral situation in society, with the neglect of the poor in developing countries, and with the decline in religious zeal and increase of pluralism and relativism, would find these words difficult to accept.

Forsyth provided a prophetic diagnosis of the moral situation in society, and an enduring foundation upon which to build to meet the present challenges to the Church in the realm of social ethics. But the task of constructing a programme or method of application is one that remains. As John de Gruchy has argued more recently, Christianity must provide a foundation for belief, and also a means of speaking and acting prophetically in the midst of particular situations.[73] This is what it means to be committed to the 'whole gospel.' He clarifies and contemporises the spirit of Forsyth's work in a helpful way. Being committed to the whole gospel means '...a commitment to the evangelical doctrines as affirmed in early catholic tradition and retrieved by the Reformation, but also a commitment to the biblical prophetic witness to God's purposes of justice and equity within society.'[74] This means that 'while a tradition can wither and die - or worse, become an albatross around our necks - it can also be retrieved as a source of empowerment in the present, providing the symbols not only for its own revitalisation and renewal, but for society at large.'[75]

Forsyth recalled for his day, as he recalls for ours, the foundation of moral theology, in God's gracious, holy, loving act in the Cross of Christ. He represents the thoughtful side of Christianity, which does not jump onto every socio-ethical bandwagon, sometimes poorly disguised in theological clothing, without seeking first to understand the premises upon which any form of praxis must rest. While the age determines the application of moral theology, Forsyth reminds us that moral theology should not be determined by every wind and breeze of the age. He has helped to remind the Church of the stones laid for a Christian social ethic which is evangelical, ecumenical, teleological, and prophetic. In his words, 'I have found my rock, my reality, my eternal life in my historic Redemption. And what is moral rock, real existence, and spiritual master for me is also the authority and charter of the Church, the living power in all history, the moral foundation of Society, and the warrant of an infinite future for the human race.'[76] The building of a method of socio-ethical application and praxis upon this rock-solid foundation is the challenge left by Forsyth to each generation, and such is the task for ours.

Notes:

1   Alistair McGrath, *Three Evangelical Voices*, Themeliosa 22, April 1997, p 22-24.
    McGrath offers his own evaluation of such advice: 'As one looks at the sustained
    gains made by liberalism in German Protestantism up to the eve of the First
    World War, the wisdom of Ritschl's advice is clear. To win the long-term
    victories, you have to influence the way in which a rising generation thinks.'
    Forsyth sought to meet the challenge recognising that the critical call to access
    and impress the mind of each generation is one that stands perennially before the
    Church's theologians. He argued: '...if the Church is in spiritual and mental
    health, it must prize its theological centres quite as highly as it prizes its
    philanthropic. The Church is on the down grade which cares more for the
    hospitals than for its colleges and staffs them better.' P T Forsyth, *Theology in
    Church and State*, London, Hodder and Stoughton, 1915, p 113.

2   Even Walter Rauschenbusch, the social gospel's foremost advocate in America,
    is studied now more for historical importance than for contemporary theological
    application.

3   Apart from scattered references in books and articles, the most helpful critical
    analysis of Forsyth's social ethics to date is found in Trevor Hart (ed*), Justice the
    True and Only Mercy,* T & T Clark, Edinburgh, 1995. See especially, *P T Forsyth:
    a Political Theologian?* by Keith Clements and helpful references in *P T Forsyth
    on the Church* by Stephen Sykes, and *P T Forsyth as Unsystematic Systematician*
    by Alan P Sell.

4   References to social ethics, and comment on Forsyth's contemporary social
    crisis, are found throughout his major and minor works. See especially *Church,
    Gospel and Society, Socialism, The Church and the Poor, Positive Preaching and
    Modern Mind, Justification of God, Christian Aspects of Evolution, Theology in
    Church and State, The Work of Christ, Faith Freedom and the Future.*

5   Although W A Visser T'Hooft described early the social gospel as a distinctively
    American movement, the social Christianity forming in this period on both sides
    of the Atlantic had shared origins, goals and philosophical bases. For that reason
    I will use the term 'social gospel' interchangeably with 'social Christianity'. For
    a recent examination of these similarities and connections, see Paul T Phillip, *A
    Kingdom on Earth: Anglo-American Social Christianity 1880-1940,*
    Pennsylvania State University Press, 1996. Cf. Willem Aldoph Visser T'Hooft,
    The Background of the Social Gospel in America, Harlem, 1928.

6   The lack of gender balance in not using the term 'sisterhood' is acknowledged.
    The terms 'brotherhood', 'man', and 'fraternity' are used in this paper as they
    occur in direct quotations from authors of the time period involved. Otherwise
    gender-inclusive language is employed.

7   See for an example of this later edition, Herbert Spencer, *The Data of Ethics*,
    Williams and Norgate, London, 1907.

8   Hugh Price Hughes, *The Philanthropy of God,* Hodder & Stoughton, London,
    1890, p 296. These words are taken from *Titus 3: 4*. See the introduction of this
    book for Hughes' comments on Spencer.

9   Ibid, p xi.
10 Spencer, *The Data of Ethics*, op cit, p 53.
11 Ibid, p 30.
12 See for example, Thomas H Huxley, *Evolution and Ethics and other essays*, Macmillan and Co, London, 1894. For a searching critique see A G N Flew, *Evolutionary Ethics*, Macmillan, London.
13 Spencer, *The Data of Ethics*, op cit, p 53.
14 See Walter Gladden's critical interpretation of this aspect of Spencer's ethics in *Ruling Ideas and the Present Age*, James Clarke and Co, London, 1895, p 74.
15 Hughes, for example had a personal relationship with Green. See Phillips, p 179; Alan P F Sell, *Philosophical Idealism and Christian Belief*, University of Wales, Cardiff, 1995, pp 54-5, 251.
16 See Green's critique of Kant, and proposal of a modified utilitarianism in T H Green, *Proleomena to Ethics*, 3rd ed, A C Bradley (ed), Clarendon Press, Oxford, 1890. For a critical comparison of Spencer and Kant, see Jacob Gould Schurman, *Kantian Ethics and the Ethics of Evolution*, Williams and Norgate, London and Edinburgh, 1881.
17 Bernard M G Reardon, *Religious Thought in the Victorian Age: a survey from Coleridge to Gore*, 2nd ed, Longman, London and New York, 1995, p 152ff.
18 Ibid, p 150.
19 See F D Maurice, *Social Morality*, Macmillan and Co, London, 1872.
20 Bernard M G Reardon, *Religious Thought in the Victorian Age: a survey from Coleridge to Gore*, op cit, p 154.
21 P T Forsyth, *The Church, the Gospel and Society*, Independent Press, London, 1962, p 110. This book is comprised of two papers presented earlier by Forsyth, in 1905.
22 It has been noted that Forsyth was not alone in his reservations over these social issues, including his negative response to the growing sentimentality of liberalism, espoused by R J Campbell in *The New Theology*, Chapman and Hall, London, 1907. Forsyth opposed Campbell adamantly, as he fused God and humanity in an extreme immanentism. Bradley suggests that many ministers agreed with Forsyth, but they did nothing about it. W L Bradley, *P T Forsyth: the Man and his Work*, Independent Press, London, 1952, p 62.
23 P T Forsyth, *Socialism, the Church and the Poor*, Hodder and Stoughton, London, 1908, p 1.
24 P T Forsyth, *The Church, the Gospel and Society*, op cit, p 110
25 Ibid.
26 Walter Rauschenbusch, *Christianizing the Social Order*, Macmillan and Co, New York, 1919, pp 106-107. Rauschenbusch explains that some who have left will return, others who have questions will find answers, and still others who have gone may genuinely have outgrown their Christian faith.
27 See Clements, P T Forsyth: a Political Theologian? in Trevor Hart (ed*), Justice the True and Only Mercy*, op cit, p 146. In his article Clements makes it clear that socio-political commitments 'were clearly manifest in his twenty-five years of local Church ministry when his practical concern for the poor and his sympathies

with working-class and trades union movements were outstanding features of his pastoral work.'

[28] Forsyth admonished his hearers with his own testimony, 'I pray you do not be impatient when I speak so much of reality. And do not suspect a flavour of philosophy instead of contact with facts. Do not take my arm and lead me away to the pound-a-weeks and the nothing-a-weeks and tell me if I want realities to consider there. Long ago I was there, and worked there, and considered there, and have been considering it ever since.' *The Church, the Gospel and Society*, op cit, p 96.

[29] Ibid, pp 96-97.

[30] Some argue that Forsyth's theology 'should best be studied in its relation to the theology of Albrecht Ritschl... and in its reaction to the critical interpretations of Harnack, for whose work, widely though he differed from his theological conclusions, he had a profound respect.' Gwilym O Griffith, *The Theology of P T Forsyth*, Lutterworth Press, London and Redhill, 1948, p 7.

[31] See Robert McAfee Brown, The 'Conversion' of P T Forsyth, *The Congregational Quarterly* 30, July 1952, pp 236-244. Brown argues that a full understanding of Forsyth's theology hinges on a clear grasp of his theological 'about face', whereby 'Forsyth somehow changes so completely that he left his own generation far behind and emerged as a thinker who anticipated many of the insights represented... by such men as Barth, Brunner and Niebuhr.' A M Hunter explains that 'though Forsyth had repudiated the errors of Liberalism... he retained all that was best in the Liberal approach to theology and the Bible.' A M Hunter, *P T Forsyth : Per Crucem and Lucem* , SCM Press, London, 1974, p 18.

[32] P T Forsyth, *Christian Aspects of Evolution*, Epworth Press, London, 1950, p 9. [Originally published as, Some Christian Aspects of Evolution, *London Quarterly Review* 104, October 1905, pp 209-239.]

[33] Ibid, p 31.

[34] Ibid, p 33.

[35] Gladden, *Ruling Ideas and the Present Age*, op cit, p 35ff.

[36] Ibid, p 25.

[37] Rauschenbusch, *Christianizing the Social Order* op cit, p 90.

[38] J S Seeley, *Ecce Homo: A Survey of the Life and Work of Jesus Christ*, 2nd ed, Macmillan & Co, London and Cambridge, 1866, p 126.

[39] P T Forsyth, *Socialism, the Church and the Poor,* op cit, pp 6-7.

[40] P T Forsyth, *Theology in Church and State*, op cit, pp 4-5.

[41] Ibid, pp 92-93.

[42] P T Forsyth, *Socialism, the Church and the Poor,* op cit, p 6.

[43] P T Forsyth, *Christian Aspects of Evolution,* op cit, p 8.

[44] Ibid, p 15.

[45] Ibid, p 37.

[46] Ibid, p 11.

[47] Ibid, pp 11-12.

[48] P T Forsyth, *Socialism, the Church and the Poor,* op cit, p 55.

49 Ibid, p 56.

50 P T Forsyth, *Christian Aspects of Evolution,* op cit, p 38.

51 P T Forsyth, *Psitive Preaching and the Modern Mind*, Hodder and Stoughton, London, 1917, p 173.

52 P T Forsyth, *The Church, the Gospel and Society*, op cit, pp 110-111.

53 Forsyth suggested that we learn more from eighteenth-century Calvinists than from modern social prophets that, 'a creed which starts from the glory of God has more power for man's welfare than one that is founded on the welfare of man alone.' *Justification of God: Lectures for War-Time on a Christian Theodicy.* Later Edition, Independent Press, London, 1948, p 83. [First published 1917.]

54 Ibid.

55 Forsyth saw the church in danger of 'losing the Gospel in the Gospel's humane law.' As he warned, 'We make the mistake of thinking that the Kingdom of God was set up in the ideal precepts of Jesus instead of His Cross. But it is by the Cross we are to read all the precepts, and, if necessary, to revise them.' P T Forsyth, *The Church, the Gospel and Society*, op cit, p 17.

56 Maggie Gee, 'Suffer our children and other species', *The Daily Telegraph,* 7th February 1998, Section 2 p 2.

57 P T Forsyth, *Positive Preaching and the Modern Mind,* op cit, pp 169ff.

58 A F Simpson, *P T Forsyth: The Prophet of Judgement* in *The Scottish Journal of Theology* 4, June 1951, p 151.

59 Cf Ronald Preston, *Confusions in Christian Social Ethics*, SCM Press, London, 1994.

60 P T Forsyth, *The Church, the Gospel and Society*, op cit, p 82.

61 Cf, Discussion of post-liberal narrative approaches, based on the thought of George Lindbeck and evangelical foundationalism, in Timothy Phillips and Dennis Okholm, (eds), *The Nature of Confession: Evangelicals and Postliberals in Conversation*, Intervarsity Press, Downers Grove, Il, 1996.

62 B G Worrall, *The Authority of Grace in the Theology of P T Forsyth,* in *The Scottish Journal of Theology,* 25th February 1972, p 70.

63 P T Forsyth, *The Principle of Authority*, Hodder and Stoughton, London, 1912, p 52.

64 Alan Sell has argued strongly for increased theological reflection prior to theological action, by those representing both sides of Christian ethical issues. See Alan P F Sell, *A Renewed Plea for Impractical Divinity*, in Studies in *Christian Ethics* 8, 1995.

65 See for example, Jurgen Moltmann, *Jesus Christ For Today's World*, trans Margaret Kohl, Fortress Press, Minneapolis, 1994, pp 24ff. Moltmann's description of realising the Kingdom of God sounds remarkably similar to Rauschenbusch's process outlined in *Christianizing the Social Order.*

66 Sell, *A Renewed Plea for Impractical Divinity,* op cit, p 70.

67 P T Forsyth, *Socialism, the Church and the Poor,* op cit, p 70.

68 P T Forsyth, *The Church, the Gospel and Society*, op cit, p 83.

69 B G Worrall, *The Authority of Grace in the Theology of P T Forsyth,* op cit, p 72.

70 P T Forsyth, *The Church, the Gospel and Society*, op cit, p 59.

71 P T Forsyth, *Socialism, the Church and the Poor,* op cit, p 59.

72 P T Forsyth, *The Church, the Gospel and Society,* op cit, 25.

73 See John de Gruchy, *Liberating Reformed Theology*, Eerdmans, Grand Rapids, 1991.

74 Ibid, p 40.

75 Ibid, p 39.

76 P T Forsyth, *The Church, the Gospel and Society*, op cit, p 127.

9.

P T Forsyth

Theologian for a New Millennium?

Alan P F Sell

In a letter to the experimental philosopher Robert Hooke, the eminent man of science Isaac Newton (1642-1727) declared, 'If I have seen further it is by standing on ye shoulders of Giants.[1] [2] We may feel that during this conference we have been standing on the shoulders of a theological giant, though we may hesitate to say that we have seen further than he did. We may feel that we have learned much from him, and we may be ready to go on our theological way rejoicing. Let us then beware of the shower of cold water waiting to be directed upon us by those post-modern literary theorists who deny that we can ever discover what a past author's intentions were. The meaning of a text, they say, resides in itself. Having no access to the author's intentions, we simply have to ask what the text in its present shape says to us now. This is not the time of the place to embark upon a thorough analysis of this view, but I think it important that we briefly adjust ourselves to it, so that we can see what kind of guidance we may expect from Forsyth as we enter a new millennium.

On the one hand, it is clear that when reading any text we do come to it with presuppositions, convictions, expectations; and we come bringing our own personal history - some of it lumber - with us. On the other hand, notwithstanding the opacity which some have found in Forsyth's epigrammatic style, I believe that a reader would have to work very hard to exit from a Forsyth text in absolute ignorance of the author's intention. That intention is generally placarded on every page. It is, theologically, of the greatest importance that we are able to sustain this position, otherwise we can no longer speak of the apostolic succession in the Gospel, or of the guidance of the Holy Spirit through the ages, or of the ongoing providence of God. The 'fellowship of Christian minds' which is 'like to that above' would be ruled out; our forebears would be quite unable to acquaint us with their meanings; our appreciation of past writings would be exclusively instant, as if they emerged from no context whatsoever; and the value judgements we passed upon past texts might then be made in accordance with the degree to which they appeared to accord with our own socio-political platforms or other interest.

None of this is to deny that, if humility forbids us to say that we see further than the giants, we frequently see different things. Since we can be only creatures of our time, this is what we should expect. Consider, for example, John Howard (1726-1790). He was a pioneer of prison reform, whose investigation of the dire conditions of gaols in Britain and Europe did much to shame society into taking appropriate action. He was a man ahead of his time, and we applaud him. But this same John Howard one day wrote to his recently-wedded wife as follows: 'My dear, for the prevention of those discords which I have observed to prevail among married people, it is my wish that in case of any disagreement between us my will should prevail.'[2] How benighted, we may nowadays feel! However, there is no point in getting Cross with John Howard; his attitude was not sexist, he was simply being conventional. The Church is always catching up with the Gospel, and where the place of women is concerned it still has a long way to go. May point is that the giants of the past are not infallible; we must expect that with the passage of time and with dramatic advances in knowledge and changes in society, our articulation of the Gospel cannot be exactly theirs (though I gather that it is still possible to stumble aCross clones of C H Spurgeon and even of Martyn Lloyd-Jones); and we are called upon to communicate the Good News in circumstances which they could not have envisaged and to which, therefore, they could not directly speak. But none of this means that we cannot learn from them, though we may need to modify and supplement their views. It does suggest, however, that in our assessments we should proceed with a certain humble caution. There is a wilful blindness which will not allow us to accept the truth when it stares us in the face; but there is also a non-culpable cultural myopia which should caution us that in two hundred years time people will say of us what T H Huxley said of himself when, in 1859, Darwin revealed natural selection as the explanatory principle of evolution: 'How extremely stupid not to have thought of that!' We simply do not know what those things are about which we shall be deemed to have been extremely stupid, but that there will be such matters we need not doubt.

Against this background, I shall attempt to illustrate how we may learn from, modify and supplement Forsyth's writings by briefly examining four of his major claims. (You will understand that my greatest difficulty in preparing this paper on so fruitful a writer was to limit myself to just four significant claims.)

I

First, God's love is holy love. The thought did not originate with Forsyth. In their different ways the Scots A B Davidson and Robert Flint, and the German Rudolf Otto, were elucidating the holiness of God, and Forsyth's contemporary James Denney did likewise. But none majored on the theme to the degree that Forsyth did. Partly this is because he was a convert from a liberalism which he came to regard as too humanitarian, too optimistic concerning human progress, and too sentimental concerning God's love. Partly it is because, though urgent in addressing the concerns of his day, he was rooted in the broad Christian tradition - not least the Puritan strand of it; and from Thomas Goodwin, whom he called 'the apostle and high priest of our [Congregational] confession,'[3] he could hardly have failed to catch the emphasis upon the holiness of God. Above all, he found the concept of God's holiness in the Bible:

> The New Testament name and idea of God is not simply 'Our Father', but 'the God and Father of our Lord and Saviour Jesus Christ.' And Christ's own prayer was 'Holy Father.' That was Christ's central thought of God, and he knew God as he is.[4]

It is not too much to say that whenever Forsyth speaks of the love of God it is holy love that he has in mind. That is, he thinks of the one whose love stands over against us in judgement and mercy. There can be no doubt that this note needed to be struck at a time when more extreme liberal theologians were muffling it. But there is something more to be said, and here we may need to supplement Forsyth. Listen to his contemporary, D W Forrest, who was no way-out liberal:

> Nothing is plainer in the whole Gospel story than that Christ personally had a great charm for men. The lowest and most despised of the people gathered around Him. They were not won by simple graciousness… What attracted them was the union in Him of holiness with love and gentleness.[5]

Now while I am the first to agree that an exclusive emphasis upon what the evangelical hymn calls 'the sympathising Jesus' can coddle the saint and cheat the sinner, it may be that Forsyth, with his strong emphasis upon the majesty of God's love, and his conviction that it is in the epistles rather than the gospels that the Gospel is fully to be seen, needs to be supplemented at this point.[6] We need to reverence the holy, but also to heal and encourage the human by proclaiming the holy as close: and is not this at least part of what incarnation means? And is it not why God, in Christ, reaches out to those who are hurting: the poor, the marginalised, the sick, the rich fool? I do not think for one moment that Forsyth would have disagreed with this: indeed, he clearly portrayed the perils on all sides:

> To preach only the atonement, the death apart from
> the life, or only the person of Christ, the life apart
> from the death, or only the teaching of Christ, His
> words apart from His life, may all be equally one-
> sided, and extreme to falsity.[7]

It is, however, sometimes easier to give advice to others than
consistently to take it ourselves.

Nevertheless Forsyth's emphasis upon God's love as holy
must be preserved at all costs; and in our time and in our
culture its implications must be worked out afresh not least,
perhaps, in our worship. Forsyth said,

> The grace of God cannot return to our preaching or to
> our faith till we recover what has almost clean gone
> from our general, familiar, and current religion, what
> liberalism has quite lost - I mean a due sense of the
> holiness of God. This sense has much gone from our
> public worship, with its frequent irreverence…[8]

Would it not be true to say that today it is not only liberal
Christian worship which lacks 'a due sense of the holiness of
God,' or what R W Dale had earlier called a 'sense of the
divine greatness'?[9] Indeed, may it not be that in some
contemporary liberal worship, with its ecological concern for
the environment and its deep grasp of the sanctity of life,
coupled with an active concern for human well-being, there is
a good deal of reverence - even if on some occasions it may
seem to be more a reverence for nature than for nature's God?
Is it perhaps some of the evangelical or theologically diverse
middle-of-the-road groups which need to ask questions of
their worship? In the house of the Lord today do we feel
solemnised?

On our return to this country following nearly a decade abroad, my wife and I discovered that whilst our backs had been turned some Churches had made two liturgical discoveries: first how to open worship in 'wake-up-happy-campers-style' with a jolly 'Good morning everybody: how are you feeling today?': secondly, how to project banal little ditties, often sung to dirge-like tunes, on the walls for all to sing. The first directs the congregation to their own feelings and away from the majesty of God, and overlooks the fact that if the saints have been busy sinning all the week they ought not to be feeling too good until after the prayer of confession! The second frequently empties the Gospel of its transcendent dimension, denudes it of its challenge, and cosily sentimentalises it, sometimes to the point of blurring the distinction between a heavenly friend and a dear old pal. I do not wish to be interpreted as having antediluvian tendencies; I value many modern hymns and tunes (though how quickly dated imitation 'pop' becomes!); and I have never thought that all expressions of Christian worship should, or could, be identical in shape and content. But where the basic liturgy of Word and Sacrament is concerned I plead for reverent, joyous, duly proportioned praise; for by the content and manner of our most characteristic worship we display our doctrine of God - and our opinion of ourselves.

But we have to do more than remind those who conduct worship of the doctrine of God and the prerequisite of humility - and if need be pull the plug on projectors. We are called to worship God in the midst of a society which emits contradictory signals. On the one hand, to a greater degree than Forsyth's, large tracts of our society seem unaware of or inimical to the sacred. I do not overlook the satires written against the Puritans, or the caricaturists and cartoonists of the eighteenth-century for whom the pretentious were fair game. But since the so-called satire boom of the nineteen-sixties, of which the late lamented Peter Cook, Willie Rushton and John Wells were such conspicuous promoters, reverence has been at a premium. Forelock touching is out; and the Victorian and Edwardian decorum of Forsyth's day - however hypocritical some aspects of it may have been - is no more. We do not trust authority figures - in particular cases with good reason; and many have become their own authorities. We do our own thing; we go for what makes us feel good; and that is right which does not hurt anyone else. I speak in universals, and clearly there are many exceptions. But I am trying to characterise a pervasive cultural mood in our land at this time, and I am ambivalent about what I see. I am glad to live in a society in which *Private Eye* and the satirists can flourish - and live. There is a place for the pricking of pretensions, and for teasing the libel laws with sentences beginning, 'It would be quite wrong to suggest that...' But if nothing is sacred, may we not have lost more than we have gained?

On the other hand, there is in our society a craving for the spiritual, which finds expression in meditation groups, anti-stress groups, spirituality conferences, New Age thought. That we do not live by bread alone is a good lesson to learn; but Forsyth would think it better that we nourish our souls at the Cross of Christ. Here should be the focus of our reverence and praise. At this point, with his talk of the holy love of God revealed and active in the Cross, Forsyth directly challenges us – and, above all, our worship. By all means let our worship be joyous: we have a grand Gospel to proclaim and a great God to celebrate. But let it be reverent too. When we contemplate God's love and think of ourselves in relation to it, how can any of us keep on our shoes on such holy ground?

But what is it, more than anything else, which prompt our reverent rejoicing? It is the Cross of Christ. And with this I come to the second of Forsyth's major claims.

II

The Cross is and must be central in our experience, our theology, our preaching, our life. It is by the Cross that God's holiness is satisfied and people are saved. Forsyth writes:

> The Holy Father's first care is holiness. The first charge on a Redeemer is satisfaction to that holiness. The Holy Father is one who does and must atone. As Holy Father he offers a sacrifice rent from his own heart. It is made to him by no third party, but by himself in his Son, and it is made to no foreign power but to his own holy nature and law.[10]

These are by no means the easiest of sentences to construe. I take them to encompass the following claims at least: the holiness of God requires to be satisfied, for God is God and sin affronts his holy love; the righteous anger of God against sin must be appeased; the redemptive initiative can come only from God's side; it is not that God requires a death before he can be merciful: on the contrary, the first word of the Gospel is grace, and it is God in Christ who renders satisfaction and reconciles the world to himself; the atoning sacrifice is made possible by God and received by him: it is not a ransom paid to anyone else - least of all to the devil (however construed), who has no rights; above all, at the Cross something is done and not simply shown.

What are we to make of this? It will sound very strange to any that do not have a sense of the reality and damaging nature of sin. As in Forsyth's day, so in ours: there are those who so sentimentalise the love of God that one wonders why the Cross should have been necessary. They preach a 'there, there - God knows you couldn't help it' message which at one and the same time demeans God and human beings too. We are responsible people; we do sin. God's response to our sin is wrathful; but note this: it is not that God is first loving and then decides to be merciful. God's holy love is graciously judging love. As Forsyth's contemporary Robert Mackintosh said, 'God's love is not mere benevolence. He will judge sin because he loves righteousness... Grace includes morality within itself; love is justice at white heat.'[11] Forsyth drew the consequence: 'The one thing [God] could not do was simply to wipe the slate and write off the loss. He must either inflict punishment or assume it.'[12]

On the other side are those who have a sense of sin which is acute to the point of being almost pathological. They belabour themselves because of their offences; they maintain a rigorous and regular programme of self-examination to the point that they turn inward, they take their eyes off the Saviour, and are for ever taking their own spiritual temperature to see if they are worthy of God's grace. Well, none of us is; but still God comes, and that is what makes grace grace. There are even those whose proudest boast is that they are the greatest sinners imaginable; and for them the Methodist philosopher T E Jessop has a little rhyme:

> Once in saintly passion I cried with desperate grief:
> 'O Lord, my heart is black
> with guile, of sinners I am
> chief!'
> Then stooped my guardian
> angel and whispered from
> behind,
> 'Vanity, my little man, you're
> nothing of the kind!'[13]

I trust I do not need to say that a sense of sin is not something to be whipped up by doom-laden, threatening preachers. It is the work of God the Holy Spirit to convict us of sin; and this frequently comes when the Gospel of God's grace has been so winsomely proclaimed that we, as sinners, can bear it no longer. Remember: Jesus did not lambast Zacchaeus; it sufficed that Zacchaeus was in his loving presence.

But this reference to preaching pushes us on to ask how our sermonising stands up against Forsyth's position on the relations of holy love, sin and atonement. There would seem to be two respects in which he would weigh some current preaching and find it wanting. The first is perhaps more of a pitfall for evangelicals. (I have serious reservations concerning the wanton labelling of one's fellow Christians, but I here use shorthand. For myself I am happy to be described as evangelical, provided that I am also described as liberal, catholic and Reformed, and I find this to be neither paradoxical nor the mental habit of one whose security resides in the adage, 'You can't hit a moving target'.) To return: there is a type of evangelical preaching which majors on sin, and on God's 'plan of salvation' whereby sin is dealt with. And the entire emphasis is upon what has to be done, and has been done, to put us right with God. The virtue here is that these preachers know that something has been done for us. The pitfall is that they do not seem always to grasp the point that something had to be done for God. The result is that a truncated doctrine of the atonement is proclaimed.

So it is by those liberals for whom the Cross only exemplifies God's love. They rightly understand that the Cross shows us that God suffers alongside us, but they play down the ideas of sin and satisfaction, and of God's redeeming and victorious action. Forsyth was quite clear:

> Christ came not to *say* something, but to *do* something. His revelation was action more than instruction. He revealed by redeeming. The thing He did was not simply to make us aware of God's

> disposition in an impressive way. It was not to *declare* forgiveness. It was certainly not to *explain* forgiveness. And it was not even to *bestow* forgiveness. It was to *effect* forgiveness, and to set up the relation of forgiveness both in God and man.[14]

Elsewhere I have had the temerity to suggest that this note was muffled, if struck at all, by some of the contributors to *The Myth of God Incarnate*. For example, John Hick, in a follow-up volume on the *Myth* debate asks, 'May we not say that although the Cross, and the incarnation as a whole, whilst not exclusively constituting God's co-suffering with humanity, nevertheless *reveals* that co-suffering and so enables us to believe it?'[15] To which I reply, 'It may all be said; it must all be said; [but] is God, at the Cross, merely showing us something about himself as fellow-sufferer, or is he vanquishing once and for all everything that would keep us apart from him?'[16] With Forsyth, I believe that the Cross is more than a visual aid concerning God's character and demeanour. It is the place where atonement is made and the once-for-all victory wrought.

In playing down God's saving action at the Cross (though by focusing on the suffering of God rather than the immanentist dying and rising motif of Edward Caird and others) the mythographers, as they came to be called, are, in this respect, in the line of those incarnational theologians and idealist philosophers contemporary with Forsyth who did likewise.[17]

III

The third of Forsyth's claims to which I would draw attention is that concerning the necessity and inescapability for Christians of the Church. Even as I specify this third claim I am conscious of the risk of falsifying Forsyth. Least of all theologians does he parcel up his doctrines into separate bundles. On the contrary, no matter with what doctrine he purports to be dealing, all of this thought is governed and guided by deep reflection upon the holy love of God supremely revealed and active at the Cross.[18] So when he thinks of the Church he thinks of it as rooted and grounded in the saving, victorious work of God in Christ at the Cross. On the basis of this event the Church is called out by the Spirit: 'It is primarily a divine creation and not a voluntary association',[19] and it is one people: 'what the Gospel created was not a crowd of Churches but the one Church in various places.'[20] Because it is one, our sectarianisms and schisms must be dealt with; because it is a people, individualism is ruled out: as he said, 'To be in Christ is in the same act to be in the Church.'[21] Fellowship in the Church is essential because 'Salvation is personal, but it is not individual.'[22] Or again, 'it was a race that Christ redeemed, and not a mere bouquet of believers. It was a Church He saved, and not a certain pale of souls.'[23]

I like to think that the majority of those in our tradition have, during what has been called 'the ecumenical century', taken the point concerning the unity of the Church. We know that the Church is one; that its unity has been given by God; and that the challenge before us is so to dismantle Churchly sectarianisms on all sides whilst at the same time offering the gifts we have received, that the given unity may be ever more fully manifested, especially at the table of the Lord. We also know just how difficult it is to do this; but under God we know we must press on.[24]

It may be that what we need to learn at our end of the twentieth century is how to react to the diverse and sometimes contradictory voices which tell us today how the Church should be in the world. Listen first to an American United Methodist Church Planner, Lyle Schaller:

> The emergence of the megachurch is the most important development of modern Christian history... big Churches are more attractive to young people... People today expect to make choices about things - about a new TV, an automobile, what they eat, their housing... Parents and grandparents stayed with their denomination, but people from age 40 down to 25 don't have that denominational loyalty. They shop around... [Even large congregations in mainline denominations have declined]: Like the mom and pop grocery store, they can't compete with the 'supermarket' churches... To be competitive you have to do a better job. That's free-market competition. I have no problem with it.[25]

If we would succeed, then, we must build megachurches. And it is undeniably the case that in many largely attended conventicles the parking, child care facilities and gymnasia are all admirable. And before we thank God that we in Britain are not like other people, or even as those Americans, let us note that Walter Hollenweger, no less, who once sojourned among us, declared, 'Religion can be "sold" if it is marketed properly.'[26] In the same paper Hollenweger speaks of what he calls a 'floating Christianity' which may even comprise the majority of Christians; it is outside our buildings but not uninterested in the faith - at least for discussion purposes; and its members are full of good works.

Perhaps a difference between Schaller and Hollenweger is that Schaller's floating Christians have found a roof under which to settle whereas Hollenweger's have not (yet). The question which neither writer addresses in the articles cited is, 'Who are the Church'? Hollenweger is surely right to say that if local Churches are apostate God will bypass them and work in other ways - he can ever work through Cyrus, as the Old Testament reminds us. But have we really served the floating Christians if all we have done is either to have corralled them within the ancillary regions of our megabuildings, or to have deemed them Christian whilst they repudiate Church fellowship?

Our present context could hardly be more different from that of Forsyth. He was writing in the numerical heyday of the Free Churches, when their combined numbers equalled those of the Church of England, when the disabilities against them were tumbling away, and when they were becoming a force to be reckoned with in society. We live in a time of numerical decline when many main-line Churches hardly have the resources to maintain their current programmes, still less to augment them. Yet Forsyth can still help us, for none knew better than he that more numbers do not necessarily mean more of the Church. Why, otherwise, did he so insistently try to recall ministers, members and all that would listen, to the Gospel of God's grace? Who knew better than he how easy it was, amidst the numbers, to sacrifice the Gospel to the Church programme? He waxes eloquent on this point:

> Recently I read a complaint from a large County Union that they were not getting the young into the Churches, and that, too, while the Churches were going to unheard-of lengths in providing cricket, football, draughts and dominoes, dancing classes, and pierrot troupes. I agree with the protests made on the occasion, and should say that that was just the way not to fill Churches, except with burdens.[27]

(Perhaps, in self-justification, I should here explain that my early heroic efforts to teach the members of a youth fellowship the Boston Two-step and the St Bernard's Waltz were undertaken with a view to varying the programme, and not under the illusion that droves of young people would, on hearing of these occasional Terpsichorean excitements, come flooding into the Church!)

But the general message is plain: in a time of numerical decline the worst thing we can do is to panic, to tone down the Gospel, to reduce the challenge of the way of the Cross, and to tempt people into the Church by all possible means.

But Forsyth knew something deeper too. He asks, 'What is the change that takes place when we are converted? Our change is really from one membership to another, from membership of the world to membership of the Church.'[28] However disconcerting it may be to us, for whom the term 'born again believer' has been hijacked by a particular party within the Church, this is precisely the phenomenon to which Forsyth refers. The New Testament and Church polities of the congregational type insist that the Church comprises believers, and that there is a distinction of eternal significance between those who are 'in Christ' and those who are not. Do we any longer believe this? Do we feel at ease with it? Or have we become so identified with our culture that we are comfortable with all and an irritant to none? I do not plead for our Churches to become ever more obnoxious to those around them. But listen to a rather differently-minded United Methodist minister, William Willimon:

> I believe that the day is coming, has already come, when the Church must again take seriously the task of making Christians, of intentionally forming a peculiar people... A stark reality for many of us liberal, mainline Churches is that there is no way for us to form people into a body that has no boundaries, no integrity of its own. We must define our beliefs and attitudes, the integrity of our community. No one ever lived or died for 'pluralism'... One reason why formation has been deemed unimportant by many of our Churches is that we assumed that our community was roughly continuous with the society as a whole.[29]

Did not Forsyth himself lament that the Church 'is established on good terms with its world instead of being a foreign mission from another?[30]' He also said,

> I am afraid we must part with the idea that there is no narrowness in Christianity. There must be. We can only take care that it is the right kind. Strait is the gate and narrow the way that leads to life.[31]

Do not misunderstand me. I am not suggesting that we should retreat from the world never to go into it again. Rather the crusade must be for genuine Churches composed of genuine Christians who are rejoicing in the Gospel; who will really forsake all (even their Church buildings!) if this should be God's will; who are learning their faith; and who, under the guidance of the Spirit, own the Lordship of Christ in all their affairs, and not least in connection with their mission. It seems to me that, unless we are clear on the nature of the Church, we shall be all at sea as to its mission. But, with the mention of the word 'mission', I come to the last of Forsyth's claims with which I am here concerned.

IV

Forsyth was convinced of the urgency of Christian mission. But he was most anxious that Christians should view missions in a proper way. The objective is not primarily numerical, it is theological. Missions, he declares,

> are a dispensation of the Spirit. So entirely are missions supernatural in their nature that they must rise and fall with our faith in the supernatural, with the reality of the Cross to us, and of the resurrection, and of our relations with the living Christ.[32]

Hence, with reference to those who feel that the objective of mission is to save perishing souls before the judgement come, he insists that the motive for mission 'is not pity but faith, not so much pity for perishing heathen, but faith and zeal for Christ's crown rights set up for ever in the deed decisive for all the world.'[33] Not, indeed, that 'we must always go straight to the heathen, at home or abroad, and assail them with these truths. They are the deep motive of the Church rather than the first method of the missionary.'[34] Conversely,

> A Church cold to missions is a Church dead to the Cross. It may have religion, but not the Gospel. It may have Christian sympathies, good music, intelligent views, social friendliness, excellent intentions, but not the power of the Gospel.[35]

> … It is not that Forsyth minimises the importance of the Church's social programmes. He does, however, fear for those who 'lose the soul in serving Christ - like Martha,'[36] and he is convinced that 'missions have more to hope for from a narrow creed which remains great than for a wide humanism that runs thin.'[37] Why? Because 'The basis of a social salvation is the final redemption in one act of the total race. And that act was the Cross of Christ.'[38]

There is the anchorage in the Cross, once more. And in that Cross Forsyth finds also the clue to the method and manner of mission:

> The Cross was not only His message, it was His method. Oh! Why does our method not oftener preach our message? His way was the way of service, not dominion; of sympathy, not suppression; of healing, not harrying; of atonement, and not exaction; of affinity, not of Empire[39]

- points on which he proceeds to contrast Islam unfavourably with Christianity. But he is no less critical of a Christianity gone astray, as when he regrets that all too often, 'when we have not persecuted, or neglected, the heathen we have exploited them. We have been careless what became of them, provided we have made fortunes out of them.'[40]

It is time to take stock. As to the motive of mission it seems to me that Forsyth is sound, and in our culture with its tendency to commercialise the Gospel we should do well to heed him on mission as the proper response to the reception of the Gospel of grace. What he says concerning the manner and method of mission is also instructive - indeed, he is here more tender than we saw him to be when speaking in a dogmatic context about God's holiness. But, no less than we ourselves, he was a child of his age. We should not speak in terms of the 'heathen' or of 'inferior races' as he did; we should be more discriminating concerning Islam; and, after two World Wars and many wars since, we may feel that he was over-optimistic in thinking that, provided individuals were free to find the Word of God in the Gospel, society would, in due course find it too.[41]

I suspect that Forsyth would rejoice that in many places the understanding of mission itself has become more Churchly. That is to say, instead of being almost an optional extra, supported by the gifts of those who are interested in that sort of thing, mission is now integral to Church budgets, as it should be. What is more, it is mission in partnership with other Churches around the world; it is no longer a few sending to the many; rather, it is recognised that all need to receive and to share. This is as it should be, given that for all mission partner-Churches mission is mission at home as well as abroad. If we think of our own society from this point of view, we cannot escape the fact that the world has come to our doorstep in ways of which Forsyth could hardly have dreamed. I do not think I saw a black person until I was eighteen (or a Mennonite, come to think of it, until I was in my forties!). But we now live in a multi-faith society with all the opportunities and challenges that this brings. We have to learn afresh who our neighbour is; we have to learn how to engage in constructive dialogue with those whose views in some cases differ widely from our own - and in this connection we have to maintain the important distinction between faithful witness in dialogue and evangelistic proclamation. This dialogue room is no more a mission hall than the state school classroom is.[42]

What, finally, of those who have not believed? If the Church has failed them, great will be the judgement of God upon a faithless people. But what if people refuse the Gospel? Here Forsyth offers a helpful clue: 'We do not say they will be damned if they do not believe, but we do say that they will be blessed if they do.'[43] Why? Because Christ 'is not the exclusive possession of a sect; He is the exclusive possession of all mankind.'[44] Moreover, God's mission cannot finally fail, for it is the work of his triune self. While it is our privilege to testify and to serve, God alone is Lord of the harvest. As Forsyth explained, the Father sends the Son; the Son sends the Spirit into all the earth; and the Church is the fourth missionary,[45] called by the Spirit through the Word to be an earnest of, and a witness to, that kingdom life which is eternal.

V

I have tried to show that, although our context is in many ways different from Forsyth's, we should do well to heed many reminders from him which tumble off his pages. Among these reminders are that God's love is holy love; that the Cross, understood as the fount of our salvation and the source of our new life, does and must hold central place; that fellowship in the Church is inescapable for Christians, because God calls a people for his praise and service; and that mission, conceived in the first place as a grateful response to God's unmerited grace, is an urgent matter.

On all of these points Forsyth can stimulate, encourage and challenge us. To this extent he qualifies as a theologian for the new millennium. However the appropriation and application of these insights must be our own. Where Forsyth is least able to help us directly is in connection with those distinctly novel aspects of our society and intellectual environment of which he could not have been aware. For example, he had nothing to say about Third World debt, or the reform of the welfare state. While contending earnestly against the liberal doctrines of inevitable progress and the perfectibility of human nature, and, where the heart of the Gospel was concerned, mightily opposed to post-Hegelian pantheising immanentism, he did not have to face the rebuke of Michel Foucault that claims to truth are nothing but disguised bids for power, or answer the case that religious language has no cognitive import.

Yet even in connection with matters of which he could not have been aware, I should be surprised if Forsyth's fundamental principles were not among those parameters within which we need to move if our witness and apologetics are to be recognisably Christian. At the very least he poses the claimant question of starting-points which is crucial to witness and apologetics alike:

> Do we start from the world or the Word? Are we to demand that Christ shall submit to the standard of certain principles or ideals which we bring to him from our human nature at its heart's highest and its thought's best? Or as our new creator is he his own standard, and not only so, but both judge and king,

and redeemer of human nature, and the fountain of a new life, autonomous in him, and for all the rest derived?[46]

Forsyth leaves us in no doubt concerning his starting-point. From whence shall we set out as the new millennium dawns?

Notes:

1   *Isaac Newton to Robert Hooke, 5 February 1675/6*, in H W Turnbull, ed., *The Correspondence of Isaac Newton*, CUP for the Royal Society, Cambridge, 1959, vol 1, p 416.

2   I regret that I no longer have to hand the source from which, long ago, I copied this.

3   P T Forsyth, *Faith, Freedom and the Future*, Independent Press, London, (1912), 1955, p 118 Cf. Goodwin's *Exposition of that Famous Divine Thomas Goodwin, DD., on the Part of the Epistle to the Ephesians and on the Book of Revelation*, 1842-1844, p 4-59.

4   Idem, *God the Holy Father*, (1897), Independent Press, London, 1957, p 3.

5   From a sermon on 'The redemption of pity,' (*Isaiah 53: 9*) in J H Leckie, ed., *David W Forrest D.D. ...Memoir, Tributes, Sermons and Theological Lectures*, Hodder and Stoughton, London, 1919, p 144. For Forrest see Alan P Sell, *Defending and Declaring the Faith. Some Scottish Examples 1860-1920*, Paternoster Press, Exeter and Helmers & Howard, 1987, Colorado Springs, ch.8.

6   Cf. the criticism of Forsyth's colleague A E Garvie in '*Placarding the Cross: the theology of P T Forsyth*,' *Congregational Quarterly*, XXI, October 1943, p 352. It remains the case, however, that Forsyth was correct in writing 'The Cross was not central to Christ's teaching as the kingdom was; but it was central to what is more than His teaching - to His healing, to His person, work and victory.' See *Missions in State and Church*, Hodder & Stoughton, London, 1908, p 11.

7   P T Forsyth, *The Cruciality of the Cross*, (1909), 4th impression, Independent Press, London, 1957, p 42.

8   Ibid, p 22.

9   R W Dale, '*On some present aspects of theological thought among Congregationalists,*'*Congregationalist,* January 1877, p 6.

10 Idem, *God the Holy Father*, Independent Press, London, 1957, p 4.

11 Robert Mackintosh, *Essays Towards a New Theology*, Maclehose, Glasgow, 1889, p 332.

12 P T Forsyth, *The Cruciality of the Cross*, p 98.

13 T E Jessop, *Law and Love. A Study of the Christian Ethic*, SCM Press, London, 1940, p 37.

14 Idem, *God the Holy Father*, Independent Press, London, 1957, p 19.

15 Michael Goulder, ed., *Incarnation and Myth*, SCM Press, London, 1979, p 82.

16 Alan P F Sell, *Aspects of Christian Integrity*, (1990), Wipf & Stock, Eugene, Oregon, 1998, p 44.

17 For a selection of whom see Idem, *Philosophical Idealism and Christian Belief*, Cardiff: University of Wales Press and New York: St Martin's Press, 1995. I do not deny the justice of J K Mozley's criticism that Forsyth is too disjunctive *vis à vis* incarnation and atonement. As Mozley points out, Forsyth contrasts 'an act largely metaphysical, like the Incarnation' with 'the moral Act of Atonement' (see *The Justification of God*, (1917), Independent Press, London, 1948, p 92. But elsewhere, especially when treating of kenosis in *The Person and Place of Jesus Christ,* Forsyth is more than a little aware of the ethical value of the incarnation.

See J K Mozley, *The Heart of the Gospel*, PCK, London, 1925, p 94. This book was dedicated to the memory of Forsyth and also to G A Studdert-Kennedy.

[18] For a fuller exposition of this point see Alan P F Sell, 'P T Forsyth as unsystematic systematician', in Trevor Hart, ed., *Justice the True and Only Mercy*, T & T Clark, Edinburgh, 1995, especially pp 144-145.

[19] P T Forsyth, *The Church and the Sacraments*, (1917), Independent Press, London, 1964, p 60.

[20] Ibid, p 68.

[21] Ibid, p 62.

[22] Idem, *The Work of Christ*, (1910), Independent Press, London, sixth impression, 1958, p 119.

[23] Idem, *The Church and the Sacraments*, p 43.

[24] See further Alan P F Sell, *Aspects of Christian Integrity*, ch. 4.

[25] Quoted by George Cornell in 'More megaChurches foreseen', *Calgary Herald*, 19th January 1991.

[26] Walter Hollenweger, 'The Christian and the Church of the future.' *Audenshaw Papers*, no. 39, 1973, [3].

[27] P T Forsyth, *Missions in State and Church,* p 92.

[28] P T Forsyth, *The Work of Christ*, p 120.

[29] William Willimon, 'Making Christians. The Fox Theater and Christian formation.' *Canada Lutheran*, February 1990, pp 15, 17. Alongside this we may place some remarks of the New Testament scholar, Eduard Schweitzer, here discussing Romans 12: 1ff: 'Just because there are no more strict borderlines between holy and profane places, just because God is no longer enclosed in a holy temple or a group of holy men separated from an unholy world, it is even more important to find God in the world by very clearly distinguishing between his will, his promise, his gift and that of the world. Hence, the Church is only able to render its service to the world by being definitely and unambiguously 'Church'.' See his L W Anderson Lecture for 1970: *Divine Service in the New Testament and Today*, Montreal: Presbyterian College, 1970, p 13.

[30] P T Forsyth, *Missions in State and Church*, p 37.

[31] Ibid, p 201.

[32] Ibid, p 12.

[33] Ibid p 16; cf. 96.

[34] Ibid,p 19.

[35] Ibid, pp 250-251.

[36] Ibid, p 17.

[37] Ibid, p 32.

[38] Idem, *The Work of Christ*, p 96.

[39] Idem, *Missions in State and Church*, p 22.

[40] Ibid, p 265.

[41] See his *Positive Preaching and the Modern Mind*, p 177. Perhaps considerations such as these account for the non-republication of *Missions in State and Church* in the 1950s and 1960s, when so many of Forsyth's works were given a fresh lease of life.

42 See further Alan P F Sell, *Aspects of Christian Integrity*, ch. 5.
43 P T Forsyth, *Missions in State and Church*, p 112.
44 Ibid, p 208.
45 See Ibid, pp 270-271.[46] P T Forsyth, 'Veracity, reality, and regeneration', *London Quarterly Review*, 123, April 1915, p 204.

Contributors

Clyde Binfield, OBE, MA, PhD, FSA, FRHistS, is Reader in History, University of Sheffield, and an elder and lay preacher in the United Reformed Church.

David Cornick, MA, BD, PhD, AKC, is Principal of Westminster College, Cambridge.

Richard L Floyd, BA, MDiv, Dmin, is Minister of the First Church of Christ (United Church of Christ) in Pittsfield, Massachusetts, USA.

Alan Gaunt, MA, is Minister of Carver Memorial United Reformed Church, Windermere, and a poet and hymn writer.

David R Peel, BSc, BD, STM, PhD, is Principal of Northern College, Manchester.

Anna Robbins, BA, MRE, MA, is a Minister of the Canadian Baptist Federation, and a postgraduate student at Aberystwyth.

Alan P F Sell, BA, BD, MA, DD, PhD, DD, DrTheol, FSA, FRHistS, is professor of Christian Doctrine and Philosophy of Religion, and Director of the Centre for the Study of British Christian Thought, Aberystwyth.

Kirk Summers, BA, MDiv, is Minister of Westminster Presbyterian Church, Calgary, Canada, and a postgraduate student at Aberystwyth.

W Bryn Williams, BA, BD, MTh, is Director of the Children's and Youth Service of the Presbyterian Church of Wales, Bala, and a postgraduate student at Aberystwyth.